T0317336

Pliable Pupils and Sufficient Self-Directors

Narratives of Female Education by Five British Women Writers, 1778–1814

Pliable Pupils and Sufficient Self-Directors

Narratives of Female Education by Five British Women Writers, 1778–1814

BARNITA BAGCHI

Tulika Books

Published by **Tulika Books**
35 A/1 (third floor), Shahpur Jat, New Delhi 110 049, India

First published in India 2004

ISBN: 81-85229-83-X

Designed by Ram Rahman, typeset in Sabon and Univers at
Tulika Print Communication Services, New Delhi, and printed
at Pauls Press, E-44/11, Okhla Phase II, New Delhi - 110 020

FOR MY PARENTS
sine qua non

Contents

Contents

Acknowledgements

Most narratives of female education, including the ones analysed in this book, seem to revel in wandering between the diverse spheres, spaces and realms of knowledge that women (great amphibians as they have to be) make integral parts of their self-construction. The path I have traced is no exception. I composed the bulk of this work as a doctoral dissertation at Trinity College and the Faculty of English, University of Cambridge, between 1997 and 2001. It was finished at the Indira Gandhi Institute of Development Research in Mumbai, India, where I currently teach and research issues at the interface of gender, education and development.

I am grateful to many individuals and institutions who have made this journey and process such a stimulating and generative one. Trinity College, Cambridge funded my research through an External Research Studentship, and the Cambridge Commonwealth Trust provided some financial support during the last months. The Indira Gandhi Institute of Development Research, in particular its computing and administrative staff, provided efficient and helpful infrastructural support. I thank its Director, Prof R. Radhakrishna, for giving me the freedom and space to finish the book.

I have been fortunate in having been trained successively in educational institutions that have fostered and showcased women's intellectual achievements. In India, I thank my A-level teachers at the pioneering women's institution Lady Brabourne College in Kolkata, my much-admired teachers (especially Supriya Chaudhuri, Sajni Mukherji, Swapan Chakravorty and Malini Bhattacharya) at the Department of English, Jadavpur University, and the intellectual and political richness of the interdisciplinary School of Women's Studies at Jadavpur University. In England, I am grateful to those who taught me at St Hilda's Collge, now sadly the only women's college in Oxford. In particular, Dr Sally Mapstone's encouragement has remained unstinting. In a sense, this book began at St Hilda's, as an extended essay on Jane Austen and Mary Wollstonecraft.

Dr Caroline Gonda's love and intricate knowledge of eighteenth-century and Romantic-era British women's writing, as well as her critically acute, painstaking but unjudgmental scholarly supervision during the Ph.D., proved to me yet again that feminist pedagogy can be both educative and unoppressive.

Conversations, laughter, food, drink, lazy days on the grass, stemming bouts of despair and imminent dementia – friends provided all these and more, in Kolkata, Cambridge and Mumbai. I salute in particular Rachel Foxley, Natalie Tchernetska, Subha Mukherji, Santanu Das, Jamey Leifer, Jeff Vernon, Kasturi Banerjee, Jayeeta Bagchi, Deepkanta Lahiri Choudhuri, Suchetana Chattopadhyay, Barbara Graziosi and Johannes Haubold.

I thank my sister Tista, whose nine years' seniority made her the obvious recipient of my anxieties and worries about life in academia, a situation she dealt with admirably, both sympathizing with me and offering me wonderful stories from her own narrative of development. My greatest debt is very inadequately acknowledged in the dedication. Jasodhara Bagchi's lifelong commitment to women's writing and education has made her perhaps the most sensitive reader of this work so far. Amiya Bagchi has helped me to better understand and fight the disjunctions and inequalities that are so much and so unjustly a feature of life in general, as well as a powerful theme in the writing I look at in this book.

Introduction

Some women use their tongues – she look'd a lecture,
Each eye a sermon, and her brow a homily,
An all-in-all sufficient self-director . . .
In truth, she was a walking calculation,
Miss Edgeworth's novels stepping from their covers,
Or Mrs Trimmer's books on education,
Or 'Coelebs' Wife' set out in quest of lovers,
Morality's prim personification,
In which not Envy's self a flaw discovers;[1]

The female character should possess the mild and retiring virtues rather than the bold and dazzling ones; great eminence in almost any thing is sometimes injurious to a young lady, whose temper and disposition should appear to be pliant rather than robust; to be ready to take impressions rather than to be decidedly mark'd; as great strength of character, however excellent, is liable to alarm both her own and the other sex.[2]

Pliable pupils and autonomous self-directors: the two passages above present two recurring poles in images of female pupils and female education in British life and writing in the eighteenth and early nineteenth century. In *Don Juan* (1819–24), Byron, satirizing an entire generation of strong-voiced, intellectual, self-directing, educative British women writers, recognizes, with humorous disapproval, the close relationship between women of letters, female education and fiction[3] in the late eighteenth century and early nineteenth century. Far more unthreatening and socially acceptable is Erasmus Darwin's ideal of the pliable, receptive female pupil (found in his *A Plan for the Conduct of Female Education in Boarding Schools*, 1797). A readiness to be 'impressed' by the lessons that the pedagogical figure deals out adapts age-old notions of female passivity to a relatively new situation in which the education of young girls and women is becoming common, in a period in which women have a close and anxious relationship to education.

It is the triangle formed by the intersection of women writers, fiction and representations of female education that this book analyses. I examine the writings, primarily fiction but also some non-fiction, of five representative British women writers who flourished between 1778 and 1814: Lady Mary Hamilton, Clara Reeve, Elizabeth Hamilton, Mary Brunton and the early Jane Austen, with close readings of these writers' narratives about the growth and evolution of adult or near-adult women. It is important that these writers are, by virtue of social and political beliefs, categorizable as 'conservative', for I go on to show that their treatments of female education and development unsettle categories of 'radical' and 'conservative'.

In a climate in which female education was a subject of great anxiety and discussion in print culture, in which fiction was also a relatively low genre and a site of contestation, and in which women were emerging as major producers both of educational writing and of ostensibly didactic fiction, such writers as the ones I focus on produced fictions of female education which were pioneering *Bildungsromans*. Highly gendered, these fictions explore key tensions and questions generated by the theme of education, including a dialectic between formal and experiential education; between the pliable, receptive pupil obedient to pedagogical authority figures and the more autonomous, self-sufficient auto-didact; and between a desire for greater institutionalization of education and a recognition of the flexibility or freedom that distancing from established structures gives.

The Writers

The oldest of the writers I examine, Clara Reeve (1729–1807), the daughter of an impoverished Ipswich clergyman, started publishing in 1769, although the three works I primarily examine were published between 1785 and 1792. Mary Hamilton (1739–after 1818), ten years younger than Reeve, came from an aristocratic Scottish background. I discuss her before Reeve because while Lady Mary's English novels were all published in the late 1770s, Reeve continued to publish into the 1790s. Elizabeth Hamilton (1758–1816), born into a Scottish Presbyterian background, started writing in the 1780s, first published in 1796, established herself as an anti-Jacobin novelist between 1796 and 1800, and later gained even more fame as an educational writer and popular-izer of philosophy, continuing to publish until her death. Mary Brunton (1778–1818) was the youngest of the writers I discuss. A minister's wife, she, like the Hamiltons, belonged firmly to a Scottish milieu. Her brief literary career began late in her short life, with her two major novels published in 1810 and 1814. I conclude with a chapter on Jane Austen (1775–1817), where I analyse early pieces of short fiction written between the 1790s and the first decade of the nineteenth century: these works bear the imprint of the mid to late eighteenth-century tradition of women's writing on education in more direct ways than her later oeuvre.

Why have I chosen to write author-based chapters? Why have I chosen these particular writers? Why have I focused on fiction? What has governed my choice of dates? Let me answer these methodological questions. I have deliberately chosen to write author-based chapters. If the development of the fictional heroines of my writers is the main subject of attention in this book, a related area of interest is the development, self-construction or biographical construction of their creators as authors, as pupils and as educators. Mary Hamilton's comments on women hazarding the notoriety of publication, and her private comments on how seriously she took her own writing; Clara Reeve's self-presentation as female author and educator in *The Progress of Romance*; Mary Brunton's development from hesitant, fumbling writer to a confident awareness of her own membership of the republic of letters; Elizabeth Benger's account of Elizabeth Hamilton's negotiation of the burden and responsibility of female authorship; Jane Austen's representation of herself as an ignorant, unlearned female author, and her simultaneous elevation of the novel and female novelists – such narratives show that many women writers selling their works in the marketplace were simultaneously seeing themselves, most often with hesitation, ambivalence or cunning, as serious women of letters, educators and writers of fiction.

This is particularly significant given that, as Cheryl Turner has pointed out,[4] in the period under consideration, women novelists' freedom as literary producers was constrained both by personal and legal restrictions, such as the lack of access to property by married women, and by the power of publishers, for whom novels were usually ephemeral commodities for which the majority of authors could expect only small monetary rewards.[5]

Socially, the writers I examine have clear affinities. Three were closely connected with the clergy (Reeve and Austen were clergymen's daughters, Brunton a clergyman's wife). All, with the exception of Mary Hamilton (an aristocrat who married a commoner), were members of the gentry. Each espoused a social order firmly based on older hierarchies (peasant, farmer, yeoman, gentry and aristocrat), and displayed respect for a responsible landed gentry and aristocracy, as well as for cohesive rural communities. Politically, they were conservative, hostile to the American Revolution (Lady Mary Hamilton) or the French Revolution (the rest of the writers).

All wrote fiction interested in the education, growth and evolution of adult women. Each writer, in her different way, discussed the pains of female education: 'Female Difficulties', the sub-title of Frances Burney's *The Wanderer* (1814) could be used for all their works. They all used a moral framework that stresses reason, self-control and prudence. The same broad, miscellaneous process of education helped to form them, including such influential works as Locke's *Some Thoughts Concerning Education* (1693), Richardson's *Pamela* (1740–42) and *Clarissa* (1747–48), and Hester Chapone's *Letters on the Improvement of the Mind* (1773).

But if they are similar, the writers I look at are also diverse – a Scottish aristocrat and expatriate, an English critic and novelist who also wrote one of the first Gothic novels, a Scottish clergyman's wife, a prominent Scottish philosopher and woman of letters, and the juvenilia of a now-canonical writer of courtship novels. This diversity testifies to another argument of this book, that we need to recognize how non-monolithic a site women's writing was in this period. United as they are by chronology, genre, gender, social grouping, conservative ideology, an interest in education and cultural register, the differences and dissimilarities in the fiction of the writers I examine demonstrate the flux of late eighteenth-century and early nineteenth-century British women's fiction.

The absence of other important conservative women writers, such as Frances Burney, Jane West or Hannah More, as points of focus in my book is due partly to constraints of space, partly to already existing excellent work on some of them (notably on Burney[6] and Edgeworth[7]), partly to personal criteria (Hannah More, I feel, was manifestly uncomfortable as a writer of fiction, so that her very thinly novelized conduct book *Coelebs in Search of a Wife* is best discussed under the rubric of non-fiction), and partly to a desire to create a fresh perspective on women's writing of the period by my choice of authors and texts. The book brings together writers whose work has now become obscure (such as Mary Hamilton, and Clara Reeve as a writer of non-Gothic fiction) with (now) highly canonical ones such as Austen. It reads novelists of ideas (Mary Hamilton and Elizabeth Hamilton) and novelists of manners (Austen and Brunton) together. It collocates late 1770s writing and early nineteenth-century writing. It encompasses a wide variety of sub-genres in the fiction of the period, from the single-heroine courtship novel to the Oriental tale and Cottage tale.

I have chosen 1778 as the starting point of my work because it was a year in which both Mary Hamilton's *Munster Village* and Frances Burney's *Evelina* were published, works which exemplify two poles in fictions of female education in the period of study. Lady Mary's work, which in terms of tone and style belongs more to the mid-eighteenth century, is an ambitious novel of ideas, representing a female-founded and female-administered community, with inset stories of the struggles and self-realization of cultivated, mature women. *Munster Village* is very much in the line of such earlier British Bluestocking female utopias as Sarah Scott's *Millenium Hall* (1762). *Evelina*, Frances Burney's first published novel, on the other hand, epitomizes the single-heroine courtship novel, where, as the sub-title puts it, a young lady makes her 'entrance into the world', negotiating the pressures of prescriptive femininity *en route* to social respectability and marriage. Readers will find in this book some works which align themselves with the *Munster Village* pole, notably Clara Reeve's *The School for Widows* (1791) and *Plans of Education* (1792), and Elizabeth Hamilton's *The Cottagers of Glenburnie* (1808). These focus on or devote a great deal of attention to older women, and on women's search for vocations outside marriage. More *Evelina*-like are the novels of Mary Brunton and Jane Austen, also single-heroine courtship novels.

Another reason for my choice of starting date is that, as Cheryl Turner points out,[8] it was from the 1780s that the volume of female-authored fiction increased sharply, with that trend continuing in the following decades.

What of my choice of end-date? In 1814, Sir Walter Scott's *Waverley*

was published. If *Evelina* marks an important moment in the rise in respectability
and fame of women's fiction, the publication of Scott's work marks the beginning
of a gradual marginalization of female-authored fiction, as Ina Ferris has argued
through her analysis of periodical writing in *The Achievement of Literary
Authority*.[9] Hazlitt's scathing review of Burney's *The Wanderer*, also published
in 1814, bears out[10] that it was no longer acceptable to chart 'female difficulties',
a phrase that Hazlitt could by then use pejoratively to describe Burney's novels.
To be respectable to men of letters, the woman writer had to write miniaturized,
apparently cosy novels like Austen (whose *Mansfield Park* was published in
1814). This book shows how adventurous and disturbing female-authored fictions
of education could be, both in the preceding thirty-six years, and *simultaneously*
with the publication of Austen's works, in the writings of such women as Brunton
or Elizabeth Hamilton who wrote a very non-Austenian kind of fiction.

Female Education in the Eighteenth Century

The growth of interest in female education in eighteenth-century Britain
was a major component of what has been seen as a feminization of polite British
culture in Britain,[11] with a growing emphasis on women's influence in polite
society in such areas as print culture, parenthood, conjugality, philanthropy and
social assemblies. Lawrence Stone[12] and Randolph Trumbach[13] have argued that
one of the main reasons for this was the emergence, from the late seventeenth
century, of the modern nuclear family, the companionate ideal in marriage and
'affective individualism' between family members. In such an ideological climate,
they argue, there was a shift from an overtly patriarchal model of the family to
one where women's importance and influence were acknowledged, particularly
in the private sphere. Stone's thesis of 'affective individualism' has proved contro-
versial, with many writers questioning whether this was entirely a new phenom-
enon, or whether it was as positive and empowering for women as Stone
claims.[14] This book, indeed, shows how embattled women writers' relationship
was with such 'feminized' cultural elements as the sentimentalized family,
drawing-room sociability and negotiations of marriage.

Female education has always, perhaps, been an overdetermined area,
but this was particularly true of the eighteenth century. This was a period in
which domestic and school education for women was undergoing expansion.[15]
There was an increase in the number of female boarding schools, in the number
of women teachers and governesses, and in public concern about charity schools
for girls.[16] Although the real expansion in female literacy did not occur in the
period I focus on but a century earlier, there was nonetheless a greater increase
in female literacy than in its male counterpart in the later part of the eighteenth
century.[17]

After the mid-nineteenth century, such issues as movements for national
systems of female formal education, or institutions for female higher education,
or provisions for training women for jobs, became distinct questions, emerging
with the growth and development of national systems of education. In the period

I focus on, however, polite female education was a web in which ideological, curricular, political, pedagogical and personal issues were enmeshed.

What is most striking about eighteenth-century polite female education is the unprecedentedly large role that print culture played in it. Dorothy Gardiner, for example, argues in her still unsurpassed study of girls' education in England, that the middle of the eighteenth century was a period in which female education was shaped most powerfully by writing.[18] This is evidenced by such diverse phenomena as the popularity of Richardson's novels (*Pamela* appeared in 1740), or of Jean-Jacques Rousseau's *Emile* (1762), the social influence of the Bluestockings' public advocacy of female education, and the publication and dissemination of many treatises (usually in letter form) devoted to female education. There was, too, a rise in the number of educational and didactic women writers.[19] At that time, women were writing with enthusiasm and adeptness on topics such as political economy (Jane Marcet, *Conversations on Political Economy*, 1816[20]) and history (Catharine Macaulay, *History of England*[21]). Even if in small numbers, women of learning and letters were visible in the public sphere.

Anxieties about class and female education, about access to books and female education, about the possible goals and necessary constraints on female education – printed matter in the late eighteenth and early nineteenth century teemed with treatments of such topics. In the print culture of 'polite and commercial' Britain, commodified images of women as pupils and teachers, of female readers and writers, of accomplished young women playing the harp or drawing or singing, testified to how easily the educated woman could be turned into an eroticized, vendible object for the male gaze and in the marriage market.[22] It is in this context that we need to read the fulminations against female 'display' and 'accomplishments' found in virtually every major woman writer of the period, including the ones I analyse.

One could argue that for women of the middling classes in particular, 'education' then was a site of irreducible tension – tension between a view of education as, on the one hand, a form of social control, a way of guiding and indoctrinating the pupil into gendered social norms and acceptable models of femininity, and, on the other, a more outward-looking model of education with the stress on opening up opportunities and freedom, impelling the pupil towards a more open-ended model of development. On the one hand, the female, above all figures, was seen to be a lifelong pupil, whether as child, adolescent, girl, wife, mother or widow, imbibing ideology and wisdom from pedagogical and monitorial figures ranging from parents to tutors, guardians and husbands. On the other hand, in Britain, as in virtually every other culture, feminism first articulated itself precisely through the discursive site of education.[23] Education offered a language of meliorism as well as of critiques of existing conditions. Education directly involved questions of power, autonomy and control: what are the powers of teachers and teacher-like guardian figures in women's lives? Should women be educated to earn their own living? Should marriage be the primary goal of female education? The writing I analyse thus manipulates with great dexterity the basic discursive framework of education, so as to open out a huge variety of questions pertaining to women's experience; using the language of education, my writers argued that women can become political economists and land-owners, national saviours in times of crisis, or female philosophers.

The tensions in the notion of education that I have been describing are found in the very etymology of the word education – the emphasis on '*ducare*', or leading, on the one hand, and on '*ex*', or the movement outwards towards freedom, on the other. This was a dialectic between control and freedom, a dialectic that has further complexities in the works I look at, given that their authors routinely used a language of regulation, propriety, control and reason as a means of controlling their selves and achieving a degree of autonomy.

Didactic Proper Ladies, or Polemical Amazons of the Pen? Women Writers, Fiction and Education

Although heroine-centred fictions of education had existed before the mid-eighteenth-century (for example, the work of Jane Barker and Mary Davys[24]), it is arguable that scandal fiction, seduction fiction and other types of amatory fiction were more typical of the earlier, Restoration and early eighteenth-century period, when Aphra Behn, Delariviere Manley and the early Eliza Haywood flourished.[25] In the propriety-ridden era that followed, domesticity, self-regulation and control of sensibility became important. Paradoxically, in this later period, even as women risked being pigeonholed into a maternal, wifely, homebound, genteel role, they also came far more into the centrestage of print culture, both as readers and writers.

It was particularly after the popularity of Samuel Richardson's female-centred fictions, *Pamela* (1740–42) and *Clarissa* (1747–48), that education, female selfhood and fiction became peculiarly intertwined. Fiction took on a powerful educative function, including that performed by advice literature or conduct books for women.[26] The heroine as exemplary figure; the novel, situated in contemporary or near-contemporary settings, describing her development, education and experience; the reader participating in this experience and learning from her example – this configuration of didactic relationships between the protagonist, her education and the potential education of the reader was well-established in the period.

A strikingly large number of women wrote such fictions of education after 1740, many of them creating heroines belonging to a line of what Jane Spencer has called the 'reformed heroine' tradition:[27] Charlotte Lennox's *The Female Quixote* (1752) and Eliza Haywood's *The History of Miss Betsy Thoughtless* (1751) are well-known early examples. In the period I focus on, it became a commonplace that 'amazons of the pen' (Samuel Johnson's term) had become major players in the market of fiction. In 1773, *The Monthly* wrote of novel-writing: 'This branch of the literary *trade* appears now, to be almost entirely engrossed by the ladies.'[28] I take this quotation from Terry Lovell's *Consuming Fiction*, where the period between 1770 and 1820 is described as one 'during which the literary credentials of the novel were at their lowest point. It was denounced not only for its lack of literary merit, but also for its alleged effects on morals.'[29]

The novel was more of a site of contestation than Lovell's summary assessment would indicate, but there is no doubt that in the history of the cultural institutionalization of the novel, this was a transitional period. The deluge of acclaim that a Richardson or a Fielding received was a thing of the past. The novel, by the 1770s, was not as novel. Popular fiction continued to be viewed with great suspicion by the majority of critical reviews. After the removal of perpetual copyright in 1774, one sees tentative spurts in the publication of works which were coming to be considered classics of fiction (by authors such as Goldsmith or Fielding).[30] The tail-end of the period began to witness the very beginnings of the canonization of the novel as part of the heritage of English literature, through enterprises such as Anna Barbauld's British Novelists series (first edition, 1810).[31]

Fiction, as the legions of eighteenth-century writers holding forth on the dangers of novel-reading were all too aware, was an ambivalent instrument of education. Michael Mckeon has argued[32] that the eighteenth-century novel mediates questions of truth and questions of virtue, and that the evolution of the genre follows a dialectical pattern of constant redefinition, showing how contested such a claim is. Gender played a key role in such contestation and mediation during the late eighteenth and early nineteenth century. There was a close connection between, firstly, the status of fiction as a contested genre (both morally and epistemologically), secondly, women writers as producers of fiction, and thirdly, representations of female education. Women writing fictions of female education were representing and vindicating tension-ridden patterns of female development, and simultaneously trying to negotiate the problem of fictional truth: is fiction a site of alternative knowledge, different in kind from older, established kinds of knowledge with their claims to truth-value, or is it a lying, corrupting genre?

Women obviously had a double-edged position with regard to the novel in this period, with women readers and writers routinely associated with the feminized genre of fiction, frequently viewed as a corrupting, illicit form. There was great anxiety about women's reading, particularly their reading of fiction. The possibility of private, freely chosen reading raised the spectre of autodidacticism, of 'sufficient self-direction'. This possibility was enhanced when fictions charted the education of women through the hard school of experience, so that the practice of reading led to a vicarious experience of reality.

Charges or objections to fiction – that novels may teach young ladies the pleasures of love, encourage them to lead a vicarious, fictional existence, or produce ennui – were ones that all novelists of the period intent on presenting an educative model of the novel needed to confront. There were many attempted resolutions to this problem, as well as examples of patently unresolved tensions (Mary Wollstonecraft would be a good example). Whether the writer was a

Wollstonecraft,[33] a Catharine Macaulay[34] or a Lady Sarah Pennington,[35] the reading of fiction in this period cannot be taken for granted: even those speaking in defence of novel-reading, such as Erasmus Darwin,[36] or Mary Hays,[37] or Clara Reeve in *The Progress of Romance*, did so after a debate. Recent empirical studies have argued that women readers did not necessarily read more fiction than other genres, or more than men did:[38] the continual discussions about women and their relationship with fiction must be related to cultural *anxieties* about women.

Such anxieties and ambivalence about the literary and epistemological status of fiction, and about the relationship of women to fiction, recur in the fictions I analyse. Austen's confident vindication of the novel in *Northanger Abbey* occurs before a novelistic purging of the excesses of the Radcliffean Gothic, in a work that was considered minor until recently and which remained unpublished until after her death. I argue that Austen's economical, 'realistic' model of the novel is deliberately self-circumscribed, eschewing the breadth, ambition and confident intellectualism of many earlier and contemporary female-authored and female-centred fictions that depict the education of heroines.

In *The Progress of Romance*, Clara Reeve's female critic Euphrasia defends the much-derided genres of novel and romance, and invokes the educative function of fiction – here, too, cultural anxieties about the immorality of fiction, its value as compared with the Classics, and the special relationship that women have with fiction, figure as prominent issues. Elizabeth Hamilton (*Translation of the Letters of a Hindoo Rajah*) and Mary Brunton (*Self-Control*) wrote fiction that itself preaches against the potentially dangerous effects of fiction-reading for women. Throughout her career, however, Elizabeth Hamilton kept returning to fiction to discuss educational, historical and philosophical ideas, even while believing that historical and philosophical biography is superior to fiction as a literary form.

Reeve, Elizabeth Hamilton, Brunton and Austen, all argued in their fiction against the stereotypical idea that only women read novels and are corrupted by novels, with Hamilton and Brunton presenting particularly corrupt male novel-readers. These writers, then, while being very aware that the association between women and fiction can further women's literary and educative roles, also viewed this association with scepticism, and worried about what kind of ethics and pleasure they were purveying by choosing to write in the form most readily available to them, a form which the majority of them filled with many and miscellaneous domains of knowledge.

Fictions of Female Education: Compendiousness and Miscellaneousness

Didactic heroine-centred fictions authored by respectable, proper eighteenth-century ladies were highly compendious, bringing into one discursive site diverse genres, modes and styles, such as prescriptions and advice literature, Enlightenment educational writing, politics, personal or subjective polemics, the fable, romance and letter. The various ideological and rhetorical elements that went together to form notions of fictional education jostled each other in works that did not conform to a realist model of the novel (this is true also of Jane Austen's early writing).

The often-proclaimed didactic and educational purpose of fiction in the period had much to do with this compendiousness and miscellaneousness.[39] History, botany, biography, politics, economics, theology and speculations about ideal communities – a whole host of extra-fictional fields of knowledge crowded the world of fiction. Long passages of advice, polemics, historiography, fable, romance, personal reminiscence and prescriptions about female curricula co-habited the same space. The theme of education created, on the one hand, an emphasis on controlled development, on the acquiring of various sorts of knowledge and self-regulation; on the other hand, the miscellaneousness of fiction worked against the grain of such attempts at imposing structure and control.

Such fiction both feminized the Enlightenment and assimilated Enlightenment thought and knowledge into the miscellaneousness of fiction. Education was *the* Enlightenment theme par excellence, offering a language of improvement and controlled development and progress. Recent scholarship has demonstrated that the category of 'woman' played a major role in mainstream masculine Enlightenment thought, including historical and educational writing such as Diderot's and Rousseau's.[40] Equally, it has been argued that women writers, from Madame d'Epinay to Stephanie Genlis, Mary Wollstonecraft and Mary Hays were extending the Enlightenment stress on cultivation, self-improvement and amelioration to discussions of their own gender.[41]

Most of the writers discussed in this book wrote in an Enlightenment mode, privileging reason and controlled, regulated development:[42] as Aidan Day has argued in a recent critical reader on Romanticism, the late Enlightenment strand in late eighteenth-century and early nineteenth-century writing is far more pervasive than has been recognized.[43] In the case of four of the writers discussed here (Mary Hamilton, Clara Reeve, Elizabeth Hamilton and Mary Brunton), Enlightenment philosophy played an obviously important role in their conception of education, most importantly for their notion of the human mind, seen as a dynamic entity with its own processes and laws. Locke, the main source for their notions of the human mind, was also important for them as an educational thinker: his Empiricist emphasis on the power of environment, habit and other social processes in the development of human beings was a major source of intellectual support for Mary Hamilton and Elizabeth Hamilton. (Despite the fact that Locke's *Some Thoughts Concerning Education*, 1693, was written for a gentleman's son, the Lockeian pupil is curiously feminized, with a long adolescence, a constant attention to the cultivation of virtue and an emphasis on domestic education.)

Elizabeth and Mary Hamilton and Mary Brunton belonged to Scottish Enlightenment formations. Mary Hamilton used Enlightenment histories of women (by writers such as Antoine Thomas), shared an Enlightenment interest in non-European cultures and, while she criticized his scepticism, quoted him approvingly on taste. Elizabeth Hamilton was close to Dugald Stewart, Thomas

Reid's disciple and popularizer, and to Scottish Common Sense philosophy in general.

Christianity was as important a shaping force for these writers' fictions of education as any abstract or secular notion of Enlightenment. Their interest in the dynamism of the female mind, conceived of in Lockeian or Reidian terms, was complemented by a belief in the Protestant woman's vocation, her struggles and achievements. *The Pilgrim's Progress* as much as Locke's *Essay Concerning Human Understanding* shaped the fictions I look at: from Reeve's *The School for Widows* to Elizabeth Hamilton's *Translation of the Letters of a Hindoo Rajah* and Mary Brunton's *Self-Control* and *Discipline*, Protestant, Miltonic notions of virtue needing to confront adversity to prove itself combined with the topos of the school of adversity, with both of these represented as narratives of 'female difficulties'. Hamilton's eulogy of women mathematicians and politicians, Reeve's account of an unhappy wife's struggles to become a successful teacher, or Elizabeth Hamilton's application of 'the science of the human mind' to the efforts of a Scotswoman who wants to improve female education – shaping all these narratives was a Christian narrative of backslidings, confrontation of adversities and fulfilment of a spiritual vocation through good works.

Eclectic resources yielded by contemporary print culture were, for these writers, as valuable for their heroines' evolution as high philosophy. In the case of Austen (easily the most distanced of all my writers from the world of high philosophy and 'masculine' learning), poetry, periodical essays, conduct literature and novels – in short, the world of miscellaneous print culture that women like her devoured[44] – figured as important resources for her heroines. Austen's characters inhabit the world of Fordyce's *Sermons*, of Hannah More's *Coelebs in Search of a Wife*, of Charlotte Smith's novels, and of Cowper's and Crabbe's poetry. An abstract notion of 'Enlightenment' thus combined with older Protestant ideas as well as a more random field of knowledge and reading practices for such writers – giving a new dimension to our emerging notions of a feminized Enlightenment.

'Fiction', rather than the 'novel', is my preferred term and category: I am not positing a monolithic site called 'the novel'. Critics such as Clifford Siskin have pointed out that from the end of the eighteenth century to the early decades of the nineteenth, the novel begins to be classified and idealized as a well-formed artefact, and fiction takes an inward-looking 'lyric turn' in its delineation of character.[45] Siskin has also seen in this period the birth of what he calls 'novelism', or a subsuming of writing under the category of the novel, with the category of the novel undergoing a 'taming or 'naturalization' in the 1820s and 1830s.

My contention is that late eighteenth-century and early nineteenth-century female-authored conservative fictions of female education overturn such neat theses as Siskin's about the naturalization of fiction and the idealization of the novel. The fictions I analyse embody the fact that 'the novel' in this period encompasses a huge variety of sub-genres of fiction, ranging from the long tale (the Cottage tale and the Oriental tale, for example) to epistolary fiction, from fictionalized plans of education to single-heroine courtship novels. The works examined in this book, representative of their period, do not consistently or primarily privilege an inward turn in characterization. Far from idealizing the category of the novel, they create internal debates about the value and status of fiction. They unsettle distinctions between the categories of 'radical' and 'conservative', as well as between those of the 'residual' and the 'emergent' or 'modern'. The constant see-saw between various styles and registers in these works, too, prevents our seeing them as well-wrought urns, corresponding to the neatly formed subjects such works might be seen as representing. This is fiction in a state of transition, a site where women writers tried out fictional patterns of female education with a diversity of intention and effect.

Female Traditions and Female Communities
in Fictions of Female Education

The reader of this book will soon realize that there is a rich eighteenth-century tradition of women's educational writing, in which figures such as Mary Astell, Sarah Scott, Elizabeth Carter, Sarah Fielding, Stephanie de Genlis, Frances Burney and Mary Wollstonecraft are prominent names. Writing in 1791, for example, Elizabeth Benger, the poet, novelist and biographer (whose biography of Elizabeth Hamilton I discuss in this book), was very aware of Astell's important role in the advocacy of female learning:

> Astell and Masham female learning fir'd,
> Their bright example every breast inspir'd.·
> Note: Mary Astell and Damaris Lady Masham, were adepts in philosophy, divinity, etc. and discussed the abstrusest subjects; they were both great advocates of female learning.[46]

Astell,[47] herself one among a host of late seventeenth-century writers advocating a better female education[48] (others are Bathsua Makin, Hannah Woolley and Judith Drake), was a potent though subterranean influence for many eighteenth-century women writers, among them Mary Hamilton and Clara Reeve. Astell's *Serious Proposal to the Ladies for the Advancement of Their True and Greatest Interest* (1694) describes a female community and seminary where the women inhabitants devote themselves to improving their own minds and to educating younger gentlewomen. It is the first in a line of eighteenth-century British women's utopias, most notably Sarah Scott's *Millenium Hall* (1762) Mary Hamilton's *Munster Village* (1778), and Clara Reeve's *Plans of Education* (1792).

In *Literary Women*, in an excellent chapter entitled 'Educating Heroinism',[49] Ellen Moers has shown how influential another such late eighteenth-century female educator, Stephanie de Genlis, was on contemporary European women writers. Governess to the children of the Duke of Orleans, Genlis wrote a host of educational books, most of them in fictional form, meant for parents and for children alike, which made her a celebrity. Mary Hamilton's *Letters from the Duchess de Crui* (1776), which describes maternal educators every bit as active and determined as Genlis's characters, in fact appeared well before Genlis's famous *Adèle et Theodore* (1782). But the spirit is strikingly similar. Clara Reeve acknowledged Genlis fulsomely, while Austen, as Moers has shown, was sceptical about but very aware of the influence of her distinguished predecessor.

As important for the writers I look at, particularly for Mary Hamilton and Clara Reeve, were the 'Bluestockings' and their contemporaries,[50] a large if loose grouping of eighteenth-century women writers. Elizabeth Carter, Elizabeth Montagu, Sarah Scott, Hester Chapone, Charlotte Lennox and Sarah Fielding belonged to this group, while influential contemporaries included Elizabeth Griffith, Frances Sheridan and Frances Brooke. Clara Reeve's *The Progress of Romance* (1785) conveys the excitement of reading the novels of this generation of women, with their deep interest in education.

The Bluestockings, as well as Griffith and Brooke, showed through their life and writings that it was permissible and possible for gentlewomen to have a life of the mind. The learned Elizabeth Carter, famous particularly for her translation of Epictetus, became a byword for female excellence, and was eulogized by Mary Hamilton and Benger, among others. Elizabeth Montagu's sister Sarah Scott wrote *Millenium Hall* (1762), eloquent about the difficulties that many of her contemporary gentlewomen faced, especially from family pressures and in love and marriage. *The History of Sir George Ellison* (1766), the sequel to *Millenium Hall*, connects women's education and the amelioration and education of slaves. Sarah Fielding, translator and novelist, praised by Reeve particularly for her pioneering educational novel for adolescent girls, *The Governess* (1749), anatomized, in the same way as Mary and Elizabeth Hamilton later in the century, the difficulties faced by women interested in cultivating their minds.

The censoring of female learning, the exercise of authority to curtail female education, the problematic relationship between women's education and marriage, and attempts to delineate a female curriculum – such issues were accorded extended fictional discussion and criticism for the first time in English writing by the mid-eighteenth-century generation of writers. In their novels, women aspire to and achieve self-cultivation, correspond about female learning and become authors. In Sarah Fielding's *The Adventures of David Simple* (1744), Cynthia describes the immense parental resistance she faces when she wishes to cultivate her mind.[51] The heroine of Frances Brooke's *The Excursion* (1777) arrives in London determined to publish or sell for performance the novel, epic poem and tragedy, all written by herself, that she carries in her luggage.[52] In Charlotte Lennox's *The Life of Harriot Stuart, Written by Herself* (1750), the eponymous heroine is a gifted poet.[53] One could multiply these examples, which demonstrate that a strong tradition of women's fiction highlighting the role of education in women's lives had evolved in an astonishingly short time in eighteenth-century Britain.

A look at such mid-eighteenth-century women writers and their influence on later writing suggests that it is time to recognize the continuities between women's fiction written before and after the post-French Revolution era of crisis and reaction. A distinguished line of criticism on late eighteenth-century and early nineteenth-century British women's writing takes as a starting point the fact that this was a period of political and cultural revolution. Marilyn Butler,[54] Claudia Johnson[55] and Gary Kelly[56] have seen the French Revolution and its aftermath, the period of reaction in Britain, as crystallizing, even causal, factors in women's writing on education. 'Radical' or 'Jacobin,' 'reactionary' or 'anti-Jacobin' have been useful ways to understand the polemical female fictions of education that were produced in the last decade of the eighteenth century and the first decade of the nineteenth.

However, pre-revolutionary and post-revolutionary women's fictions of education are also deeply connected. Clara Reeve's 1790s novels are indeed anti-Jacobin, but the ideal of fiction they embody is spelt out in her earlier critical work, *The Progress of Romance* (1785), which invests heavily in mid-eighteenth-century female author–educators, with whom her 1790s heroines have strong affinities. *Plans of Education*, too, is as much, if not more, a successor of the mid-eighteenth-century *Millenium Hall* as it is a 1790s conservative novel. Reeve and Elizabeth Hamilton offer the most overtly politicized and public treatments of female education among all my writers – yet, writing in the 1770s, Mary Hamilton offers equally bold, polemical defences of women's political roles. The two most intellectually ambitious and wide-ranging among my writers, Mary and Elizabeth Hamilton, one pre-French Revolution and the other post-French Revolution, show a very similar interest in how women can use the science of the mind to gain greater agency.

Much of the fiction I look at shows a rapprochement between conventionally categorized radical and conservative women writers (such as between Clara Reeve and Elizabeth Hamilton, on the one hand, and Mary Wollstonecraft, on the other) – a rapprochement that has been noticed in the context of non-fictional writing by Mitzi Myers, in an article on the similarities between Hannah More's and Mary Wollstonecraft's views on female education.[57] My analysis of the five writers shows that the paucity of paid trades for women preoccupied writers throughout that period. In the 1790s radical, pro-French Revolution women writers (such as Mary Hays, Mary Anne Radcliffe and Mary Robinson[58]) chimed with conservative, anti-French Revolution women writers, such as Reeve and Hamilton, on this issue. And while Mary Hamilton in 1778 commends one of her characters for daring to use her 'good sense' and 'talents' to sell her paintings, in 1814 Mary Brunton's creation Ellen Percy asks, like Reeve, Hays and Mary Anne Radcliffe in the 1790s: 'What channel had the customs of society left open to the industry of woman?'[59]

Readers will have noticed that the one writer I focus on who did not share this concern for the paucity of paid trades for women is Jane Austen. I argue that as far as breadth and range in treatments of female education go, Austen was far *more* conservative than such 1790s conservative writers as

Elizabeth Hamilton, Jane West, Hannah More and Clara Reeve, even though she was radically critical of the pressures of education as ideology operating on young women. The confusion of the categories 'radical' and 'conservative' thus holds good for Austen's treatment of female education as well.

Fictions of Female Education as *Bildungsromans*:
The Tensions in Female Education

A recent study of the *Bildungsroman* as a literary form has provocatively argued that it is a 'pseudo-genre', an ahistorical category and a post-nineteenth-century construct.[60] It does seem clear that there is no one kind or form of the *Bildungsroman* – but the term remains a fruitful way of approaching very diverse European fictions of education and development. Considered as *Bildungsromans*, the female-centred fictions I examine challenge post-Romantic views of education which privilege and mystify interiority and an organic notion of the self. The process of 'Bildung' at the heart of the *Bildungsroman* was seen by critics such as Wilhelm Dilthey (the man who singlehandedly brought the category into the mainstream of literary criticism) as natural and organic, created by the self (perceived in idealistic, Kantian terms) out of its difficult negotiation with the world. Mystification of the self is a danger in this sort of critical enterprise.

Unlike in such classic canonical *Bildungsromans* as *Huckleberry Finn* or *Great Expectations*, one cannot see the growth and development of the female subject in the fictions I analyse primarily as an organic or natural process of evolution. The overt external authority of didacticism, the presence of stock topoi such as virtue in distress, and the use of the prescriptive register foreground the complexity and *constructedness* of the process of female education in these works. From Mary Hamilton's romance-like, 'improbable' style to Elizabeth Hamilton's mixing of psychology, philosophy, caricature and fiction, or Austen's parody of earlier fictions of female development in her juvenilia, the literary and ideological building-blocks of the female self are firmly in evidence in these writers' works.

The fictions I examine also represent constitutive tensions in the educative process, such as between formal and experiential education, between pedagogical authority and auto-didacticism, between control and randomness or excess, and between amateurism and incipient professionalism. Such apparently prim, respectable writers, therefore, delineate some of the most potent tensions in post-Enlightenment subject formation.

Each of the writers I examine problematizes the relationship between women's formal and experiential education. Mary Hamilton asks whether women's limited access to the traditionally defined system of formal education in the period is in fact a way into a richer experiential education, or whether this is making a virtue of necessity. Hamilton's characters worry about the fact that the 'destination' of women is uncertain and random, making it particularly important but difficult that they receive a rigorous education which allows them to know their own minds. Elizabeth Hamilton tries to formulate an educational plan based on the principles of the science of the mind that will make women's mental faculties more alert and active, and which will enable them to cope with the vicissitudes of their lives. The 'school of adversity', a phrase that Clara Reeve uses in *The School for Widows*, is one that all the heroines discussed in this book go to: in the process, they also learn mathematics or paint semi-professionally, act as governesses or school teachers, set up libraries and schools, superintend estates and educate their own children and wards.

Many of the writers I examine (especially Mary Hamilton, Elizabeth Hamilton and Mary Brunton, who are, perhaps not coincidentally, part of Scottish Enlightenment formations) make women learners and practitioners of all sorts of disciplines, some of them emerging at this time, such as the science of the mind, botany, physics, chemistry and mathematics. Older disciplines such as history and biography are also made part of women's intellectual horizons by each of the writers: Mary Hamilton's use of Enlightenment historiography, Clara Reeve's evocation of the historical figure of Madame de Maintenon, a pioneer in female education, Elizabeth Hamilton's deep interest in historical biography, and Austen's heroines' interest in the discipline of history, all come readily to mind.

Equally, women demand an education to train them for well-defined social vocations, ranging from philanthropy to paid work – a strand of profession-alism[61] and institutionalization. However, the term 'profession' should be applied with extreme caution to women's work in this period. None of the paid 'trades' (the term women in the period most often used to describe paid work) open to women had an iota of the status and money associated with the professions, in the older and still established sense of the word, referring to the clergy, medicine and law. Teaching was the only non-menial occupation open to women, and the indignities and poverty of the woman teacher or governess taxed writers such as Reeve and Maria Edgeworth.

Given the paucity of paid trades for women, it is natural that in these fictions women should hover on the edge of being perpetual amateurs, conversant with many disciplines but in danger of being adept in none. Jane Austen, for example, who was the most sceptical among my writers about formal education, shows that heroines such as Kitty Percival and Catherine Morland make original, eclectic and often critical use of the very miscellaneous formal education they receive. Yet they do not aspire to any degree of command over the various domains of learning they come into contact with. Mary Brunton's Laura's attempts to be a professional painter are discouraged by the men in her life. In other areas, such as in her successful attempts to pick up mathematics, she is depicted very much as an amateur. Even her perseverance in mastering this subject is more a marker of her moral steadfastness than of her intellectual competence. One could argue that such notions of amateurism have close links with, and are sometimes identical to, emerging notions of a liberal education,[62] as the wide-ranging, unspecialized curriculum in Hester Chapone's *Letters on the Improvement of the Mind*, for example, suggests. To be a successful domestic woman possessed of such a liberal education might be said to be the 'profession' of most such women. But this is not all the story. Female authors, philanthropists, philosophers, landed owners, servants, teachers, governesses, shopkeepers, and the work they do, also take centrestage in the works I examine, creating an ongoing and unresolved tension between professionalism and amateurism.

The fictions of female education I look at are eclectic, unpredictable, disconcerting, disturbing and eccentric, their surface primness and didacticism serving to make their adventurousness all the more striking. However, even in very valuable recent work, such as Alan Richardson's chapter on women's educational writing in *Literature, Education and Romanticism*,[63] the analysis of a female-authored Romantic-era novel focusing on female education, like *Belinda*, makes the fictional education of heroines with 'well-regulated minds' seem tame and unadventurous. Women's writing is seen as particularly weighted by notions of education as discipline, control and regulation, buttressed by reason, prudence and the suspicion of passion – with a few exceptions being made for radical 1790s writers such as Mary Wollstonecraft and Mary Hays, in whose world sexuality and sensibility are seen to play more positive roles.

This book, on the contrary, will show that self-regulation and self-control function unexpectedly in female-authored fictions of female education. In such works, the selfhood of the heroines is represented in a constant state of see-saw, under siege by elements, both from within and from without, that threaten their ability to govern themselves. Faced with such threats, the heroines, struggling to govern their own selves, make regulative moral elements such as 'self-control', 'discipline' or 'prudence' integral parts of their self-construction.

Clara Reeve's unhappily married Mrs Darnford uses a controlled language of reason and prudence to protest against her husband's excesses. Mary Hamilton's unhappy wife Mrs Lee also uses Lockeian, contractarian arguments and adduces the authority of her own reason to break out of the tyranny of her marriage. There is a complex dynamic constantly at play in these works between the broad poles of controlled reason/sense/strong government of self and mind, on the one hand, and play of emotions/sensibility/a letting go of controlled selfhood, on the other. On the whole, it would be true to say that *no* late eighteenth-century or early nineteenth-century British woman writer privileged the latter pole over the former. What one gets is a charting of the heroines' development in which a susceptibility and receptivity to emotion is overlaid by an educative process in which reason, self-control, prudence, fortitude and control give a patterned, cohesive subjectivity to these fictional selves. Yet, the underlying emotional vulnerability and near-abjection are never lost sight of in these narratives of education, as we shall see time and again. In Brunton's *Discipline*, for example, the mentor-figure Miss Mortimer recognizes that Ellen's greatest weakness – an impulse to do anything that she thinks will win her the affection of those she loves – is also one of her greatest strengths. Ellen must learn how to govern and channelize her desire for affection.

This desire for control over one's self cannot be written off as a purely repressive attempt to chain the heroines' subjectivity, given that there is no such thing as free, untrammelled subjectivity. Thus, while loss, pain and thwarted vocations form one pole in fictions of female education in this period, achievement, self-sufficiency, auto-didacticism and unusual or surprising episodes or ends in the educative process form the other pole, and are constructed over the underlying level of difficulty, pain and frustration.

Just as it is mistaken to straitjacket such fictions as narratives about disciplined female selves, so too it is incorrect to assume that most late eighteenth-century and early nineteenth-century fictions of female education are courtship novels about young heroines. Young ladies making their entrance into the world, unhappy wives, widows, single women, female authors and educationists, peasants, middle-aged and young servants or housekeepers, governesses – the age, marital status and social status of women undergoing fictional education are very varied indeed. Elizabeth Hamilton's creation Betty Mason is an unmarried servant-turned-governess. Mary Hamilton's Lady Frances Finlay is a landowner. Frances Burney's Juliet Granville, besides being the heroine of a courtship novel, is also a seamstress, a milliner and a paid companion. Mary Hamilton's Lady Filmer is a middle-aged married woman, mother and educator. Equally, a strikingly large number of female characters who educate others are neither biological mothers nor married women, but single or widowed – Reeve's Mrs Darnford, Mary Hamilton's Lady Frances Darnley, Elizabeth Hamilton's Mrs Fielding and Mrs Mason, and Mary Brunton's Miss Mortimer are cases in point. Such figures show what varied fictional forms the eighteenth-century ideal of the female educator could assume.

Self-realization or self-fulfilment, thus, does not necessarily come from marriage and the heterosexual family in the fictions I look at. When the category *Bildungsroman has* been applied to British women's fiction written in this period, it has usually been used to discuss courtship novels.[64] In *Unbecoming Women*, for example, Susan Fraiman,[65] analysing the novels of Burney and Austen among others, has argued that the female *Bildungsroman* inevitably shows, along with the development of the heroine, a simultaneous loss or deformation related to the gender of the protagonist. My book shows that in many late eighteenth-century and early nineteenth-century fictions of education, marriage, instead of being the ending or the end of female education, is rather a site of crisis – [66] as in the works of Mary Hamilton and Clara Reeve, where marriage most often thwarts female education and development, and where the education of many characters continues outside, after and beyond marriage.

Indeed, the fictions of education I examine show the fissuring of any simple category of 'conservatism' as regards the representation of same-sex bonds between women.[67] Caroline Gonda, while analysing the greater freedom from heterosexual ideology that Brunton the conservative shows, compared to Inchbald the radical, has remarked: 'In sexual politics, as in novels of education, the radicals and conservatives don't always line up as you'd expect.'[68] All the writers I look at privilege the educative and affective value of bonds between women, cutting across class, age and marital status. Two of the writers, Clara Reeve and Elizabeth

Hamilton, themselves single women, are the most explicit in their vindication of single women who act as educators, as well as the boldest articulators of the view that one should formulate plans of education for women without husbands. Elizabeth Hamilton's writing gives us a sense of female education as a process that occurs in a 'female world' (her own words), inhabited by female educators and pupils who are 'sisters adept in . . . free-masonry'. The reader of this book, and of the fictions I analyse, will have little sense of men as important figures in the process of female education; when she does encounter them, it will usually be in a context where they pose difficulties for the heroines – near-consistently, lovers, husbands, fathers and even mentor-heroes are shadowy, absent, ineffective or damaging educative presences in these works. This is equally true of courtship novels such as Brunton's, where the self-willed, self-regulatory heroines spend much of their time adventuring and wandering away from their prospective husbands in the public sphere.

The Female in the Public Sphere: Between the Private and the Public

Jürgen Habermas's work on the eighteenth-century public sphere saw the literary public sphere (unlike the political public sphere, which was far more exclusionary) as an arena in which women played a major role (although he made little of the fact); feminist scholarship has pursued this line of inquiry vigorously, even positing a female 'counter-public sphere' created by women writers.[69] Indeed, more and more recent work (such as that of Amanda Vickery[70]) has been breaking down the notion that the eighteenth century was characterized by the presence, real and representational, of completely separate spheres of the public and the private, and the stereotype that women were confined to the private sphere. My book adds to such work by showing the continual see-saw between public and private in fictions of female education.

The status of the writers I analyse is somewhere between the professional and the amateur, the domestic and the public, between the 'proper lady' and the 'woman writer', to use Mary Poovey's terms.[71] In their varied ways, all these writers show that propriety and gentility are no bar to their advocating women's greater participation in public affairs and trades of various sorts. Education, again, is a key term in this bridging of the public and the private.

Fiction, too, situated itself between the public and the private. Women writers produced their work in the private sphere, then saw their works circulating in the market – when readers bought or borrowed such fiction. They then read them in the domestic sphere, and found such works, as in the case of my authors, discussing history, politics and philosophy, while narrating patterns of female education and development. Mary Hamilton, for example, started off by claiming to write her book in her nursery as an aid to her daughters; yet, just some pages onwards, she was undertaking a sweeping survey of history. We also see her women characters holding public salon-type conversations on ambitious intellectual subjects. Clara Reeve wrote anti-abolitionist polemics in the 1790s. Elizabeth Hamilton, equally, also writing in the 1790s, opposed slavery, as did

Brunton in the post-revolutionary period. Elizabeth Hamilton saw women becoming rigorous and adept philosophers using their vantage point in the home, where, she argued, human nature is seen in its nakedness. And when she advocated greater female responsibility and involvement in philanthropic activities such as the running of charity schools, she saw such public work as benefiting from women's knowledge of domestic management.

Between Pliability and Self-Direction: Finding a Space

The most deep-seated tension in these works is the one I began this chapter with, between pliability and autonomy or self-direction in the process of education. Every one of these writers is showing ways in which their female characters learn to govern their own selves and find a place in the world, the school of adversity. Their heroines use such external elements as their reading, prescriptions, religion and morality to construct their selves, and they respect the authority of fathers, of the church, of established precepts of various sorts. And yet, again and again, we see strange and surprising uses of such forces and authorities operating on them. A daughter fallen on hard times remembers with gratitude how her mother had taught her to use Locke's *Essay Concerning the Human Understanding* to gain power and control over her own self. Another daughter tells her father that the suitor whom he would like her to marry is a rake, and invokes Christianity to question his acceptance of the sexual double standard. Another heroine, this time a married woman, repulses another rake by carrying on a learned argument with him on the illegitimacy of concubinage. Repeatedly, we see good daughters, good wives and good heroines using the miscellaneous resources yielded them by their education in ways that allow them, if in highly limited ways, to develop their own sense of autonomy – and all the while, they remain within a conservative framework, maintaining the hierarchies of society.

Straitjacketing Romantic-Era Women's Fictions of Education?
Complicating Categories

Eighteenth-century women writers' advocacy of better formal education for women has led Clifford Siskin to argue (using Mary Astell's *Serious Proposal*) that these writers 'engender' the modern disciplined subject, one of whose defining traits is the ability to cultivate herself and her mind. Education, and women's writing about it, is a marker of modernity for Siskin: 'Although this was certainly not the only factor, education could be said to assume its modern form only when women came to desire it.'[72] The novel too becomes, Siskin argues, a powerful instrument for the creation of the modern individual, who is disciplined, self-regulatory and cultivated – and from the mid-eighteenth century to the early nineteenth century, the novel is a feminized genre. By the beginning of the nineteenth century, according to Siskin, the novel, as part of the emerging discipline of English literature, starts to buttress English nationalism, the profession of letters and a remasculinization of the literary arena. This book, focusing on a transitional period when fiction was beginning to be recognized as respectable, shows that female-authored conservative fictions of female education were powerfully fissured at this time, resisting absorption into such neat disciplinary narratives.

In her influential work *Desire and Domestic Fiction: A Political History of the Novel*,[73] Nancy Armstrong also sees female-authored domestic fiction as a disciplining form, creating female subjects who epitomize and uphold the emerging bourgeois order. It is in the late eighteenth and early nineteenth centuries that Armstrong sees this process beginning. Implicit in Armstrong's work is a sense of the linear development of history, of transitions from the semi-feudal/courtly/aristocratic to the industrialized/bourgeois liberal order of the nineteenth century. For Armstrong, such 'professional' literary women as the ones I analyse are key agents in the change, veering more towards the emergent order.

I argue, however, that it is incorrect to see representative writers and heroines such as the ones I examine as hegemonic bourgeois subjects, or as agents of a middle-class cultural and professional revolution: such terms are blanket, facile categories that come nowhere near to capturing the strange disjunctions, alliances and congruences thrown up by these fictions. These writings complicate notions of what is residual and what is emergent, what is conservative and what is radical. And it is their writers' gender that unsettles such categories.

The writers I analyse did not have the obvious modernizing thrust that writers such as Mary Wollstonecraft, belonging to anti-Jacobin, pro-French Revolution radical formations, had. All of them believed in an older, hierarchical society, with the aristocracy, clergy and gentry playing an important part in the social order. They espoused an ideology of benevolence and paternalism. At the same time, they advocated female public vocations, including landowning, teaching and other paid trades. It would be incorrect to categorize such advocacy and representation of women's public vocations as 'middle-class professionalism', since these writers' social milieux, and the worlds they evoke in their fiction, are not categorizable as 'middle class'. Mary Hamilton's fictional world is full of duchesses and marchionesses, aristocratic spectacle, and masque-like entertainments reminiscent of Stuart times. Elizabeth Hamilton created an idealized vision of Scotland melded together by good landlords and an independent-minded, yet happily subordinate peasantry. Mary Brunton evoked a utopian, feudal Scotland. Each of these 'residual' worlds is crucial in the development of these writers' heroines.

Again, many of the ways in which my writers resisted the pressures of patriarchy drew on older formations: Reeve's idealization of Madame de Maintenon and her *ancien régime* female community of St-Cyr is a case in point. In Reeve's planned female community, written during the crisis-ridden 1790s, poor gentlewomen are trained in paid trades which were already becoming residual because of industrialization. Or consider the importance of loyal, rural mistress–servant relationships in Reeve and Hamilton. Such alliances enable the gentry-born or aristocratic or peasant heroines to evade marriage, to earn their own living, to find spaces for female solidarity and cohabitation, or exercise female authority.

Frances Darnford, who finds fulfilment in escaping marriage and setting up school with a carpenter's widow; Betty Mason, the peasant heroine with a limp who does not marry and devotes her energies to renovating a Scottish Highland village; Ellen Percy, who finds refuge and fulfilment in another Scottish village with strong feudal loyalties and structures – such heroines do not fit Armstrong's model. These fictions do not create heroines who are good domestic women reinforcing a new middle-class order from their position in the private sphere. On the contrary, they trouble it, in ways that are deeply uncomfortable. This book does not tell a celebratory story: rather, it asks that we see such disturbing passages as Clara Reeve's racist, anti-abolitionist polemics, or the hostility towards class mobility found in all of these writings, as symptomatic of the disjunctions that are built into our post-Enlightenment legacy of education.

Romantic-Era Conservative British Women's Fictions of Female Education as Cruxes of Historical and Social Tensions

Such fictions of education unsettle linear narratives of literary history and development. Like the fictional narratives of development this book analyses, the narrative of development that we as readers and critics construct for late eighteenth-century and early nineteenth-century women's writing proves to be riddled with tensions and ambulatoriness, rather than telling a story of blanket disappearances and emergences.

Inscribing such disjunctions and non-linearities into our map of Romantic-era Britain, in turn, creates a more intellectually rich and complex, more politically unsettling picture of the period and the country. We enter a world where, for example, a learned, poor Suffolk clergyman's daughter, feeling let down by the masculine aristocracy of her country, returns to a seventeenth-century French aristocratic woman as the norm for a feminized educative ruling class. We grapple with a Scottish female philosopher taking a position against the ongoing triumphal march of industrialization and against its prophet Adam Smith, and instead, positing rural Scottish kirk schools as the ideal locus for creating good Scottish citizens, men and women. These individual cases, and the positions of contestation that such writers adopt, are symptoms of deep-seated tensions and fissures in these women's contemporary culture and society.

More than this, I would argue that such tensions and contests are consummately foregrounded *precisely* by writers such as the ones I look at, because they were at one and the same time members of the gentry or the aristocracy *and* women, and because they wrote in fiction, itself a site of contestation for legitimacy, while making education, yet another concept constituted by tensions, a discursive node in their work.

This book complicates many categories and makes many uncomfortable claims – about feminism, about the Enlightenment, about Romanticism, about notions of education and development, and about Britain in the age of the

Industrial and French Revolutions. It argues that it pays to take seriously women who were not supporters of the French Revolution or of the emerging Industrial Revolution, and who did not exhibit obvious pro-democratic or emergent bourgeois notions. It shows that such women wrote passionately and polemically on issues of national, social and political import, most importantly through the guiding notion of education, and that such writing defamiliarizes and questions our notions of what is 'progressive', what is 'pre-modern', what is 'emergent bourgeois' and what is 'feminist'. Deeply old-fashioned in some ways, the writers we shall encounter asked fundamental, uncomfortable questions about their world order, plotted surprising and strange paths of growth and education for their heroines, and keep us alertly poised on the edge of the constitutive dialectics of education.

Notes and References

1 'Don Juan' Canto I, stanzas xv–xvi, in *Complete Poetical Works of Byron* (Oxford and New York: Oxford University Press, 1970), pp. 638–39.

2 Erasmus Darwin, *A Plan for the Conduct of Female Education in Boarding Schools* (London: Joseph Johnson, 1797), p. 10.

3 He refers to the work, both fiction and educational writing, of the celebrated Anglo–Irish woman of letters Maria Edgeworth, and to *Coelebs in Search of a Wife* (1808), the only novel by the Evangelical conservative social and educational reformer, Hannah More.

4 Cheryl Turner, *Living by the Pen: Women Writers of the Eighteenth Century* (London and New York: Routledge, 1994), p. 60.

5 John Feather, *A History of British Publishing* (London: Croom Helm, 1988), pp. 96–97.

6 For example, Margaret Anne Doody, *Frances Burney: The Life in the Works* (Cambridge: Cambridge University Press, c.1988); Julia Epstein, *The Iron Pen: Frances Burney and the Politics of Women's Writing* (Bristol: Bristol Classical Press, 1989).

7 See, for example, Marilyn Butler, *Maria Edgeworth: A Literary Life* (Oxford: Clarendon Press, 1972); Mitzi Myers, 'The Dilemmas of Gender as Double-Voiced Narrative; or, Maria Edgeworth Mothers the *Bildungsroman*', in *The Idea of the Novel in the Eighteenth Century*, edited by Robert W. Uphaus (East Lansing: Colleagues Press, 1986), pp. 67–96; Mitzi Myers, 'Romancing the Moral Tale: Maria Edgeworth and the Problematics of Pedagogy', in *Romanticism and Children's Literature in Nineteenth-Century England*, edited by James Holt McGavran (Athens and London: University of Georgia Press, 1991), pp. 96–128; Mitzi Myers, 'We Must Grant a Romance Writer a Few Impossibilities': "Unnatural Incident" and Narrative Motherhood in Maria Edgeworth's "Emilie de Coulanges"', *The Wordsworth Circle*, 27:3 (Summer 1996), pp. 151–57.

8 Turner, *Living by the Pen*, p. 39 and passim. Turner studies the period from 1770 to 1800. For the next thirty years, when the volume of women's fiction continued to rise, see Peter Garside and Anthony Mandal, 'Producing Fiction in Britain, 1800–1829', Cardiff Corvey website, http://www.cf.ac.uk/uwcc/secap/corvey/articles.html, accessed 15 April 1998.

9 Ina Ferris, *The Achievement of Literary Authority: Gender, History and the Waverley Novels* (Ithaca and London: Cornell University Press, 1991).

10 William Hazlitt, unsigned review of *The Wanderer*, *Edinburgh Review*, 24 (1815), pp. 320–38.

11 See, for example, Paul Langford, *A Polite and Commercial People: England 1727–1783* (Oxford and New York: Oxford University Press, 1989), pp. 109–16; G.J. Barker-Benfield, *The Culture of Sensibility: Sex and Society in Eighteenth-Century Britain* (Chicago and London: University of Chicago Press, 1992).

[12] Lawrence Stone, *The Family, Sex and Marriage in England, 1500–1800* (Harmondsworth: Penguin Books, 1979).

[13] Randolph Trumbach, *The Rise of the Egalitarian Family: Aristocratic Kinship and Domestic Relations in Eighteenth-Century England* (New York: Academic Press, 1978).

[14] See, for example, Susan Moller Okin, 'Women and the Making of the Sentimental Family', *Philosophy and Public Affairs*, 11:1 (Winter 1982), pp. 65–88.

[15] See Susan Skedd, 'Women Teachers and the Expansion of Girls' Schooling in England, c. 1760–1820', in *Gender in the Eighteenth Century: Roles, Representations and Responsibilities*, edited by Hannah Barker and Elaine Chalus (London and New York: Longman, 1997), pp. 101–25.

[16] For an overview of these trends, see Josephine Kamm, *Hope Deferred: Girls' Education in English History* (London: Methuen and Co, 1965), pp. 83–151.

[17] According to the records provided by marriage registers, in 1754, 60 per cent of males and 35 per cent of females could sign their names. By 1800, the percentage of men was unchanged, while 45 per cent of women could now sign their names. Thus, three out of every four women were illiterate in the early Hanoverian period, two out of every three by the accession of George III. Rosemary O'Day, *Education and Society 1500–1800: The Social Foundations of Education in Early Modern Britain* (London and New York: Longman, 1982), p. 190. See also J. Paul Hunter, *Before Novels: The Cultural Contexts of Eighteenth-Century English Fiction* (New York and London: W.W. Norton and Co., 1990), pp. 69–72.

[18] Dorothy Gardiner, *English Girlhood at School: A Study of Women's Education through Twelve Centuries* (London: Oxford University Press, 1929), pp. 393–438.

[19] For an overview of women's non-fictional didactic writing in the same period, see Ruth Alexandra Symes, 'Educating Women: The Preceptress and Her Pen, 1780–1820' (unpublished D.Phil. thesis, University of York, 1996).

[20] Jane Marcet, *Conversations on Political Economy* (5th edn, London: Longman etc., 1824).

[21] Catharine Macaulay, *The History of England from the Ascension of James I to that of the Brunswick Line* (London: Nourse, Dodsley, Johnston and others, 1763–83).

[22] Ann Bermingham, 'Elegant Females and Gentlemen Connoisseurs: The Commerce in Culture and Self-Image in Eighteenth-Century England', in *The Consumption of Culture 1600–1800*, edited by Ann Bermingham and John Brewer (London and New York: Routledge, 1995), pp. 489–513.

[23] See Jane Rendall, *The Origins of Modern Feminism 1780-1860: Women in Britain, France, and the United States, 1780–1860* (Basingstoke and London: Macmillan, 1985), pp. 108–49.

[24] Jane Barker, *The Galesia Trilogy and Selected Manuscript Poems*, edited by Carol Shiner Wilson (Oxford: Oxford University Press, 1997); Mary Davys, *The Reform'd Coquet, Familiar Letters Betwixt a Gentleman and a Lady, and The Accomplish'd Rake*, edited by Martha Bowden (Lexington: University Press of Kentucky, 1999).

[25] Ros Ballaster, *Seductive Forms: Women's Amatory Fiction from 1684 to 1740* (Oxford: Clarendon Press, 1992).

[26] Nancy Armstrong, *Desire and Domestic Fiction: A Political History of the Novel* (New York and Oxford: Oxford University Press, 1987).

[27] Jane Spencer, *The Rise of the Woman Novelist: From Aphra Behn to Jane Austen* (Oxford: Basil Blackwell, 1987), pp. 140–80.

[28] John Tinnon Taylor, *Early Opposition to the English Novel* (New York: 1943), p. 84, quoted in Terry Lovell, *Consuming Fiction* (London: Verso, 1987), p. 9.

[29] Lovell, *Consuming Fiction*, p. 8.

[30] William St Clair, 'The Explosion of Reading in the Romantic Period', lecture series, Faculty of English, University of Cambridge, Michaelmas term 1997; forthcoming as a book.

[31] Anna Laetitia Barbauld, ed., *The British Novelists: with an Essay, and Prefaces, Biographical and Critical*, 50 vols (London: Rivington, 1810).

[32] Michael McKeon, *The Origins of the English Novel, 1600–1740* (Baltimore: Johns Hopkins University Press, 1987).

33 'Novels, music, poetry, and gallantry, all tend to make women the creatures of sensation, and their character is thus formed in the mould of folly while they are acquiring accomplishments.' Mary Wollstonecraft, *A Vindication of the Rights of Woman*, edited by Carol H. Poston (New York and London: W.W. Norton and Co., 1988), p. 60.

34 Macaulay argues that children and adolescents shouldn't read novels, but that adults could learn a great deal from the best examples of the genre. Catharine Macaulay, *Letters on Education* (London: C. Dilly, 1790; rpt, Oxford and New York: Woodstock Books, 1994), p. 145.

35 Pennington hopes that her daughters will 'scarce ever meddle' with novels or romances, her one major exception being *The Vicar of Wakefield*. Lady Sarah Pennington, *An Unfortunate Mother's Advice to Her Daughters*, in *The Young Lady's Pocket Library, or Parental Monitor*, with a new introduction by Vivien Jones (Dublin: John Archer, 1790; rpt, Bristol: Thoemmes Press, 1995), p. 88.

36 While Darwin prohibits young ladies from reading 'amorous' novels or romances, he allows 'serious' (including Burney and Charlotte Smith) and 'humorous' varieties to be read. Darwin, *Plan for the Conduct of Female Education in Boarding Schools*, pp. 33–37.

37 Mary Hays, 'Letter to Mrs—, on Reading Romances', in Mary Hays, *Letters and Essays, Moral and Miscellaneous* (London: T. Knox, 1793; rpt, New York and London: Garland Publishing, 1974), pp. 86–98.

38 Jan Fergus, 'Women Readers: A Case Study', in *Women and Literature in Britain 1700–1800*, edited by Vivien Jones (Cambridge: Cambridge University Press, 2000), pp. 155–76.

39 Didactic fiction creates a very particular kind of multiplicity of registers, more specifically knowledge-oriented than Bakhtin's influential notion of 'heteroglossia' (a continual collision of different kinds of linguistic register and social discourse) as a defining characteristic of the novel. For Bakhtin's term, see, for example, 'From the Pre-history of Novelistic Discourse', in M. M. Bakhtin, *The Dialogic Imagination: Four Essays*, edited by Michael Holquist, translated by Caryl Emerson and Michael Holquist (Austin: University of Texas Press, 1981), pp. 41–83.

40 See, for example, Rendall, *The Origins of Modern Feminism*, pp. 7–32; Sylvana Tomaselli, 'The Enlightenment Debate on Women', *History Workshop Journal*, 19 (1985), pp. 101–24; Dena Goodman, *The Republic of Letters: A Cultural History of the French Enlightenment* (Ithaca and London: Cornell University Press, 1994); Joel Schwarz, *The Sexual Politics of Jean-Jacques Rousseau* (Chicago: University of Chicago Press, 1984).

41 Cf. Dena Goodman, 'Enlightenment Salons: The Convergence of Female and Philosophic Ambitions', *Eighteenth-Century Studies*, 22:3 (Spring 1989), pp. 329–50; Mary Trouille, 'Sexual/Textual Politics in the Enlightenment: Diderot and D'Epinay Respond to Thomas's *Essay on Women*', *British Journal for Eighteenth-Century Studies*, 19:1 (Spring 1996), pp. 1–15; Roland Bonnel and Catherine Rubinger, eds, *Femmes Savantes et Femmes d'Esprit: Women Intellectuals of the French Eighteenth Century* (New York: Peter Lang, 1994); Burton Pollin, 'Mary Hays on Women's Rights in the *Monthly Magazine*', *Etudes Anglaises*, 24:3 (1971), pp. 271–82.

42 Anne K. Mellor, 'A Criticism of Their Own: Romantic Women Literary Critics', in *Questioning Romanticism*, edited by John Beer (Baltimore and London: Johns Hopkins University Press, 1995), pp. 29–48.

43 Aidan Day, *Romanticism*, The New Critical Idiom (London: Routledge, 1996), pp. 126–82.

44 See Jacqueline Pearson, *Women's Reading in Britain 1750–1850: A Dangerous Occupation* (Cambridge: Cambridge University Press, 1998).

45 Clifford Siskin, *The Historicity of Romantic Discourse* (Oxford and New York: Oxford University Press, 1988), pp. 90ff; Clifford Siskin, 'Epilogue: The Rise of Novelism', in *Cultural Institutions of the Novel*, edited by Deidre Lynch and William B. Warner (Durham and London: Duke University Press, 1996), pp. 423–40.

46 Elizabeth Benger, *The Female Geniad* (London: Hookham and Carpenter, 1791; reprinted with repagination, Providence: Brown Women Writers Project, 1993), pp. 7–8.

[47] Ruth Perry, *The Celebrated Mary Astell: An Early English Feminist* (Chicago and London: University of Chicago Press, 1986).

[48] For discussions of such writers, see, for example, Elaine Hobby, *Virtue of Necessity: English Women's Writing 1649–1688* (London: Virago, 1988), pp. 190–203; Hilda Smith, *Reason's Disciples: Seventeenth-Century English Feminists* (Urbana: University of Illinois Press, 1982).

[49] Ellen Moers, *Literary Women* (London: W.H. Allen, 1977), pp. 211–42.

[50] See Sylvia Harcstark Myers, *The Bluestocking Circle: Women, Friendship, and the Life of the Mind in Eighteenth-Century England* (Oxford: Clarendon Press, 1990); *Bluestocking Feminism: Writings of the Bluestocking Circle, 1738–1785*, general editor Gary Kelly, 6 vols (London: Pickering and Chatto, 1999).

[51] Sarah Fielding, *The Adventures of David Simple*, edited with an introduction by Malcolm Kelsall, Oxford World's Classics ([1744] Oxford and New York: Oxford University Press, 1994), p. 101.

[52] Frances Brooke, *The Excursion*, edited by Paula R. Backscheider and Hope D. Cotton ([1777] Lexington: University Press of Kentucky, 1997).

[53] Charlotte Lennox, *The Life of Harriot Stuart, Written by Herself*, edited with an introduction by Susan Kubica Howard ([1750] Madison: Fairleigh Dickinson University Press; London: Associated University Presses, 1995).

[54] Marilyn Butler, *Jane Austen and the War of Ideas* (Oxford: Clarendon Press, 1987).

[55] Claudia L Johnson, *Jane Austen: Women, Politics, and the Novel* (Chicago and London: University of Chicago Press, 1988).

[56] Gary Kelly, *Women, Writing and Revolution, 1790–1827* (Oxford: Clarendon Press, 1993); Gary Kelly, *Revolutionary Feminism: The Mind and Career of Mary Wollstonecraft* (Basingstoke: Macmillan, 1992).

[57] Mitzi Myers, 'Reform or Ruin: "A Revolution in Female Manners"', *Studies in Eighteenth-Century Culture*, 11 (1982), pp. 199–216.

[58] Mary Hays, *Appeal to the Men of Great Britain in Behalf of Women*, in *The Radicals: Revolutionary Women*, edited by Marie Mulvey Roberts and Tamae Mizuta, with an introduction by Marie Mulvey Roberts (London: Joseph Johnson, 1798; rpt, London: Routledge/Thoemmes Press, 1994); Mary Anne Radcliffe, *The Female Advocate; or an Attempt to Recover the Rights of Women from Male Usurpation*, in *The Radicals: Revolutionary Women*, edited by Marie Mulvey Roberts and Tamae Mizuta, with an introduction by Marie Mulvey Roberts (London: Vernor and Hood, 1799; rpt, London: Routledge/Thoemmes Press, 1994).

[59] Mary Brunton, *Discipline*, introduced by Fay Weldon ([1815]; rpt, London: Pandora Press, 1986), p. 211.

[60] Marc Redfield, *Phantom Formations: Aesthetic Ideology and the Bildungsroman* (Ithaca and London: Cornell University Press, 1996). Fritz Martin shows that, much before Dilthey's famous use of the category in his *Das Leben Schleiermachers* (1922), Karl von Morgenstern had used the term in a course of lectures in 1819–20. Fritz Martin, 'Bildungsroman: Term and Theory', in *Reflection and Action: Essays on the Bildungsroman*, edited by James Hardin (Columbia: University of South Carolina Press, 1991), pp. 1–25.

[61] Gary Kelly highlights the thrust of professionalization in revolutionary and post-revolutionary women's writing, in his *Women, Writing and Revolution*.

[62] See my chapter on Reeve, in particular my discussion of the letter Mary Anne Radcliffe quotes in *The Female Advocate*.

[63] Alan Richardson, *Literature, Education and Romanticism: Reading as Social Practice, 1780–1832* (Cambridge: Cambridge University Press, 1994), pp. 167–212.

[64] Mitzi Myers, however, convincingly analyses Edgeworth's children's stories as *Bildungsromans*. Myers, 'The Dilemmas of Gender as Double-Voiced Narrative'.

[65] Susan Fraiman, *Unbecoming Women: British Women Writers and the Novel of Development* (New York: Columbia University Press, 1993).

[66] 'How women are to exist in that state where there is to be neither marriage nor giving in marriage, we are not told.' Wollstonecraft, *Vindication of the Rights of Woman*, p. 34.

[67] On eighteenth-century female same-sex bonds, see Betty Rizzo, *Companions without Vows: Relationships among Eighteenth-Century British Women* (Athens and London: University of Georgia Press, 1994); Emma Donoghue, *Passions between Women: British Lesbian Culture, 1688–1801* (London: Scarlet Press, 1993).

[68] Caroline Gonda, *Reading Daughters' Fictions 1709–1834: Novels and Society from Manley to Edgeworth* (Cambridge: Cambridge University Press, 1996), p. 202.

[69] Jürgen Habermas, *The Structural Transformation of the Public Sphere: An Inquiry into a Category of Bourgeois Society*, translated by Thomas Burger (Cambridge: Polity Press, 1989); Johanna Meehan, ed., *Feminists Read Habermas: Gendering the Subject of Discourse* (New York and London: Routledge, 1995); Joan B. Landes, ed., *Feminism, the Public and the Private* (Oxford and New York: Oxford University Press, 1998); Anne Mellor, 'Joanna Baillie and the Counter-Public Sphere', *Studies in Romanticism*, 33:4 (Winter 1994), pp. 559–67. .

[70] Amanda Vickery, 'Golden Age to Separate Spheres? A Review of the Categories and Chronology of English Women's History', *The Historical Journal*, 36:2 (June 1993), pp. 383–414; Amanda Vickery, *The Gentleman's Daughter* (New Haven and London: Yale University Press, 1998).

[71] Mary Poovey, *The Proper Lady and the Woman Writer: Ideology as Style in the Works of Mary Wollstonecraft, Mary Shelley and Jane Austen* (Chicago and London: University of Chicago Press, 1984).

[72] Clifford Siskin, *The Work of Writing: Literature and Social Change in Britain, 1700–1830* (Baltimore and London: Johns Hopkins University Press, 1998), p. 56.

[73] Armstrong, *Desire and Domestic Fiction*.

CHAPTER ONE
'The difficult study of others and herself':
Lady Mary Hamilton

'My mind is amphibious, and can subsist in different elements', wrote Lady Mary Hamilton[1] to her nephew, the Earl of Leven, at the age of seventy-five, from an estate in Jamaica.[2] Nor was her claim unjustified: in the course of a varied and eventful life, she had played the roles of an earl's daughter, a commoner's wife, an abandoned wife with children to bring up, a British novelist, an expatriate in France, a writer in French and an absentee estate owner in Jamaica. Both aristocratic and marginal within that order because of her gender, beliefs and personal circumstances, Hamilton also knew well that women are *the* great amphibians. Her novels, most of them written in the 1770s (*Letters from the Duchess de Crui*, 1776; *Memoirs of the Marchioness de Louvoi*, 1777; *Munster Village*, 1778), contain some of the most wide-ranging and eloquent eighteenth-century fictional discussions of female education.

Lady Mary argues for the cultivation of the female mind and, at the same time, that such cultivation should also prepare women for lives where 'amphibious' minds are indispensable to cope with vicissitudes. Yet this does not entail any weakening of rigour or scope: on the contrary, whether in the study of literature in leisure hours, or in writing books, or in coping with difficult marriages, women are asked to live by principles based on both intelligence and ethics. The letter in which the quotation I began with occurs, for example, shows that Hamilton is by no means meekly submissive to the pressure of circumstances. She has left France, her residence for over two decades, to collect rents in person from an estate in Jamaica, because she had not been receiving the full amount. Once she has received the money, she cannot return to France, where the Napoleonic War is in full swing: her letter is dated three days before Waterloo. Hamilton may well have been a slave owner in Jamaica – showing, as readers will find throughout this book, that categories of inequality such as gender, race and class are often disturbingly aligned in the life and works of these conservative women writers. Yet Hamilton also finds the white population in Jamaica obsessed with money-making, devoid of mental energy: 'I think, of all the places I have seen, one may live there at the smallest expense of wit, as by all rules of economy, the disbursements bearing proportion to the receivings, one ought to lay out very little. My mind was in a palsy, and its faculties benumbed.'[3] Such frugality in the economics of wit being unacceptable, Hamilton decides to return to London. Her life, like her books, is full of the conviction that one must, as a woman, be prepared for changes in circumstances, but not give in blindly to them.

Of Hamilton's 1770s novels, two are epistolary. The authorial voice does not appear directly; instead, it is split into a number of female voices, each interested in female education, generating a polyphony of perspectives. While the authorial voice *is* heard directly in *Munster Village*, here too letters play an important role. Lady Mary's fictions of education are situated firmly in a post-Bluestocking era where female intellectual and literary achievement are beginning to be celebrated in some quarters. She uses Hester Chapone's enlightened conduct book for women (*Letters on the Improvement of the Mind*, 1773), as well as Enlightenment treatises on the history of women being published at this time. Hamilton has an unabashedly intellectual tone in much of her fiction, with long sections expressing outrage at the denial of female education, using the language of Lockeian Empiricist psychology. She praises such Bluestocking figures as Elizabeth Carter, as well as mid-eighteenth-century writers of fiction, such as Frances Brooke and Elizabeth Griffith. In my second chapter, on Clara Reeve, we shall see that Reeve is also a great admirer of such novelists and other Bluestocking novelists like Sarah Scott and Sarah Fielding, whom she places in her canon of fiction and praises as public educators. Reeve sees fiction as a form of knowledge, with women having a privileged role in the production and dissemination of such knowledge. Hamilton's fiction exemplifies Reeve's ideal of educative fiction – Hamilton uses the form of the epistolary novel with multiple voices, male and female, to create a theoretical debate on female education, as well as to exemplify through her characters the possibilities, frustrations and intransigences of female education.

As my introduction points out, it has been argued that the second half of the eighteenth century sees a 'feminization' of polite British culture,[4] with the hallmarks of refinement, sensibility and an acknowledgement of women's important role in this polite order. Lady Mary's fiction might seem on a cursory reading to exemplify this period, with her glamorous, intellectual and benevolent aristocratic heroines, her love of the cultivation of fine arts, her depiction of *salon*-type *conversaziones* with learned women at the centre, and her emphasis on the graciously powerful women's role in the improvement of female education and in the 'circulation of social kindness'.

On the contrary, Hamilton uses the language of cultivation, refinement and politeness to create women characters and paradigms of female education which are resistant to established notions about marriage, the limits of feminine influence and the goals of female education. Hamilton's world is also one of despotic or capricious husbands, of trials and adventures for her heroines, of dark, bleak perspectives on marriage, of intelligent, quirky old maids and exemplary seduced maidens. Quintessential exemplars of a culture of politeness, refinement and feminization, Hamilton's fictions also continually show up the rifts, shadows and contradictions in this culture.

Biographical Details

Lady Mary's novels are peopled mainly by aristocratic personages: the Duchess de Crui, Sir Robert and Lady Filmer, the Marchioness de Louvoi, Lady Frances Darnley and so on. This is not accidental. Lady Mary Leslie (later Walker, still later Hamilton) was the youngest daughter of Elizabeth Moneypenny and of Alexander, fifth Earl of Leven and fourth Earl of Melville. Again, the large number of intelligent maternal or quasi-maternal educators in her works (Mrs Trueman, Lady Filmer, Mrs Pierpont, Mrs Harris, the Marchioness de Louvoi) seems to have had a real-life counterpart in her own much-admired mother, of whom she wrote in 1779 that she was 'the best of mothers, whose whole life has been a pattern of unerring excellence'.[5]

From her father, Lady Mary would appear to have inherited respect for a useful, professional education, and for the world of letters in general (both expressed frequently in her novels). Her father had been a younger son, who had succeeded to the title only after the deaths of his brother and nephew. He had been bred for a profession, completing his study of law at Leiden. Charles Mackay, later professor of civil history at Edinburgh, the Earl's erstwhile tutor, was a life-long friend of the family. The Earl also appears to have been an active patron of intellectuals and men of letters, obtaining a post for the famous Scottish intellectual Hugh Blair in a parish near him in 1742. The Edinburgh intelligentsia, then, were no strangers to Lady Mary's family. Her writings, in fact, show marked traces of the Scottish Enlightenment: she was familiar with Hume's philosophy, criticizing his scepticism and atheism, and praising his writings on taste. Her interests in history and the science of the mind, too, bear the imprint of an Enlightenment formation.

Hamilton's private life was bedevilled by unhappiness. While Lady Mary's sisters both married earls, she married a certain Dr James Walker, of her home county of Fifeshire, and had four children by him. The repeated anatomizing in her works of women's unhappiness in marriage obviously had a personal charge. In another letter to her nephew, Lady Mary ascribes her career as author to economic necessity, as a result of being abandoned by her husband. She writes that she had recourse to literature when she found herself unhappy in marriage; she 'hazarded' the 'effronterie' of publication 'to clothe, feed and educate' her children, all the while aware that '[n]otoriety to women is destructive, at least collectively and generally speaking'. Characteristically, however, this apparently reluctant entry into authorship becomes a successful *intellectual* exercise: '. . . there are few persons so weak as to be incapable of understanding a subject if they devote their constant and undivided attention to it.'[6]

Lady Mary continued her literary activities all her life (her last novel, *La Famille du Duc de Popoli*, written in French, was published in 1810[7]). She took pride in her authorship, though she was both resigned to and critical of the fact that most women authors do not, because of their gender, receive fame, seen as a masculine prerogative:

Ladies in this age have greatly distinguished themselves in literature, and there can be no reason why they should not soar above vulgar conceptions, as well as the men. Knowledge, like the cheery light, and genial warmth of the sun, may be participated [*sic*] by numbers, without the least diminution of the influence shed upon a few, why then should it be refused to women? A woman truly virtuous, in the utmost extent of this expression, has virtue of a purer kind than any philosopher has ever shewn. Since she knows, if she has good sense, and without which there can be no virtue, that mankind is too much prejudiced against her sex, to give her any degree of that fame, which is so great a spur to their greatest actions.[8]

The constellation of terms in this passage – an emphasis on virtue, defined in a way that has nothing to do with the conventional meaning of sexual chastity, and on knowledge, good sense and the denial of fame to women – is typical of Hamilton. Women's reputation or fame, whether in their personal life or for their achievements, is a persistent concern of hers: while she criticizes the way women's reputations can be destroyed by the world (Miss Harris and Lucy Lee in *Munster Village*, Miss N– in *Letters from the Duchess de Crui*), she also gives fame to the most powerful of her women characters (in particular Lady Frances Darnley in *Munster Village*), creating a gallery of what I analyse as 'female virtuosos'.

In real life, too, Hamilton cultivated herself as a serious woman of letters. From the memoirs of the French Romantic intellectual Charles Nodier, who acted as secretary to Hamilton and her friend Sir Herbert Croft, we gain a picture of a woman in her seventies who worked with enthusiasm and diligence at a French novel she was writing. Nodier describes his employer in near-rhapsodic terms: 'Plùs que septuagénaire, mais . . . fraîche et presque jolie . . . un esprit riche, cultivé, ingénieux, fécond et peut-être trop fécond.'[9] ['More than seventy, but . . . still fresh and almost pretty . . . a rich, cultivated, ingenious, fecund spirit, perhaps too fecund.'] Hamilton apparently started writing at four in the morning, her day finishing with a reading out of what she had written in the evening.[10] In 1818, at the age of nearly eighty, she was trying to procure copies of her English novels from the circulating libraries, claiming that the different editions had all been sold out within three years.[11] In 1815 she was thinking of publishing a work in French, and in 1818 offering to send her French novel, *Duc de Popoli*, to her nephew, telling him also that *Munster Village* was her best work. Authority, then, whether literary or otherwise, was something she willingly took on.

In the 'Address to the Public' in her earliest work, *Letters from the Duchess de Crui* (1776), Hamilton uses a female and domestic author-persona. Claiming a vantage point from her 'nursery', surrounded by children, she claims that her writings are intended for her children – she represents herself as another of the maternal educators that crop up in her work. She adduces for her writing the authority of life rather than books ('not . . . *opinion* but *experience*, not . . . *logic* but . . . *life*'[12]). Throughout her oeuvre, she condemns the pedantic, authoritative but ultimately useless knowledge that men often receive in formal education from 'logic' or the 'opinion' of scholastic wrangling. This is at least partly a defensive position, but it also contains a serious plea that the knowledge women gain from life should be considered an integral part of their education. Here, the theme of the conflict between formal and experiential education comes up, as it will for the rest of the writers I analyse.

Later, in the voice of the Duchess de Crui, Hamilton argues for her right to use her 'commonplace book', so often the repository of randomly culled knowledge for women. She explicitly claims to write a work for her own sex: the full title is *Letters from the Duchess de Crui and Others, wherein the Character of the Female Sex, with Their Rank, Importance, and Consequence, Is Stated, and Their Relative Duties in Life Are Enforced.* Conservatism seems the hallmark of the title, with the stress on hierarchies and on already established relative duties,[13] to be 'enforced'. This is a morally charged project very aware of taxonomies and social hierarchies – an old-fashioned conduct book for women. The conservatism is deceptive, however, as the dedication itself makes clear, saying in forthright terms that this will be a work which will try to advance female knowledge.

> The author has ever lamented the fate of her sex being condemned to ignorance, or prevented from exercising their noblest mental faculties. . . . It cannot be unattended with advantage, to open our minds to the accession of new ideas . . . to reflect, and to distinguish, in order to enlarge the sphere of our knowledge, and enoble [*sic*] our intellects.[14]

The Female Mind

The groundwork for Hamilton's framework of ideas lies in her view of the human mind, seen as a fascinating object: '. . . to trace the origin of my ideas, would be an endless task, and would be a history of itself; it would be no unentertaining, no unsuccessful enquiry to examine the progress of our minds.'[15] In arguing for the intrinsic interest of the origin and association of ideas in the human mind, in a context that upholds her right to use passages from that miscellany of female knowledge, the commonplace book, the Duchess de Crui is also giving dignity to the worth and capacity of the *female* mind. A child of a post-Lockeian age and a contemporary of Hume, Hamilton believes (like Elizabeth Hamilton) that, particularly for women, the science of the mind is of great importance. One of her characters, the Marchioness de Louvoi, a powerful maternal educator, teaches her daughter the importance of Locke in this regard:

> she recommended to my frequent and careful perusal Mr Locke's admirable *Essay on the Understanding*, which she said would teach me a true use of books, and a right method of managing our own thoughts. She also recommended to me, as a rational being, the study of morality . . . and of the frame and constitution of the human mind, its powers, capacities, passions, and the end of its existence, a most ample field for the exercise and improvement of my reason![16]

For women, the human mind has a dual interest, according to Hamilton. At a purely intellectual level, it gives women systematic knowledge of ethics and psychology. One is reminded of Mary Astell, and her linking of women's reason and the imperative to gain knowledge with their status as Christians. The intellectual and ethical exercise of one's faculties has the practical advantage, too, of giving women some amount of control over their own selves and lives. One cannot underestimate the value Hamilton places on 'right method' – the study of the mind gives method and control to women's self-management.

The other importance of attention to the human mind is that it grants gender equality: 'had women the same advantages of education as men, there would be no room to doubt but that they would be equal to them, in the sciences, and every branch of useful knowledge.'[17] The knowledge that an educated woman aspires to is not passively acquired, nor unrelated to experience; women can lay claim to 'every branch of *useful* knowledge' (emphasis mine), as well as the 'sciences', signalling the realm of more institutionalized forms of knowledge: many of Hamilton's women characters are knowledgeable in the sciences, in the modern sense, such as botany and physics.

For Hamilton, cultivation of female knowledge, cultivation of female virtue (not, we remember, synonymous with female chastity) and cultivation of female talents are parts of an integrated ideal of female selfhood. Even Mrs Pierpont, a character contemptuous of established systems of formal education, defends 'learned ladies':

> What a mistaken idea do the men form of a learned lady: the only fault which a woman, that has abilities and a fluency of words, is likely to fall into, is an impertinence or affectation of distinction. Where talents are given, should we wish them either to be *uncultivated*, or *unacknowledged*? . . . Virtue, truth, and knowledge, are the only objects worthy of our being solicitous after; and these we have minds capable of reaching in the most perfect manner.[18]

Once the female mind is given its due dignity, it is a short step to espousing an ambitious view of woman's role in general. She should have the highest aims (virtue, truth and knowledge), and her talents should be acknowledged and cultivated: a strongly meritocratic charge here.

Women in the Public Sphere

Enlargement of the sphere of women's knowledge brings with it the potential enlargement of all spheres of women's lives. One clear indication of this potential enlargement is Lady Filmer's long argument (encompassing two letters to Sir James Bruce) in *Letters from the Duchess de Crui*, that throughout history women have played a prominent role in the public sphere: in politics, governance, learning and oratory. The main work that she uses (and acknowledges) for her argument is a translation of an important Enlightenment text on women, Antoine Thomas's *Essay on the Character, Manners and Genius of Women in Different Ages* (1772; translated 1773).[19]

Thomas's work aims to present 'a historical picture, an assemblage of facts and observations, which may serve as the elements of a didactic work', which 'will perhaps show, that women are susceptible of all the qualities which religion, society, or government would choose to assign them'.[20] He presents a progressive, and in many ways positive, picture of the position of women in history; yet, his ultimate standpoint is a combination of *galanterie* and pessimism:

> If we take a survey of ages and of countries, we will find the women – almost without exception – at all times, and in all places, adored and oppressed. Man, who has never neglected an opportunity of exerting his power, in paying homage to their beauty, has always availed himself of their weakness. He has been at once their tyrant and their slave.[21]

Thomas, one of the creators of what Sylvana Tomaselli has called the Enlightenment 'science of woman', thus ends up presenting a picture of women as inevitably disempowered – a picture which neither Hamilton nor the French Enlightenment educationist Madame d'Epinay (who had also read Thomas attentively) approve of.[22]

Lady Filmer begins her correspondence with Sir James Bruce by arguing for the intellectual and moral equality of men and women. She then argues that 'modesty, meekness, humility, and reserve, which are such necessary ingredients in a complete female character, are no arguments of women's wanting sense, courage, conduct, and spirit, to act in a superior sphere, if occasion should call them to it.'[23] Her tone is not always as concessional as this, however; she makes an impressive argument, beginning from the notion that it is education which shapes so-called 'natural' traits such as weakness, and extends this to the larger notion of public power:

> Mr Locke insists on a hardy education, as improving the faculties of the mind by invigorating the body. . . . It is not nature which condemns women to a retired idle way of life, but the abuses of the world, not to say the tyrannic power of the men, who will not divide the authority with us. Give to a woman the education of a man, and she also will be able to make a glorious figure in the world.[24]

Hamilton's long narration of 'female worthies' who have made a 'glorious figure in the world' ranges from Amazons and Druidesses to Boadicea and Semiramis, to the Duchess of Newcastle and Elizabeth Carter. Particularly important in her catalogue is the display of civic virtue and patriotism by women: we hear of the Spartan woman who, after enslavement, was asked what she knew, and answered, 'To be free.'[25] Some of Hamilton's examples come from her native Scotland – for example, the story of the wife of the governor of Warwick Castle, whose sons are taken hostage. Threatened with the loss of his sons unless he surrenders, the governor is about to give in, but his wife says, 'You may have other children; your honour once lost can never be regained.'[26] Or take the lady at Perth, who, faced with assassins about to enter the monarch's chamber, 'supplied the want of a bolt to one of the gates of the house, with her delicate arm, which was instantly shattered in pieces'.[27] The grim courage presented in such historical anecdotes foregrounding women as public agents is very far removed from any notion of women as soft and retiring.

In the realm of letters, prominent women are adduced from among Hamilton's contemporaries and others from the recent past. Apart from the Duchess of Newcastle and Miss Carter, Hamilton also praises a woman doctor and a woman mathematician (again, examples of Hamilton's interest in women of science):

> Signora Bassi at Bologna . . . was presented with a doctor's physical degree, and . . . gives public lectures . . . Signora Agnese, so famed in the literary world for a treatise on Analyses, in consideration of which, besides panegyrics from all the learned bodies in Europe, a professorship of mathematics has been conferred on her, in the University of Bologna.[28]

Hamilton here shows herself remarkably knowledgeable about Laura Bassi and Maria Agnese, two contemporary learned women. A distinguished historian of women scientists writes thus about Bassi:

> Laura Maria Catarina Bassi (1711–78) was a child prodigy. She was educated in mathematics, philosophy, anatomy, natural history and languages. . . . At the age of 21, she engaged in a public debate with five philosophers. Bassi went on to receive her doctorate in philosophy from the University of Bologna in 1733. . . . She eventually became a professor, publishing many papers on Cartesian and Newtonian physics.[29]

About Agnese, the same historian writes,

> It was Maria Gaetana Agnese (1718–99) who was to become the most celebrated woman of the scientific revolution. . . . Agnese completed her most important mathematical work while still in her twenties. Written in Italian as a text for her younger brothers, *Analytical Institutions* was a clear and concise synthesis of the new mathematics. . . . Fifty years later it was still the most complete mathematical text in existence.[30]

Hamilton also offers a sharp criticism of Salic Law (which denies royal succession to women), with a stinging description of the way religious sophistry is used to deprive women of power:

> When the succession of the French monarchy fell to a woman, after the death of Louis X, his brother Philip . . . gained over to his interest the greatest preacher of his time. . . . This prelate, preaching before those who were to decide this controversy, took for his text, 'The lilies neither toil nor spin': these being the arms of France, he most learnedly proved, and you may suppose, Sir, by what strong arguments, that God having declared the lilies did not spin, they could not without sin give the crown to the distaff.[31]

The power of women in politics, despite such underhand measures, has been great, she argues: the Gaulish women, for example, who had been powerful in government, are praised for having resisted the Romans.[32] The conclusion Lady Mary draws is: 'If wisdom proceeds from a clear apprehension, distinct judgment, and cool deliberation, why should women be excluded from state affairs? It is not by corporeal strength and activity that momentous affairs are conducted, but by prudent and sage counsel, and that authoritative influence which ever attends on public esteem.'[33]

'Influence' is a favourite term for describing the *indirect* power of women, and 'esteem' is also a trait indicating the respect that a good domestic woman can lay claim to – yet the subtle addition of 'authoritative' and 'public' serves to transform woman's role into one of active exercise of power in public affairs. Lady Filmer strikingly argues that women should act as 'thinkers' in the public sphere, like the Thinkers in the Chinese empire who 'have no other occupation than to form projects, or examine those that are offered to them'; men would then be 'Expeditors', 'charged with the detail and dispatch of business', answerable to 'our common statesmen'.[34] Hamilton thus neatly uses women's so-called physical weakness: implicitly, by her argument, women are all brain, men mostly brawn. If women *were* given this important public role, Lady Filmer continues, perhaps there would be fewer examples of blatantly ignorant remarks by male politicians, made in the context of the recent North American wars: 'I am serious in advancing that had certain honourable gentlemen consulted their wives on speeches they were to make in the House, it is probable that the one would not have talked of the *island* of Pennsylvania, nor the other of the *continent* of Newfoundland.'[35]

Lady Mary does not support the Americans' struggle for independence. Paradoxically, though, the self-same writer sharply criticizes British imperialism in the Caribbean, and sees this as causally related to masculine brutality: Hamilton's character Mrs Pierpont argues that women, endowed with 'humanity', would not, if given power, have committed such acts of barbarity as the extirpation of the race of indigenous Caribbeans, or 'Caribbees', a process that we think of as mainly due to Spanish imperialism but one which Hamilton sees her own country as also being responsible for:

> Errors accumulated through many centuries have never yet been exposed by ascending to general principles, nor has the force of acknowledged truths been ever opposed to the unbounded licentiousness of ill directed power, which has so continually produced so many authorized examples of the most unfeeling barbarity. Such was the extirpation of the poor Caribbees, an innocent and un-offending race. . . . Their rights of inheritance had never been called in question: but had there been a surmise of that nature, every treaty of peace in which they were included was a new grant to them: and a security on the faith of Great Britain. . . .
>
> Each case is ours: and for the human mind

'Tis monstrous not to feel for all mankind . . .

In this manner, I am very apt to believe, women would have acted, if they had been at the helm of affairs; humanity belongs to the sex.[36]

This viewpoint grounds political action on the principle of humanity, sees this as an integral part of the human mind, of which feeling is an integral part, and ascribes this faculty to women. How far Hamilton's espousal of the female mind has taken her!

Women and the 'Circulation of Kindness':
Bridging the Public and the Private in Munster Village

In *Munster Village*[37] Hamilton creates, in the character of Lady Frances Finlay, later Darnley, a heroine who undertakes public activities born out of an ideal of humanity and benevolence. She starts with building a village which she designs herself,[38] and proceeds to organize every aspect of it. T.C. Smout has shown that there was a real-life trend in eighteenth-century Scotland of building planned villages. Hamilton offers a feminized fictional utopia based on this practice. Munster Village is a strange combination of the fantastic, the speculative and the practical, an arena where an eighteenth-century female virtuoso expresses her projects for ordering, improving and beautifying life. My analysis of Clara Reeve's female utopia, *Plans of Education* (1792), in the next chapter will show how stark and functional Reeve's female community and seminary is, designed to train indigent gentlewomen in paid trades. Hamilton's utopian village is by far more colourful and ambitious.

At one level, Munster Village originates from an Enlightenment ideal of benevolent sociability, and the belief that the various parts of society are mutually dependent: thus, 'society is manifestly maintained by a circulation of kindness';[39] 'we are all of us, in some way or other, wanting assistance, and in like manner qualified to give it.' Some of Lady Frances's projects are straightforward charitable ones: a hospital for incurables, for example, and private donations to families on the brink of becoming beggars.

But most of her other projects assume that the circulation of social kindness is a sophisticated, long-term and many-sided business. They include her regulation of trade and industry, showing her interest in rudimentary political economy:

The streets, which were built on each side of the Tribuna, were uniform, and the houses ornamented with emblematical figures of the different trades intended for the possessors. She permitted them to live rent-free for the two first years, and admitted none but such who excelled in their art. This was certainly very political – By encouraging them in this manner, it enabled them at first to work, and sell their manufactures at a moderate rate; which insured them the business of the neighbouring counties that would otherwise have sent at a greater distance, for what could be equally produced at home.[40]

Nor is this the only way she experiments with the circulation of wealth and with economic production: she grows such new crops as rice, india corn and cork, and practises the cultivation of silk. And then there are her many projects encouraging learning and the arts. At the centre of her village is a splendid library, built to remedy the lack of a proper public library in the United Kingdom (some scathing remarks there on the paucity of printed books and the lack of public accessibility in the British Museum). There is also an astronomical observatory, an amphitheatre for the study of anatomy, academies for the study of painting and sculpture, facilities for the study of architecture, and museums for the natural sciences and antiques.

Education is thus an important part of Lady Frances's programme. She maintains an academy with male and female students. An issue that preoccupies her is how best to educate the young men so that they follow their natural bent or vocation:

> The young gentlemen in the neighbourhood are permitted to receive instructions from the several professors – and a day is set apart, when they examine young people, in order to discover wherein their genius consists, and to what kind of studies or employments they are naturally suited. Every man finds in himself a particular bent and disposition to some particular character.[41]

But that is for the boys. How much thought is given, in Lady Frances's scheme of things, to bringing out the natural propensities and talents of the girls? One is disappointed at the slight provision made for the education of girls in Munster Village. First of all, the ratio of girls to boys is one to ten: two hundred boys to twenty girls. Both the boys and the girls are of genteel birth – no provision for even basic education of the lower classes.[42] Moreover, priority is given, when selecting the female students, 'to those who labour under any imperfection of body – endeavouring, by increasing their resources *within* themselves, to compensate for their *outward* defects.' Female education, in other words, becomes not essential but compensatory.

This is not all the story, however. Some attempt *is* made to discover the inclinations and vocation of the girls: whenever any young lady is found to 'have a taste for any manual or mental art', the teachers 'cultivate it . . . and by various little attentions confirm these inclinations'.[43] An attempt is made also to give the young women a useful education. At first, Lady Mary's tone sounds more than a little condescending, as she contrasts the Munster school with the French aristocrat Madame de Maintenon's famous seventeenth-century Catholic seminary for women, Saint-Cyr, 'where the young women, who should have been instructed in rural labours, and economy in the duties of a family . . . by their education, were only fit to be addressed by men who were rich enough to require in a wife nothing *but virtue*.'[44]

Clara Reeve, we shall see, takes a far more positive view of Madame de Maintenon's educational project at St-Cyr. (This might seem surprising, given that Reeve's plan of female education is by far more austere than Hamilton's. But we shall see that Reeve finds in the disciplined *structure* of St-Cyr a model that could be emulated by her community.) The eagerness and knowledgeableness with which such women as Hamilton and Reeve are engaging with and evaluating models for the advancement of female education created by earlier women are remarkable.

But Hamilton's view of female education in *Munster Village* seems to limit what women learn, and also participates in that late eighteenth-century obsession analysed by Peter Miller – the fear of educating women above their station.[45] However, what is distinctive about Hamilton's perspective is the way she dignifies and justifies the accent on usefulness: the women educated in Munster Village are seen to conform to a classical ideal, since the Greeks and Romans 'esteemed it an honour to understand the making of every thing necessary for life one's self, without any dependence on others'.[46] The same principle of accenting the useful is also followed with the boys and even in Lady Frances's own family, where she chooses to educate her nephew in Holland to be a merchant, perhaps not the most obvious vocation for a very rich young nobleman.

The young ladies thus educated at Munster Village become 'infinitely . . . useful and interesting companions to those they afterwards associate with, whether in the character of wives or friends'.[47] The combination of 'useful' and 'interesting', together with the space left open for women to be not merely wives but also friends, adds a broader, more positive charge to Hamilton's scheme of female education – a charge enhanced by the fact that characters such as Miss Burt, Lucy Lee, Lady Frances or Miss Harris, who have received an advanced education, also pride themselves on having useful skills that can be, and are, used for the 'natural purpose' of earning one's living.

Female Virtuosos

The ideal of female selfhood embodied in the majority of Hamilton's characters, such as Lady Frances, Lucy Lee, the Duchess de Crui and the Marchioness de Louvoi, is that of a distinctive brand of female virtuoso, a surprising ideal given the stereotypical late eighteenth-century ideal of proper, unflamboyant femininity. For Hamilton, however, the term virtuoso goes beyond its etymological origin, the amoral Machiavellian 'virtù', and has the added connotation of moral virtue:

> Architecture, statuary, painting, and music, find in her [Lady Frances] a patroness. Refinement of taste in a nation, is always accompanied with refinement of manners. People accustomed to behold order and elegance in public buildings, and public gardens, acquire urbanity in private. The Italians, on the revival of the liberal arts and sciences, gave them the name of *virtù*; from this was derived the term *virtuoso*, which has been accepted throughout Europe. Should not this appellation intimate, to those who assume it to themselves, that the study of what is beautiful, in nature or art, ought to render them more virtuous than other men.[48]

Hamilton's female protagonists conform to this model of the exemplary virtuoso, combining the public and the private, harmonizing refinement and virtue. They bear out, and extend, Lawrence Klein's thesis of a conversational public sphere in which women participate.[49] They are antitheses to a masculinist and amoral type of the virtuoso, a type exemplified, in the Munster Village Saturnalia or masquerade, by the anti-masquerade figure of Lord C–d, or Lord Chesterfield, author of the famous book *Letters to His Son, on the Fine Art of becoming a Man of the World and a Gentleman* (an important augmented edition of which was published in the same year as *Munster Village*), a work which became a byword for masculinist, pragmatic advice literature. Lord C–d is unsurprisingly seen by Hamilton as a fop-figure who views women cynically as objects of masculine pleasure.

The masquerade itself is devised as a tribute from Lady Frances's nephew, who has now come of age, to his aunt. It elaborately celebrates the power–knowledge paradigm of Lady Frances's activities, her blending of the useful and the agreeable, the private and the public. If Praxiteles is present in the masquerade, so too is Demosthenes; if we see Michelangelo, we also see Sir William Petty, a tribute to Lady Frances's interest in political economy.

While Lady Frances is eulogized for her ability to balance all spheres of activity, from economics to art, contemporary men of public affairs are criticized because of their inability to do so. Lady Frances 'could not help questioning whether there was any minister, magistrate, or lawyer, now in Europe, who could explain the discoveries of Newton, or the ideas of Leibniz, in the same manner as the principles of Zeno, Plato, and Epicurus, had been illustrated at Rome (*by Cicero).'[50] If we bear in mind Hamilton's questioning of women's exclusion from politics in *Letters from the Duchess de Crui*, it is not difficult to see that when Lady Frances criticizes ministers or magistrates in this vein in *Munster Village*, she is also sneakily criticizing the fact that she, Hamilton's Superwoman, *cannot*, because of her sex, be a minister or a magistrate and not botch the job as the men she criticizes are apt to do.

Education, Experience and Women:
Masculine Pedantry versus Female Experience?

Hamilton obviously believes that empowering the female mind should lead to responsible female activity in the realm of experience. How best such an education, oriented towards life rather than books, is to be achieved is a matter of contention in the correspondence between the Duchess de Crui and Mrs Pierpont. The latter claims that women, while they may seek to benefit from the new, practically oriented science of the mind, should not seek the kind of formal education that most males of the day get, because such formal education tends to be divorced from experience.

> When I observe, that . . . young men are confined to studies, which are merely speculative; and that they are afterwards suddenly pushed into the world without

the least experience; I find it to be a practice, contrary both to reason and nature. . . . I have always thought our sex had a great superiority in this respect. We are taught by experience, what they learn but imperfectly from *books*. . . . Can anything be more unaccountable, than to spend so much time in teaching them things which are quite useless, whilst the great art of accommodating themselves to their situation, is quite neglected?[51]

If '*Bildung*', the process of growth through education, is as much, if not more, a result of experience as of formal education, then heroines of eighteenth-century fictions of education, by virtue of their limited access to formal education, are consummate subjects of the '*Bildungsroman*', deprived as they are of pedantic formal education but with more access to the school of life. There is a particular urgency, it appears, to women learning to 'accommodate themselves to their situation', an urgency with very personal overtones for the speaker. Mrs Pierpont has suffered years of an unhappy marriage, and the censure of the world. Education should teach women how to deal with such misfortunes – and Hamilton does not, even if she uses the word 'accommodate', principally mean that women should learn to *submit* to their situation. Mrs Pierpont is arguing, that is, that education should give women principles of selfhood which are not to be found in conventional educational texts. Her general line of argument is similar to that of the anonymous author (perhaps Judith Drake) of *An Essay in Defence of the Female Sex* (1696), yet another work in the distinguished tradition of post-Civil War British women's writing on female education.[52]

Hamilton is particularly scathing about the importance accorded to the knowledge of ancient languages in male education. This is part of a sustained attack on pedantry in her writing. Elsewhere, Lady Filmer condemns the obfuscating tyranny of technical terms:

Let us, my dear child, said she, resign the mystery of technical terms to the men, by which their ignorance is sometimes disguised, and their knowledge frequently disgraced. There cannot be a greater abuse of language, than to make use of words to which we have no fixed, or determinate ideas.[53]

Knowledge of words is the object in such learning, not knowledge of things (Hamilton thus shows an Empiricist bent):

by learning is generally meant having a knowledge of the ancient languages, that is, of *words* and *grammatical rules*, which frequently have but a very slender connection with the *objects* and *ideas* they are meant to convey. . . . Our knowledge is derived from the copious source of our senses and reason; our minds are filled with ideas that spring, not from *books*, but thought; our principles are consistent, because deduced in a regular series from each other, and not scraps of different systems, gleaned from the works of others. . . . Do we not then derive advantages from the very defects of our education? Do not our minds operate with more freedom, and with the genuine simplicity of uncorrupted nature?[54]

For Mrs Pierpont, then, the operations of the mind, including its dynamic relationship with the environment, occur naturally, giving it knowledge of things. There is a sense of freedom and freshness in this philosophical passage, with such words as 'copious source' and 'spring' figuratively evoking a sense of natural bounty (heightened by 'the simplicity of uncorrupted nature') that feeds and fills women's minds with knowledge. Mrs Pierpont is against an arid kind of education derived from 'scraps of systems' – the ultimate consideration in education should be the self and the mind, which must have the freedom to acquire principles.

To ground such principles reflection and solitude are essential, which is why Mrs Pierpont, despite being a believing Protestant, sends her daughters to a French convent, where they have 'the time solitude affords them to reflect on what they read', 'to distinguish between true rectitude, and false principles'[55] – an Astellian view of the necessity of solitude, reflection and rational contemplation for women.

This is also a tough-minded view of female education, however, and Mrs Pierpont is quite explicit on this point. Her own life has taught her to believe that women are likely to lead a life filled with sorrow and accidents. Like Mary Wollstonecraft and Elizabeth Hamilton, Mary Hamilton believes that educating women merely to be soft and delicate leaves them unprepared to cope with life:

> The only precaution a tender mother can take in her daughter's education, is to prepare her mind for all events and accidents she is liable to meet with in a life sentenced to be a scene of sorrow. But in place of this, softness and delicacy is a fault which women are generally bred up with . . . but so educated, they are sure to create in the future conduct of their lives, much uneasiness and trouble to themselves, and all about them.[56]

The Duchess de Crui agrees with her friend about the paramount importance of an education that is connected with experience. However, she disagrees crucially – women most often do not get this kind of education because their minds and their selves are not considered worthy of the serious attention that Mrs Pierpont advocates. If women have to cope with a 'life sentenced to be full of sorrow', they need *more* deliberate training than men in internal resources and strength of mind:

> Can it be denied, that the destination of our sex is so uncertain that we are bred up at random; and the sudden transitions of good or bad fortune, which daily happen to women, demand the greatest philosophy and good sense on their part, to sustain a propriety of behaviour, under such various circumstances, as require the most opposite qualifications: rendering what is praise-worthy in one situation, a defect in another, and vice versa.[57]

This is an important passage in Hamilton's work, the recognition that, because of social and legal disabilities, women's selves are not allowed to flower in the same way as men's. The 'destination' of the sex is uncertain, particularly in the field of marriage, with women expected to conform to whatever changes may befall them. Hamilton's point is that the uncertainty and randomness in women's lives need to be recognized and planned for in any scheme of female education. Yet the very idea that women may have 'destinations' or vocations is almost unheard of:

> if men are found inconsistent, or irregular in their conduct, there are much fewer excuses to be offered for them, than for women, both on account of their superior information, and because they are generally trained up from their infancy with a view to the plan of life they are destined to be in: ten years, at least, are devoted to the task of instructing them to observe, to perceive, to judge; they possess everything, they enjoy everything; the world seems made for them alone. On the contrary, a girl is condemned to silence among visitors, and seems not to be one of the company: she is hardly ever spoke [*sic*] to; or if she is, seldom is permitted to give an answer, so that her disposition and understanding are utterly unknown.[58]

Women, already barred from the professions and most other paid occupations, are not even given any training for their usual 'vocation', marriage. Such neglect is part of a wider and deeper indifference on the part of society to the female self. '[H]er disposition and understanding are utterly unknown': this sort of deliberate unknowingness on the part of society vis-à-vis women can only be countered by an equally deliberate scheme of education. Whereas, in the present scheme of things,

> if, at the age of twenty-five, a woman arrives, by the help of her own reflections, to a small degree of knowledge, it is extraordinary: and after the difficult study of others and herself, it is equally so to discover that she is formed for acquiring that knowledge, and practising those virtues, which are undoubtedly common to both sexes.[59]

The majority of women go into their commonest 'destination', marriage, with little clear idea of what they expect from it or what is expected of them from it. They are frequently brought to the 'difficult study of others and of herself' when faced with unhappiness, when it is too late to change their choice. No wonder so many fictional heroines of late eighteenth-century and early nineteenth-century women's fiction have to become auto-didacts, from Wollstonecraft's Mary and Jemima, to Elizabeth Hamilton's Betty Mason, and Clara Reeve's Frances Darnford and Rachel Strictland.

'An Unlucky Moral in the Fable': Education, Women and Marriage

Unhappy marriages are an obsession with Hamilton, and recur as a topic in the discussions between Mrs Pierpont and the Duchess de Crui. Having already agreed that women need to educate themselves to choose a partner and to survive in marriage, the friends then ask themselves how best this is to be accomplished. Hamilton is here dealing with the same sort of subject matter as treated by conduct books for young ladies such as the Scottish physician

Dr Gregory's *A Father's Legacy to His Daughters* (1774), published in Edinburgh only two years before *Letters from the Duchess de Crui*. Gregory's work has a section on 'Friendship, Love, Marriage', in which he discusses such issues as coquetry, the inadvisability of a woman showing any signs of love to a gentleman (she, after all, only has the right of refusal!), the constant vigilance that women must exert not to stray beyond propriety, and the prudence and care they should take in choosing a husband. He, as much as Hamilton, is conscious of the difficulty and importance of women knowing their own mind when they choose a husband:

> Before your affections come to be in the least engaged to any man, examine your tempers, your tastes, and your hearts, very severely, and settle in your own minds, what are the requisites to your happiness in a married state; and, as it is almost impossible that you should get every thing you wish, come to a steady determination what you are to consider as essential, and what may be sacrificed.[60]

Lady Mary Hamilton sounds similar. Since it is so important that a woman knows her own mind when she marries, she must wait and choose a partner only when her 'mind is formed'.[61]

> When a young lady is solicited to enter into this [the married] state; and various competitors of different rank and condition, possessed of the most opposite qualifications, contend for her preference, she often finds herself much embarrassed. Ambition pulls one way, inclination a second, wealth a third, and sometimes reason operates in direct opposition to them all. . . . If among the various situations which offer themselves, and the numerous inevitable evils which attend and threaten her, she be intelligent and accurate in selecting one and rejecting others, she will be at once discreet in using the means to obtain happiness, and in avoiding misery.[62]

To do this, passion must be subdued and reason allowed to be ascendant. Otherwise, women who have married with a 'complication of views' find their expectations unfulfilled. Both Hamilton and Gregory believe that women must have clear criteria about their expectations from marriage – but Hamilton, unlike Gregory, relentlessly highlights the disappointments and pains that marriage brings for most women. Hamilton describes a woman bred up in 'elegance and splendour', 'perfectly alive to the finer impressions of taste', who is confronted with a husband who tells her peremptorily to go the market and 'prove your judgment in a good penny-worth; your proper taste ought to be in distinguishing the best provision of the shambles.'[63] The Duchess and Mrs Pierpont adduce example after example of women whose expectations and taste do not tally with their husbands'. The reader is bleakly shown the effects of women's inadequate education – if these women had been taught to examine their own criteria for married happiness, they would not have married men who would not fulfil those criteria.

By the end of Hamilton's section on education and marriage, one is left asking whether women's expectations can ever be fulfilled within marriage, a question that is largely evoked by Hamilton's skilful and bitter use of myth and fable[64] to show marriage as an institution vitiated by the tyranny and caprices of men. Hamilton thus begins by writing in the prescriptive mode, changes the emphasis and writes a critique of marriage by using fable, a mode which has through the ages been used to convey coded critiques of various kinds, but equally one which was also used for prescriptive writing – Edward Moore's *Fables for the Female Sex* (1744)[65] was, after all, no less than Gregory's *Father's Legacy*, a popular prescriptive work written for women.

> Juno . . . is styled the goddess of marriage, which piece of mythology I fear is but too true; as there seems to be an unlucky moral implied in the fable, by there being few happy ones. The first match she is recorded to have made, by the poets, is that for Aeolus, the god of storms and tempests.[66]

Juno, goddess of marriage, suffers from her union with the promiscuous Jupiter; Aeolus, the first husband, aptly enough, brews up storms and tempests. Earlier, giving advice to a woman married to an unintelligent 'coxcomb', the Duchess de Crui compares the wife to a subject of an arbitrary emperor:

> An emperor of Japan, born under the supposed constellation of a *dog*, conceived such an affection for the canine species, that he ordered, that whenever a dog died, the owner of him should carry the carcass to a certain burying-ground appointed for that purpose. As a gentleman was one day sweating under the load of a dead dog, and complaining of the hardship of the order; his friend, to comfort him, said, 'We have reason to thank God, that the emperor was not born under a horse, for a horse would have been a much heavier burthen.' In this manner, a mind may be soothed in actual misfortunes. If your husband makes you *tremble*, be thankful that he does not make you *quake*.[67]

Although the ostensible message of the story tells the unhappy wife to submit to lesser misfortunes, thankful that she is not faced with a greater one, the use of the metaphor of arbitrary monarchical power over suffering subject leaves no doubt as to the capriciousness and blameworthiness of the husband. This metaphor is particularly potent in Hamilton's works: in *Munster Village*, Mrs Lee, who decides to separate herself legally from her husband, makes a radical and Miltonic argument, claiming that one's reason should be ultimate authority in all matters, including the permissibility of marital separation or divorce:

> I have consulted my reason on this subject, and when we have done so, whatever the decision be, whether in favour of our prejudices or against them, we must rest satisfied, since . . . he who follows that guide in the search of truth . . . will have a much better plea to make for his conduct, than he who has resigned himself implicitly to the guidance of others. My maxim is, our understanding, *properly* exercised, is the *medium* by which God makes known his will to us. . . . Were my marriage even to be annulled, all the theologians in the world could

not prove the least impiety in it. – Milton wrote the *doctrine and discipline of divorce*, wherein he proves, that a contrariety of mind, destructive of felicity, peace, and happiness, are greater reasons of divorce than adultery, especially if there be no children, and there be a mutual consent for separation.[68]

Lee's education has clearly given her a startling edge of Protestant individualist proto-feminism. Her anti-authoritarian stance surfaces further in her comparison of the advocacy of the husband's arbitrary power in marriage to the law of Divine Right laid down by James I:

> It is, indeed, convenient for the lords of creation to inculcate another doctrine, upon the same principles that the extreme and timorous attention to his own security made James I very anxious to infuse into his subjects the belief of divine hereditary right, and a scrupulous unreserved obedience *to the power which God had set over them.* . . . Were I to act otherwise, [that is, not separate herself from her husband] it would afford too much encouragement for the men to use their wives ill. *Too good subjects are apt to make bad kings.*[69]

Thus, criticism of arbitrary and despotic government, and criticism of arbitrary and tyrannical patriarchy come together in Lee's argument. One could call this critique Astellian, except that it goes further than the stance adopted in Astell's *Reflections upon Marriage* (1700): Astell, a Royalist, famously criticizes Milton's internal contradictions, epitomized in his refusal to extend civil and political liberty to women, but she does not advocate women's right to separate themselves from their husbands. For Astell, marriage is best avoided (with such unmarried women forming the female community envisaged in *A Serious Proposal to the Ladies for the Advancement of Their True and Greatest Interest*, 1694), but, once contracted, to be endured. By any standards, Lee's argument is subversive – advocating, as it does, marital separation on the grounds of incompatibility, that too from a woman's point of view. In *Memoirs of the Marchioness of Louvoi*, too, Lady Fanny Danvers, discussing the conduct of their future marriage to her fiancé, says, 'Now it often happens that a husband's government is nothing but the continual vexation and plague of his poor wife . . . has not a wife, under such circumstances, the same right to relieve herself, as the subject of a civil government under a tyrannical prince?'[70]

This right to rebel against a tyrannical prince is not yet explicitly formulated in *Letters from the Duchess de Crui*, but is nevertheless implicit. To underline this implicit moral, the Duchess tells another story, this time a fable of Solomon. Solomon, having had a magnificent palace constructed, finds that birds of every kind assemble there. In due course, the gift of speech is bestowed on them. Among the birds are an old sparrow and his young wife who bicker continually. One day, Solomon overhears the following conversation between them:

> the old sparrow . . . burst out in the most threatening manner, 'Wicked hussy! dread my resentment! provoke me further, and I will bring this palace about thy

head. . . .Thou knowest not the extent of my powers.' The poor ignorant female, unacquainted with the nature of things, believed what he said, trembled, and was mute. Solomon . . . beckoned the angry bird . . . and spoke to him as follows: 'Most puissant sparrow, I am as ignorant of thy power, as that little female thou hast intimidated . . .'. The sparrow, reduced to the most humiliating situation, answered thus: 'Great king, thou hast overheard a discourse I did not intend for thy ears. . . . I know perfectly well my own capacities, and that I am a small and feeble bird; but *let me, I conjure you, o king, play the bravo with my own wife!*'[71]

The implications of this account of the conning of a 'poor ignorant female' by a tyrannical husband are clear, albeit between the lines. Female knowledge, which Hamilton and her female characters have been advocating, will save many other young women from the powerlessness resulting from ignorance. Had the female sparrow been educated so that she knew, like Solomon, the real puniness of her husband's power, she would not have been reduced to silence. Nor could the husband have gone on 'playing the bravo' with impunity!

Female Selves and Fictional Dynamics

The themes I have discussed above only make full sense in the *fictional* context, with diverse views on female selfhood and education given to appropriate characters. It is no accident, for example, that the importance of women learning to adjust themselves without loss of principles to changes in circumstances should be articulated by Mrs Pierpont, who is consistently given the darkest views on women's lot in life. Like Lucy Lee in *Munster Village*, Mrs Pierpont was married when she was very young, and then falsely accused of adultery by her husband. Unlike Lee, however, Pierpont puts up with her husband for fifteen years, because it is her 'principle' that 'where duty is reciprocal, the failure of it in the one party acquits not the other for a failure in his'.[72]

Even though Mrs Pierpont stays with her husband, she is not immune from scandal. In this context, too, she follows a principle: that of being right in her own eyes, remarkable in an age where female reputation had such value: 'My husband's conduct exposed me to censure; but a censured person should first seek to be justified to herself, and give but second place to the world's opinion of her; and in all cases where the two cannot be reconciled, to prefer the first to the last.'[73]

In *Munster Village*, however, Lucy Lee, educated at the same convent as Lady Frances, in deciding on a separation from her husband, operates from another principle: that arbitrary power, whether in politics or in domestic politics, should not be tolerated. Principles, then, may vary according to the priorities of the women concerned, but you have to follow them rigorously.

Perhaps wary of the dangerous edge of Lee's argument advocating legal separation initiated by women, Hamilton makes her exemplary heroine Lady Frances disagree with Lee's stance. Despite this, in a letter to Lee, Lady Frances also expresses respect for the *principle* underlying Lee's action, i.e. that one's own reason should be the ultimate authority for action:

> I entirely agree with you in thinking that all our actions should proceed from the fixed principles we have adopted. I never pay a blind deference to the judgement of any man, or any body of men whatever. I cannot acquiesce in a decision . . . where my own reason is not satisfied. When the mind has no data, no settled principles to which it may recur as the rule of action, the agent can feel little or no satisfaction within himself, and society can have no moral security whatever against him.[74]

The rigorous intellectual and ethical register of this passage is typical of Hamilton. Everybody, man and woman alike, is seen as a moral agent, obliged to follow principles, however unorthodox they may be, in all spheres of life, including the domestic and the sexual. That half-sentence about society having no moral security against *him* has a gendered undercurrent, too, in a novel where repeatedly, in stark contrast to the women, we encounter men endowed with authority acting, in a way detrimental to women, as erratic, unprincipled moral agents: Lee's husband, Lady Finlay's father-in-law and Miss Harris's lover are only a few such examples.

Mrs Pierpont asks her friend, the Duchess de Crui, for advice about her daughters. In answer, the Duchess gives her friend a 'family narrative' in instalments, a narrative in which the commanding role is played by her stepmother, Lady Filmer, the most confident voice on education in Hamilton's work. She is one of the many older women, in their thirties or forties, in her creator's fictional universe (Lady Frances Darnley, for example) – indeed, Lady Filmer has much to say about the necessity of educating women not just for the period of their 'entrance into the world' but for middle and old age.[75]

Lady Filmer is not perfect; her faults are too great a tendency to think well of persons of rank, 'too high an idea of the prerogatives of her own sex', and a habit of 'engross[ing] the conversation, and . . . deliver[ing] her sentiments in too peremptory a manner on the subject debated'.[76] In short, Lady Filmer combines in her most of the attributes Hamilton is drawn to: powerful and intelligent women, aristocracy, and a championing of women.

Filmer's name, too, is significant, pointing as it does to Robert Filmer, author of *Patriarcha* (1680), the classic treatise defending the Divine Right of Kings. In *Munster Village*, Lucy Lee's arguments are critical, as we saw, of this political doctrine. We also saw that Lee extended this critique of the Divine Right to the private sphere, indicting capriciously powerful, tyrannical husbands. In *Letters from the Duchess de Crui*, Lady Filmer, wife to Sir Robert Filmer, is as powerful as her husband if not more: instead of the tyrannical patriarch, Hamilton presents an exemplary married couple, a partnership where the intelligent, articulate wife is as powerful as her husband.

Lady Filmer receives a shock when she encounters Lady Sophia and Lady Harriet F–, who are left in her charge after their father's death – her two charges, both in their teens when they come to her, cannot even read! The two girls are daughters of the late Earl of F–, whose parsimony made him neglect his children's education, to the regret of his wife, who is said to have died more or less as a result of her despair at her children's neglected upbringing.[77]

It is Lady Filmer who fulfils the thwarted ambitions of this frustrated maternal educator. In describing Lady Filmer's attempts to educate her wards, Hamilton also describes the problems that face a powerful, quasi-maternal educator. Lady Filmer finds that while Lady Harriet is intelligent and ready to be educated, Lady Sophia, who has spent a lot of time with her brother in his wildest phase, is not so amenable to her efforts. Throughout *Letters*, Lady Sophia is a 'problem' character – intelligent, irreverent, vivacious, intent on following a life of fashion and riches. In this didactic pairing of the two sisters, she is never, however, described as merely or even primarily the 'bad' heroine: her selfhood, in all its fascinating perversity, is given space and also respect. The depiction of Lady Sophia shows that fiction focusing on female education in this period continually shows a dialectic in the process of education, between control on the one hand, and freedom and uncontrollableness on the other.

Lady Filmer, who is often exasperated with her elder charge, tries to take account of Lady Sophia's disposition in the plan of education she draws up for her. About to send the girls to a boarding school,

> Lady Filmer privately acquainted the mistress of the boarding school . . . with her opinion of the young ladies' particular dispositions and talents. Every soil is not proper for all sorts of fruit; one ground is fit for grain, another for pasture: and so it is with the temper and disposition of children.[78]

An attempt, then, to tailor education to the specific dispositions of children. Even so, Lady Filmer readily confesses, three years after having sent the girls to boarding school, that her own disposition and Lady Sophia's are incompatible: 'Our natures . . . are not the same: my organs are incapable to convey my sentiments to her apprehension, nor can I frame a language that is intelligible to hers.'[79]

Striking here is the recognition that education has to negotiate a potentially difficult communicative process, in which the different 'natures' or selves of the educator and the pupil might pose problems. Compounding this problem, the plan of education that Lady Filmer draws up for Lady Sophia is, misguidedly, very basic, not much more than a groundwork in arithmetic, reading and writing, with a special emphasis on religion. The plan seems particularly unambitious given that Lady Sophia, who later contracts a brilliant but unhappy marriage, is unusually articulate and intelligent. She will not live by what she considers to be prim principles, because she thinks that most of the world only pays lip service to such high thinking. Faced with a husband unfaithful to her, she wants to leave him. When her brother tries to persuade her otherwise, she says:

> I always thought to be married, was to be *my own mistress*; instead of which, from the picture you have drawn, you put me in mind of the pitiable situation

of those poor men in the army, who serve under tyrannical officers. Born to the
same privileges with those who command them, and even by the same military
law entitled to good usage, it is with them often a point of prudence to put up
with the worst: to quit the service without leave, is death, to complain may be
construed mutiny, and expose a man to great danger. Now if I am under the
same unfortunate predicament, I am to have no *passions*, no *inclinations* of my
own, but am to be turned into a piece of clockwork, which my husband is to
wind up, or let down at his good pleasure.[80]

Lady Sophia, in articulating yet another metaphorical indictment of marriage, also implicitly asks whether an education oriented towards marriage takes
agency away from women. Later, when her brother criticizes her yet again, this
time for coquetry, she asks why this stock criticism against women should be
used so often by men, who pretend that they have no equivalent folly. Rather,
Lady Sophia argues, her desire to coquet proceeds from a desire for power, which
is the mainspring of many masculine actions that are often praised.[81]

Faced with the powerlessness of a piece of clockwork or a cowed soldier,
Lady Sophia's strategy is to defy the world using its own values. The authorial
voice disapproves of her, principally because of her refusal to follow reason
rather than passion, yet her critical voice is allowed much space, and importance,
in the text. Her 'salvation' comes after marriage to a man much inferior to her in
rank, a dependant of her late husband, who cures her of her attachment to the
fashionable world but whose explicit objective is, like Lady Filmer's, to make
reason ascendant in her mind.

The representation of Lady Sophia clearly shows up many of the limits
and tensions in Hamilton's work. Lady Sophia is depicted, before her marriage,
as a selfish young woman intent on a life of fashion. Once she is married to a
tyrannical husband, however, she becomes a much more striking character, articulating criticisms of marriage and double standards applied to women. Yet, Hamilton has to contain her unruly character through a second marriage in which the
husband tames the shrew. Here, as in so many other instances in the literature of
the period, the heroine is the pupil, while her lover or husband is the monitor or
teacher (examples range from Rousseau's *La Nouvelle Héloise*, 1761, or Frances
Burney's *Cecilia*, 1782, and *Camilla*, 1796, to Jane Austen's *Mansfield Park*,
1814). In such relationships, heterosexual love, male social authority and pedagogical authority mesh to form a powerful force exerted on the woman, doubly
submissive as the object of romantic and sexual love and as a docile pupil.

Lady Harriet, on the other hand, poses no such problems, and is a favourite of Lady Filmer's, receiving an ambitious education, similar to the one advocated
in Hester Chapone's *Letters on the Improvement of the Mind* (1773). She is given
a particularly wide-ranging and rigorous grounding in history and chronology,
as well as in geography, French, Italian, elocution, etymology and the study of
medals and coins. She is also taught to judge and reflect for herself, particularly
through the medium of writing:

> In Lady Filmer's absence, Lady Harriet wrote to her twice a week . . . by which
> she derived a double advantage; it accustomed her to express her thoughts
> with propriety; and by inquiring into the foundation of these maxims . . . she
> discovered a great number of arguments, which induced her to follow that
> which is good . . . and these arguments being the result of her own reflections,
> made the strongest impression on her mind. . . . Lectures on morality, by the
> instructors of youth . . . make a weaker impression on their [young people's]
> minds, than those which are the consequences of their own inquiry.[82]

The result of this education is that Lady Harriet is a modest young woman who
knows much more than she expresses in speech, is unaware of her excellence,
and by her 'unwillingness to triumph' in conversation she 'persuades people the
more'.[83] Yet the verbal articulateness of her sister is far more in tune with the
character of the main correspondents in the novel.

Hamilton justifies Lady Harriet's early marriage on the ground that it is
based on love, which furthers education if one has certain basic principles that
one can hold on to:

> The principal requisite is to get acquainted with a select number of truths, that
> their inestimable value, and divine beauty, may induce us to make them the
> constant rule of our lives. A sensible and ingenuous heart is here the most
> material point; it comes always to the assistance of the understanding: and . . .
> the examples, my dear Harriet, are not very rare, of people who, excited by
> love, have arrived at perfection in any art and science with great celerity.[84]

Love, however, is a node of irreducible ambiguity for the development of
Hamilton's women characters. Even when Lady Filmer's hope in this passage –
that love may further knowledge – is fulfilled for a time (as in Mlle le Reillet's
relationship with Mr Denham, a mentor-lover, in *Memoirs of the Marchioness de
Louvoi*), it generally brings with it unhappiness. Both Mlle le Reillet and her
mother, the Marchioness de Louvoi, another learned aristocratic female virtuoso,
suffer because of the jealousy of their lover and husband respectively.

This, despite the fact that both the Marchioness and her daughter are
exceptionally intelligent and educated women. The Marchioness, another devoted
maternal educator, is described in glowing terms by her daughter:

> She was the avowed protectress of letters and encourager of merit, and her
> house was open to the literati. She herself was highly accomplished, being perfect
> mistress of Greek and Latin, as well as the modern languages, and took great
> pains and pleasure in having me instructed in them: also in geography,
> chronology, geometry, physics, and metaphysics; in short, there was nothing
> this kind mother omitted for my improvement, as if she had had a prescience I
> should soon be deprived of her, and in consequence, obtruded knowledge on
> me superior to my years.[85]

The daughter is obviously a child prodigy. As a result of her mother's excellent education, Mlle le Reillet is able to earn her living as a governess when she is suddenly and melodramatically left without friends or fortune. It turns out later that her mother, whom she believes to be dead, has been imprisoned by villainous kinsmen. In her imprisonment, the Marchioness finds solace in study: in a little press in the wall of her cell, she finds four books – the Bible, Burnet's Theory of the Earth, a Homer, and a book on 'geometry, botany, chemistry, and science'.[86] It is geometry that proves to be her principal source of interest:

> Geometry requires the least aid from the imagination, as it continually fixes the attention to one particular object. . . . Geometry is useful to qualify and prepare our minds for the contemplation of truth, and for the profitable reading of many books. . . . I have enjoyed so much pleasure in these silent amusements, that I am no longer surprised Pythagoras, though a philosopher, was so overcome with joy, at the satisfaction he conceived in finding out his demonstrations.[87]

Science, in its most abstract aspect, becomes quasi-religious, and is seen as quite appropriate as an object of study for a woman. There is a Christianized Stoical strain in this passage, a Boethian sense of the pure, austere pleasure of contemplating knowledge.

The Marchioness's daughter is also interested in science, in the more applied forms, her interest fostered by her lover, Mr Denham, who instructs her in physics, astronomy and botany. Miss Byron, in *Letters from the Duchess de Crui*, studies botany, and is said to be familiar with the Linnaean system of classification. She is thus one of the many late eighteenth-century women whose interest in botany was making the science particularly feminized.[88] Other female exemplary figures, also interested in the sciences, are the Duchess d'Elbeuf and her sister, whose mother had taught them French, Italian, Spanish, Latin and Greek. They are *salonnières*,[89] adept in conversation on intellectual subjects:

> The Duchess has once a week a conversazione, which is much frequented by the foreigners and men of letters at Naples. This lady, besides all the virtues and graces she possesses, has acquired a knowledge above her sex; she has carried her scientifical acquisitions to the most sublime parts of geometry. These two sisters . . . talk of problems, theorems, and equations.[90]

The sisters are also adept at expounding Newton, and compel Sir James Bruce's admiration. In making the Duchess and her sister active explicators and discussants of Newton, Hamilton is going further than the usual eighteenth-century association between polite science and women: in an article on eighteenth-century Newtonianism,[91] John Mullan argues that male writers of books on Newton, such as Benjamin Martin and Algarotti, saw women as peculiarly fit recipients (pliable pupils, again), rather than active disseminators, of science. Hamilton's women (like real-life learned women such as Elizabeth Carter, translator of Algarotti) instead expound Newton to an audience.

This impression of agency is heightened by our awareness that Hamilton was very probably basing her characters on the real-life prodigy Signora Agnese, whom we have already encountered in Hamilton's fiction. Margaret Alic writes that local and visiting intellectuals used to attend Agnese's salon at Pavia 'to hear Maria expound on mathematical and philosophical subjects', with her *conversaziones*, conducted in the many languages she was fluent in, ranging from subjects such as the origins of fountains to the propagation of light and prismatic colours, and curvilinear figures in geometry.[92]

The zenith of Hamilton's ideal of the female virtuoso is Lady Frances Finlay, later Darnley. Lady Frances's personal history shows a dialectic between, on the one hand, her ambition for fame as a successful 'public woman', and, on the other, her love for Lord Darnley. Upon the deaths of her father, brother and sister-in-law, Lady Frances is left owner of the large family estate, and guardian to her nephew and niece. She decides to play a role antithetical to her late father, Lord Munster, who had ruined the happiness of his son and daughter-in-law, Lord and Lady Finlay. Legally speaking, there are no encumbrances to Lady Frances acting freely with regard to her inheritance and responsibilities, since she is a 'feme sole' – a fatherless, unmarried woman with the legal power to act independently and to administer her property herself. But she is also engaged to be married to Lord Darnley. Strikingly, she suspends her betrothal, refusing to become a 'feme coverte', her legal identity subsumed in that of her husband: freedom from the demands of marriage and sexuality thus forms the precondition for her success as founder of Munster Village:

> She [Lady Frances] remained unmoved, only assured him, that nothing but what she apprehended was her first duty, could alienate her from him, and that she would never dispose of herself to any *other*: but advised him to marry. She applied herself entirely to the care of her family, and to the improvement of that property invested in her person.[93]

There is an assured note of power in the words 'invested in her person'. The plea of 'care of her family', giving Lady Frances the stock domestic, nurturing, feminine role, is only one part of her perceived responsibilities; not only does she also perform the gentleman's task of improving the estate, she goes much farther, coming up, as we have seen, with an ambitious, almost encyclopaedic range of schemes for her property.

Despite Lady Frances's refusal to marry straightaway, however, Lord Darnley remains attached to her, and this continued attachment creates in her a tension between the demands of love and the fame she acquires as a result of her success in Munster Village. But, as the passage below attests, the two can only be reconciled in her mind with priority being given to *her*: her mind, her activities, her fame.

> It is true, the great works I have carried on, the encouragement I have given to learning, the manufactories I have introduced into this kingdom, etc. etc. have procured me the suffrage of the world, and may transmit my name down to posterity. But what flatters me most is, that if I have acquired any fame, it is

derived from the man I love. My acquaintance with him has been a happiness to my mind, because it has improved and exalted its powers. The epithet of *great*, so liberally bestowed on princes, would, in most cases, if narrowly scanned, belong rather to their ministers. . . . What is the history of Lewis XIII [sic], but the shining acts of Richelieu? . . . In all situations of life, it is of great consequence to make a right choice of those we confide in. . . . But it is still more so to princes, or to persons of large property.[94]

For Lady Frances, *she* is the 'person of large property', the prince, while Lord Darnley is her minister and confidant. He contributes to her happiness by *exalting* the *powers* of her mind; she congratulates herself on her 'right choice of confidant'. All in all, Lady Frances shows an almost exulting sense of self-worth and achievement. Her claim to fame is further strengthened in the 'Saturnalia' or masquerade towards the end of the novel, which, while ostensibly celebrating the wedding anniversary of the couple, is an exclusive celebration of Lady Frances's activities. In this context, the name Darnley is significant. Lord Darnley, after all, had been the consort of Mary Queen of Scots, although he was later, and controversially, granted the title of king; whether consciously or not, Hamilton's use of this name signals her desire to invest Lady Frances with the greater power. Hamilton would have been particularly well-acquainted with this story, given that the Earl of Leven's collection of documents included major ones related to the conferring of the title of king on Darnley.[95]

A contrast to this elevated ideal of female selfhood and education is provided by the upbringing given to Miss N–, in *Letters from the Duchess de Crui*, by her mother, who obsessively teaches her the importance of chastity and little else. Almost predictably, it is precisely in that area that Miss N– finds herself guilty:

> however deficient my mother was in inforcing other precepts, I must do her justice, in saying, she used to harangue on *virtue*, which she reduced to a *single point*. As this is the only point in which I have erred, I do not mean to condemn *her* to exculpate *myself*. The misfortunes I have met with, and the retirement I have been in, have however taught me to reflect that virtue is not wholly comprised in chastity, which is only a concomitant, and that it is necessary that a woman should have every other moral virtue.[96]

Compare this unacceptably narrow definition of virtue to Hamilton's notion of the virtuous woman, using and cultivating her talents. This broader notion of virtue may, indeed, work against the 'single point' notion of virtue. Take the case of Miss Harris in *Munster Village*, for example, an unmarried mother who has been abandoned by her lover. The reasons for her condition as an abandoned, unmarried mother have much to do with her father, who had taught her to believe that marriage was a sometimes unnecessary civil institution, and the greed of her lover, who wished not to lose his heirdom to a large estate by marrying a commoner. Well-versed in the classics, in art and in literature, Miss

Harris is portrayed as an admirable character who supports her son by making and selling artificial flowers. The history of Miss Harris's education also has in the background a mother of religious sensibility who is wounded by her husband's selfishness and scepticism. In Hamilton's world, where virtue can take the form of diverse compounds composed of very different elements, both Miss Harris's religious, delicate mother, who cannot resist her husband's beliefs, and Miss Harris herself, with her talents, education and unconventional way of life, are praiseworthy characters.

Those who censure the likes of Miss Harris and Miss N– are, in turn, condemned by Hamilton: 'Unfeeling prudes! who are virtuous from circumstances or neglect, not from principle. Do not such almost countenance another's loss of virtue, by manifesting their own want of humanity?'[97] Even after Miss N– is re-integrated into society, her selfhood must be suppressed; she must learn to be wary and cautious, and this is regarded as unfair and damaging:

> Under her unhappy predicament . . . it is most probable, that after all her care, she will be esteemed through life, either a *prude* or a *coquette*. Both of which characters are despicable; but of the two, I look upon it to be a less [*sic*] crime to go one's self, than to lead others astray; and think it much less blameable to want *prudence* than *character*; to have a weak *heart* than an impertinent and corrupt *mind*.[98]

Again, a startling conception here of the relative merits of prudence and character; even if one loses chastity, one may still have character, while prudish minds that take pleasure in condemning others' weaknesses are by far worse than coquettes (one thinks of Lady Sophia, the engaging coquette).

Not only 'seduced maidens' show want of prudence that is later forgiven, however – the eminently respectable Duchess de Crui herself confesses to such lapses in the account she gives of her own education, particularly in the near-farcical account of her aborted elopement after a masquerade. As an adolescent, the Duchess was educated by two aunts, who taught her so well that at the age of fourteen all she had learnt was to read English, to 'hammer Italian music on a harpsichord', and to read 'romances'.[99] (The Duchess's main and very conventional objection against romances, masquerade and theatre is that they touch the heart and inspire love, most often with unfortunate consequences.[100]) At this point, then, our heroine is a typical ignorant, novel-reading miss so often derided in eighteenth-century writing. She goes clandestinely to a masquerade dressed as 'Princess Iris', and meets and falls in love with a young man dressed as Mars, who claims he is a prince. In a hilariously quick sequence of events, the young man proposes that they should elope forthwith, and she agrees, only to be over-taken at Dartford (a wonderfully prosaic detail!) by the incensed tutor of 'Prince Mars'.

Once Eliza returns, she is taken in charge by her sensible stepmother, and removed from her aunts. Yet, later, fiction turns to reality as 'Prince Mars' turns out to be a real prince who manages to find his lost Iris, and the couple are married. Thus, not only has Eliza's penchant for fiction not corrupted her heart, it has in fact helped her find true love. Perhaps the clue to this apparent paradox lies in the importance of the heart itself: if this is corrupted, not the best education will improve the pupil in question; conversely, with a good heart, clandestine masquerades and loss of chastity do not impede self-cultivation and self-development. There is a stress on the innate human character in Hamilton's views on education, after all. The Duchess says, generally and about herself:

> though experience may teach us something, it can never eradicate the natural disposition. . . . The human mind is frequently retouched, but the groundwork is still the same, – I am an instance of this myself: want of education has undoubtedly made me deficient in knowledge, accomplishments, etc., but the worst examples did not corrupt my heart.[101]

In Hamilton's fiction, the balance is most definitely tilted towards the view that most people have natural dispositions that are uncorrupt and amenable to improvement. The woman publicly accused of adultery, the wife who staves off unhappiness by gambling and coquetry, and the teenager who nearly elopes with a near-stranger are only some of the host of individualized fictional women whose zest for self-cultivation and self-development is representative of Hamilton's desire to advance female knowledge and agency.

Bold, Argumentative Fictions of Ideas

Mary Hamilton is, as this chapter has argued, a dazzlingly wide-ranging and bold writer of fiction focusing on female education. She is deeply interested in the human mind and the production of knowledge, and espouses the female mind, seeing it as capable of aspiring to the highest knowledge, virtue and perfection. A Lockeian in education and politics, Hamilton combines an Enlightenment interest and faith in the capacity of the mind with a passionate argument that once developed, the female mind and female talents can be powerful and active in areas ranging from politics to fine arts and science.

Hamilton creates a vigorous debate on female education between her characters. Although never resolved, this debate sees all the participants seeking to align female education with experience. Purely speculative or pedantic or scholastic learning, seen as a large part of the established masculine model of education, cannot form the basis for a potential model for female education.

Hamilton argues that the random, fortuitous nature of women's lives requires consideration in female education. Women, like men, are argued to have vocations which they need to be educated for, the most common 'destination' being marriage. This forms the most difficult part of Hamilton's presentation of female education. On the one hand, women should marry with mature minds and clear expectations. On the other hand, even if they have done so, they may well be unhappy, given that many of Hamilton's fictional husbands are tyrants. Fable, myth and anecdotes are used to anatomise arbitrary male power in marriage. Hamilton's solution, which nevertheless fails to counter the criticisms of marriage she makes, is for women to act according to a set of principles and not give way to tyranny from ignorance.

Hamilton's analysis of history to criticize women's exclusion from the public sphere offers a complement to the many pictures she offers of disempowered and unhappy women confined to the private sphere, stifled in unhappy marriages. Women, Hamilton proves, using contemporary Enlightenment historiography, have in the past been successful in such areas as governance and public use of learning. She argues that women should function as powerful 'Chinese thinkers', a sort of decision-making think-tank, in contemporary British politics. Such bold arguments occur in the course of a domestic or family narrative, particularly in *Letters from the Duchess de Crui*, thus showing that the correspondents, mostly female friends, who are 'confined' to a domestic world, in fact engage themselves intellectually with the public sphere through their writing.

Many of Hamilton's women characters can be described as female virtuosos active in the public sphere. Her exemplary women characters, such as Lady Frances, Lady Filmer, the Marchioness de Louvoi and the Duchess d'Elbeuf, are not the young heroines of the courtship novel but more mature women eager to integrate knowledge and life. They tend to be aristocratic, and have affinities with continental *salonnières*. Lady Frances, the founder and directress of Munster Village, is, I have argued, the zenith of the female virtuoso; an educative and reforming spirit informs her activities in the village.

Powerful maternal or quasi-maternal educators (Lady Filmer, Mrs Trueman, Mrs Pierpont, the Marchioness de Louvoi) have a major part in Hamilton's *weltanschauung*. (In this context, we should remember that the work which made the model of the powerful maternal educator powerful, Stephanie de Genlis's *Adèle et Théodore*, appeared in 1782, well after Hamilton's *Letters from the Duchess de Crui*.) Hamilton is aware that educating women is not an easy task. In describing the travails of Lady Filmer with Lady Sophia, she conveys the difficulty, if not impossibility, of moulding women through education against their will: someone as intelligent, witty, irreverent, perceptive and self-willed as Sophia cannot be 'tamed' into propriety by the maternal educator, nor by Lady Sophia's jaded first husband. Her second husband, in exerting the triple authority of lover, husband and monitor in reforming her, demonstrates that the authority of the husband in marriage, an ideology of heterosexual love and female education can enmesh to form a powerful force, forcing even a self-willed adult woman to become a pliable pupil.

Lady Sophia hovers on the edge of being classed as one of the many marginal women Hamilton vindicates, old maids and ugly women (Miss Byron, Lady Anne Surry), or women who have been slandered by the world, often for loss of chastity or adultery (Mrs Lee, Miss Harris, Miss N–, Mrs Pierpont). Such women have intelligent, cultivated minds. The acerbic intelligence of Mrs Lee, for example, is sophisticated enough to make a rational and scathing critique of the husband's arbitrary power in marriage, and to apply this argument to break free of her own tyrannical husband. Hamilton moves the emphasis away from the opinion of the world and its frequent and unjust slandering of female reputation.

In *Munster Village*, a character called Miss Burt, later Lady Finlay (Lady Frances's sister-in-law), who sells her paintings to support her family, is said to have 'too much good sense to be ashamed of employing those talents, bestowed on her by nature for *so natural a* purpose'.[102] Hamilton's fictional universe depicts women with a large range of such 'natural talents', which they cultivate and use with 'good sense'. Such talents are shown to lie in a continuum: whether women sell their own paintings, or survive with dignity in unhappy marriages, or administer an estate, or educate daughter-figures – all such activities are expressions of cultivated female minds.

Hamilton is, in many ways, a conservative feminist – for example, in her views on national politics (she speaks against the American Revolution), and her choice and glamourizing of aristocratic women – though readers will have noted that many of the sympathetic characters are non-aristocratic, indigent women. At the same time, she is also a radical writer – in her views on female vocations, her critique of British imperialism in the Caribbean, her espousal of female public power in a vast array of activities from the economic to the literary and scientific, and her criticism of 'matrimonial despotism of heart and conduct'.[103]

Hamilton's range of style and literary register is wide, encompassing historical survey, philosophical writing, conversational epistolary style, prescriptive writing, romance and fable. All in all, she gives us a strikingly dynamic and dialogic view of female education, largely as a result of her manipulation of fictional characters. The correspondents have diverse viewpoints, and the stories of the different characters are also narratives of different kinds of female self-development. The debate between Mrs Pierpont and the Duchess is an example of the former. The different strategies that Lucy Lee and Mrs Pierpont use to cope with unhappy marriages are telling examples of Hamilton's ability to plead for the 'flexibility with principles' view of education, which is her hallmark. The very different paths of development followed by Lady Sophia and Lady Harriet tell the same story.

Flamboyance is very much a feature of Lady Mary Hamilton's writing, more so than any of the other writing I have examined – a flamboyance exemplified by the climactic, resplendent masquerade in *Munster Village*. If we remember that *Munster Village* appeared in the same year as Frances Burney's *Evelina, or a Young Lady's Entrance into the World*, Hamilton's distinctiveness as a writer becomes particularly clear. Rees, at the end of her chapter on eighteenth-century female utopias, compares Burney's *Cecilia* to *Munster Village* and other female utopias, and comments:

> Were she a heroine of romance, Cecilia might have been another Lady Frances, but she is not. . . . Cecilia's own utopian dream of power and benevolence . . . is doomed, if not to complete failure at least to major modification, largely by the familiar constraints of love and marriage. . . . Cecilia has to learn the hardest of lessons for a utopian reformer, intensified by the disadvantage of being a woman:

that idealistic endeavour has to accommodate itself to human society as it is actually constituted. In a sense we have come full circle, back to the domestic utopia as the centre of woman's existence.[104]

According to this reading, Burney's bleak vision of female difficulties in *Cecilia* 'realistically' exposes the impossibility of female utopian schemes, exemplified by the activities of the 'heroine of romance', Lady Frances in *Munster Village*. Rees's conclusion is wrong, even if it is partly due to her ignorance of Hamilton's other novels. As this chapter has shown, Hamilton too relentlessly shows up the limits of female aspirations, most often through the constrictions of marriage. Hamilton's bold, argumentative fictions of ideas and Burney's slyly subversive novelized versions of conduct literature offer complementary visions. While Burney acutely, and often darkly, shows the constraints of education as social control operating on young ladies entering the world, steering a difficult course to marriage, the appointed end of the courtship novel, Hamilton offers a wide vista of horizons for female education in which marriage is only a part, if a mostly painful one, of women's destinies.

Hamilton, unlike Burney, does not see marriage as the telos of female education; instead, like Bluestocking predecessors such as Sarah Scott (*Millennium Hall*, 1762, and *The History of Sir George Ellison*, 1766), she depicts women who carve out other, often public vocations for themselves, ranging from teaching, studying science and writing, to administering landed estates. In Hamilton's version of the female *Bildungsroman*, both the authorial voice and the female characters themselves are unabashedly intellectually articulate, far more so than in Burney's fiction, especially *Evelina*, where the repressions and pains of social training and etiquette often stifle female intellectualism and vocations outside marriage.

Hamilton's fiction throws up crucial issues about female subject formation and development, which recur in fictions of education through the following two centuries. Such issues include women's need for access to the privileged enclave of formal education, together with a balancing awareness that formal education in itself may be inadequate and a corresponding valorization of experiential education. She also raises the question of intransigences and randomness in education, and the impossibility of the educator achieving predictable and controllable patterns of development in the pupil.

Part of my argument in this book is that the 'conservative' late eighteenth-century and early nineteenth-century women writers I analyse must be recognized as some of the earliest and most adventurous explorers of the post-Enlightenment subject, her education, growth and development. And it is no accident that this exploration should take place in the site of fiction, still a marginal form and a site of contestation. Such fictions as Hamilton's, with their intellectualism and polemical feminism, stake a claim to the status of knowledge, and posit women as active participants and producers of knowledge – posing a challenge to the established domain of knowledge governed by the 'men of learning' whom Clara

Reeve criticized for their disdain of fiction in *The Progress of Romance*,[105] published seven years after *Munster Village*.

Notes and References

1 Hamilton was the name of Lady Mary's second husband. Her novels of the 1770s were published during her first marriage, when her name was Lady Mary Walker.

2 Letter dated 15 June 1815, from Lady Mary Hamilton to Alexander, Earl of Leven, reproduced in Sir William Fraser, *The Melvilles Earls of Melville and the Leslies Earls of Leven*, 3 vols (Edinburgh: published privately, 1890), Vol. II, p. 310.

3 Ibid., Vol. II, p. 311.

4 G.J. Barker-Benfield, *The Culture of Sensibility: Sex and Society in Eighteenth-century Britain* (Chicago and London: University of Chicago Press, 1992), and Paul Langford, *A Polite and Commercial People: England, 1727–1783* (Oxford: Oxford University Press, 1992).

5 Fraser, *The Melvilles*, Vol. I, p. 319.

6 Ibid., Vol. II, p. 329.

7 Lady Mary Hamilton, *La Famille du Duc de Popoli*, 2 vols (Paris: the author, 1810).

8 Lady Mary Hamilton [Walker], *Memoirs of the Marchioness de Louvoi*, 3 vols (London: Robson, Walter and Robinson, 1777), Vol. II, p. 176.

9 Charles Nodier, quoted in Georges Zaragoza, *Charles Nodier: le Dériseur Sensé* (n.p: Klincksieck, 1992), pp. 111–12.

10 Marguerite Henry-Rosier, *La Vie de Charles Nodier*, Vie des Hommes Illustrées, nr. 73 (Paris: Libraririe Gallimard, 1931), p. 136. Henry-Rosier writes: 'Dès quatre heures du matin, Lady Hamilton sonne pour se faire apporter la lumière et commence à écrire. Elle ne se lève qu'après avoir rédigé au moins dix grandes pages du roman en cours.' ['As soon as it was four in the morning, Lady Hamilton would ring for a light to be brought to her and kindled, and she would begin to write. She would not rise until she had composed at least ten pages of the novel she was writing.'] And again (p. 137): 'La soirée . . . Charles est chargé de lire à haute voix les pages composées dans la journée par "Milady". On critique. Chacun donne son avis. Et la nuit s'avance dans la discussion des aventures de la famille Popoli.' ['In the evening, Charles would be asked to read aloud the pages composed during the day by "Milady". They would criticize the writing. And the night would lengthen with the discussion of the adventures of the Popoli family.']

11 Fraser, *The Melvilles*, Vol. II, pp. 328–29, letter from Lady Mary Hamilton to her nephew, the Earl of Leven, dated 14 September 1818.

12 Lady Mary Hamilton [Walker], *Letters from the Duchess de Crui*, 2 vols ([1776] 3rd edn, Dublin: S. Price and fourteen others, 1779), Vol. I, p. vi.

13 See William Fleetwood, *The Relative Duties of Parents and Children, Husbands and Wives, Masters and Servants* (London: Charles Harper, 1705; rpt, New York and London: Garland Publishing, 1985), for a clear exposition of the 'relative duties' argument.

14 Hamilton, *Letters from the Duchess de Crui*, Vol. I, pp. v–vi.

15 Ibid., Vol. I, p. 2.

16 Hamilton, *Memoirs of the Marchioness de Louvoi*, Vol. I, pp. 160–61.

17 Hamilton, *Letters from the Duchess de Crui*, Vol. I, p. 38.

18 Ibid., Vol. I, p. 22.

19 *Essay on the Character, Manners, and Genius of Women in Different Ages*, enlarged from the French of M. Thomas by Mr Russell, 2 vols (London: G. Robinson, 1773). Thomas is placed in the context of Enlightenment masculine writings on the 'science of woman' by Sylvana Tomaselli, 'Reflections on the History of the Science of Woman', in *A Question of Identity: Women, Science, and Literature*, edited by Marina Benjamin (New Brunswick: Rutgers University Press, 1993), pp. 25–40, esp. p. 32. On Thomas, see also Chapter I, 'The Enlightenment and the Nature of Women', in Jane Rendall, *The Origins of British Feminism: Women in Britain, France, and the United States 1780–1860* (Basingstoke: Macmillan, 1985), pp. 7–32, esp. pp. 28–29.

20 Thomas, *Essay on the Character, Manners, and Genius of Women*, Vol. I, p. iv.

21 Ibid., Vol. I, p. 2.

22 For Madame d'Epinay's objections to Thomas's work, see Mary Trouille, 'Sexual/ Textual Politics in the Enlightenment: Diderot and D'Epinay Respond to Thomas's *Essay on Women*', *British Journal for Eighteenth-Century Studies*, 19:1 (Spring 1996), pp. 1–15. In a letter to Galiani, D'Epinay blames Thomas for ascribing the wrongs of women to nature instead of to nurture. Her argument is strikingly similar to Hamilton's.

23 Hamilton, *Letters from the Duchess de Crui*, Vol. I, p. 45.

24 Ibid., Vol. I, p. 49.

25 Ibid., Vol. I, p. 60; Thomas, *Essay on the Character, Manners, and Genius of Women*, Vol. I, p. 29.

26 Hamilton, *Letters from the Duchess de Crui*, Vol. I, pp. 60–61.

27 Ibid., Vol. I, p. 61.

28 Ibid., Vol. I, p. 66.

29 Margaret Alic, *Hypatia's Heritage: A History of Women in Science from Antiquity to the Late Nineteenth Century* (London: Women's Press, 1986), p. 136.

30 Ibid., pp. 136–37.

31 Hamilton, *Letters from the Duchess de Crui*, Vol. I, p. 71.

32 Ibid., Vol. I, p. 52.

33 Ibid., Vol. I, pp. 52–53.

34 Ibid., Vol. I, pp. 53–54.

35 Ibid., Vol. I, p. 54.

36 Ibid., Vol. I, pp. 96–97.

37 *Munster Village* is discussed in Barbara Schnorrenberg's 'A Paradise Like Eve's: Three Eighteenth Century English Female Utopias', *Women's Studies*, 9:3 (1982), pp. 263–73, as well as, at greater length, in Christine Rees, *Utopian Imagination in Eighteenth-Century Fiction* (London and New York: Longmans, 1996), pp. 227–34. Rees's discussion suffers from its inability to acknowledge the centrality of the personal life-histories of the women characters to the utopian impulse in the novel.

38 T.C. Smout, 'The Landowner and the Planned Village in Scotland, 1730–1830,' in *Scotland in the Age of Improvement: Essays in Scottish History in the Eighteenth Century*, edited by N. Phillipson and R. Mitchison (Edinburgh: Edinburgh University Press, 1970), pp. 73–106.

39 Lady Mary Hamilton [Walker], *Munster Village: a Novel*, 2 vols (London: Robson, Walter and Robinson, 1778). For the sake of convenience, I quote from the modern reprint, Mary Hamilton, *Munster Village*, introduced by Sarah Baylis (London: Pandora, 1987): here, p. 20.

40 Ibid., p. 27.

41 Ibid., p. 24.

42 In this respect, Sarah Scott in *Millenium Hall* and *The History of Sir George Ellison* is far in advance of Hamilton.

43 Hamilton, *Munster Village*, p. 25.

44 Ibid., p. 26.

45 P.J. Miller, 'Women's Education, "Self-Improvement" and Social Mobility: A Late 18th Century Debate', *British Journal of Educational Studies*, 20:3 (October 1972), pp. 302–14.

46 Hamilton, *Munster Village*, p. 26.

47 Ibid., p. 26.

48 Ibid., p. 28.

49 See Lawrence Klein, 'Gender, Conversation and the Public Sphere in Early Eighteenth-Century England', in *Textuality and Sexuality: Reading Theories and Practices*, edited by Judith Still and Michael Worton (Manchester and New York: Manchester University Press, 1993), pp. 100–15.

50 Hamilton, *Munster Village*, p. 131.

51 Hamilton, *Letters from the Duchess de Crui*, Vol. I, pp. 101–02.

52 *An Essay in Defence of the Female Sex, Written by a Lady*, in *The Pioneers: Early Feminists*, edited by Marie Mulvey Roberts and Tamae Mizuta, with an introduction

by Marie Mulvey Roberts ([1696] 4th edn, London: S. Butler, 1721; rpt, London: Routledge/Thoemmes Press, 1993), pp. 32–52, and in particular p. 50.

[53] Hamilton, *Letters from the Duchess de Crui*, Vol. I, p. 91.

[54] Ibid., Vol. I, pp. 121–22.

[55] Ibid., Vol. I, p. 106.

[56] Ibid., Vol. I, pp. 111–12.

[57] Ibid., Vol. I, p. 133.

[58] Ibid., Vol. I, p. 134.

[59] Ibid., Vol. I, p. 134.

[60] *A Father's Legacy to His Daughters, by the late Dr Gregory, of Edinburgh* (Dublin: John Archer, 1790), in *The Young Lady's Pocket Library, or Parental Monitor*, with a new introduction by Vivien Jones (rpt, Bristol: Thoemmes Press, 1995), p. 46.

[61] Hamilton, *Letters from the Duchess de Crui*, Vol. I, p. 235.

[62] Ibid., Vol. I, p. 235.

[63] Ibid., Vol. I, p. 139.

[64] In *The English Fable: Aesop and Literary Culture, 1651–1740* (Cambridge: Cambridge University Press, 1996), Jayne Elizabeth Lewis argues that while the fable as a form is an important mainstream presence in the early eighteenth century, it becomes more marginal, more used, for example, in women's and children's literature in the later part of the century.

[65] Edward Moore, *Fables for the Female Sex* (Dublin: John Archer, 1790), in *The Young Lady's Pocket Library, or Parental Monitor*.

[66] Hamilton, *Letters from the Duchess de Crui*, Vol. I, p. 263.

[67] Ibid., Vol. I, p. 246.

[68] Hamilton, *Munster Village*, p. 50.

[69] Ibid., pp. 51–52.

[70] Hamilton, *Memoirs of the Marchioness de Louvoi*, Vol. III, pp. 113–14.

[71] Hamilton, *Letters from the Duchess de Crui*, Vol. I, pp. 263–64.

[72] Ibid., Vol. I, p. 117.

[73] Ibid., Vol. I, p. 104.

[74] Hamilton, *Munster Village*, p. 54.

[75] Hamilton, *Letters from the Duchess de Crui*, Vol. I, pp. 40–41.

[76] Ibid., Vol. I, p. 10.

[77] Ibid., Vol. I, p. 4.

[78] Ibid., Vol. I, p. 35.

[79] Ibid., Vol. I, p. 73.

[80] Ibid., Vol. II, p. 81.

[81] Ibid., Vol. II, p. 108.

[82] Ibid., Vol. I. p. 93.

[83] Ibid., Vol. I, p. 151.

[84] Ibid., Vol. I, p. 165–66.

[85] Hamilton, *Memoirs of the Marchioness de Louvoi*, Vol. I, pp. 158–59.

[86] Ibid., Vol. III, p. 18.

[87] Ibid., Vol. III, pp. 34–36.

[88] See Ann B. Shteir, *Cultivating Women, Cultivating Science: Flora's Daughters and Botany in England, 1760–1830* (London: Johns Hopkins University Press, 1996).

[89] For a discussion of women and salons, see, for example, Dena Goodman, 'Enlightened Salons: The Convergence of Female and Philosophic Ambitions', *Eighteenth Century Studies*, 22 (1989), pp. 329–50; Katherine Clinton, 'Femme et Philosophe: Enlightenment Origins of Feminism', *Eighteenth Century Studies*, 8 (1975), pp. 185–99.

[90] Hamilton, *Letters from the Duchess de Crui*, Vol. II, p. 46.

[91] John Mullan, 'Gendered Knowledge, Gendered Minds: Women and Newtonianism, 1690–1760', in *A Question of Identity: Women, Science, and Literature*, edited by Marina Benjamin (New Brunswick: Rutgers University Press, 1993), pp. 41–56.

[92] Alic, *Hypatia's Heritage*, pp. 136–37.

[93] Hamilton, *Munster Village*, p. 20.

[94] Ibid., p. 57.

95 Fraser, *The Melvilles*, Vol. I, p. xxi.
96 Hamilton, *Letters from the Duchess de Crui*, Vol. I, pp. 280–81.
97 Ibid., Vol. I, p. 288.
98 Ibid., Vol. II, p. 64.
99 Ibid., Vol. II, p. 172.
100 Ibid., Vol. II, pp. 173–74. Hamilton quotes Frances Brooke and Elizabeth Griffith to support her contention that love is potentially the most powerful and dangerous of emotions.
101 Ibid., Vol. I, p. 114.
102 Hamilton, *Munster Village*, p. 16.
103 Mary Wollstonecraft, *Maria, or the Wrongs of Woman*, in Mary Wollstonecraft, *Mary and Maria*, and Mary Shelley, *Matilda*, edited by Janet Todd (Harmondsworth: Penguin Books, 1992), p. 59.
104 Rees, *Utopian Imagination and Eighteenth-Century Fiction*, p. 234.
105 Clara Reeve, *The Progress of Romance*, 2 vols (Colchester: Keymer; London: Robinson, 1785; reprinted in 1 vol., New York: The Facsimile Text Society, 1930), Vol. I, p. 112.

CHAPTER TWO

'Women of small fortunes, with cultivated minds': Clara Reeve

My father was an old Whig; from him I have learned all that I know; he was my oracle; he used to make me read the parliamentary debates while he smoked his pipe after supper. . . . He made me read Rapin's *History of England*; the information it gave made amends for the dryness. I read Cato's Letters, by Trenchard and Gordon; I read the Greek and Roman Histories, and Plutarch's Lives; all these at an age when few people of either sex can read their names.[1]

This is how Clara Reeve, in a letter quoted by Sir Walter Scott in his *Lives of the Novelists*, describes her education, and it seems a formidable one. The eldest daughter of a Suffolk clergyman, Reeve thus had an early and thorough grounding in classical and British history. She must also have learned Latin, since she translated Barclay's *Argenis* from that language. A confident writer in diverse genres, Reeve was a poet, a pioneering critic of the romance and the novel, a novelist who wrote in various sub-genres, including historical and Gothic novels, and a writer on education.

Scott's account of Reeve's education positions her as very much her father's daughter; Miriam Leranbaum has argued that the advanced education received by Reeve and nine other women writers of the time resulted in their becoming 'mistresses of orthodoxy'.[2] This chapter will show that a study of the theme of education in Reeve's writings, particularly her 1790s fiction, yields a far more complex writer. She uses the language of education to foreground women writers' public role, and to plan female communities which will train fortuneless young women in paid trades. Equally, Reeve uses the same language of education to write anti-abolitionist polemics, to exclude many social groups from the purview of education and delimit strictly the range of possibilities for female education.

Reeve is at her best when writing for and about women of her own background: intelligent, well-educated women of gentry or professional stock with few familial or material resources. If we are to believe hearsay evidence, Reeve's family was so poor that she had to work as a domestic servant: 'She was a clergyman's daughter, who had a very large family and a very small living. She, the eldest, was forced to be a common servant.'[3] One is inclined to believe this story because there is in Reeve's writing great sympathy for domestic servants,[4] and a sense of urgency whenever she talks about the need to find suitable employment for genteel but poor young women, themes which are prominent in her novels *The School for Widows* and *Plans of Education*. Reeve's writing career shows a gradual movement from a preoccupation with the role of women writers as public educators and members of the literary sphere, to a broadening perspective in which education allows women to criticize unsatisfactory marriages and forge bonds with women of other classes; concomitantly, her use of education also shows a deepening of conservatism in the arena of national politics.

'To Cultivate, to Improve and to Communicate':
The Woman of Letters and Her Public

In the 'Address to the Readers' prefacing her *Original Poems* (1769), Reeve presents herself as a 'candidate' for the favour of the reading public:

> Every man must be conscious of his talent before he can use it, and if this consciousness is free from pride . . . and self-conceit; I do not see that he is justly blameable for endeavouring to avail himself of the talents he has received from his Creator, for it is his duty . . . to cultivate, to improve, and to communicate.
>
> I formerly believed, that I ought not to let myself be known for a scribbler, that my sex was an insuperable objection, that mankind in general were prejudiced against its pretensions to literary merit; but I am now convinced of the mistake, by daily examples to the contrary. I see many female writers favourably received, admitted into the rank of authors, and amply rewarded by their public; I have been encouraged by their success, to offer myself as a candidate for the same advantages.[5]

Confidently, Reeve admits to a consciousness of talents and a religious imperative to cultivate, improve and communicate those talents. The Biblical Parable of the Talents is the obvious sub-text of the passage, which manages to combine this with an Enlightenment belief in the positive value of self-cultivation, a combination similar to that found in Mary Hamilton's writing. While in the first paragraph Reeve uses 'man' and 'he', in the next paragraph she foregrounds her gender, citing precedents and role models in other, successful women writers, and presenting herself as 'a candidate for . . . advantages' in the literary public sphere. This is the language of the literary professional seeking entry into a career open to talents. In an age when the professions, in the older sense of the term (law, medicine, divinity) are not open to women, Reeve creates fictional characters such as Euphrasia in *The Progress of Romance*, or Mrs Darnford and Mrs Gilson in *The School for Widows* – women who work for their living and enjoy it. Euphrasia is an author and critic, Mrs Darnford a teacher, Mrs Gilson a domestic servant; it does not matter what you do (and the range of occupations open to eighteenth-century women is limited anyway, a theme which crops up in Reeve's work), provided you do it well.

'All Depends on Cultivation'? *Original Poems*

One of the most striking poems in Reeve's *Original Poems* (1769) is entitled 'To My Friend Mrs–, on Her Holding an Argument in Favour of the Natural Equality of Both the Sexes'. Written in rhyming couplets, the poem is deft, light in tone, and ironic. The speaker appears to criticize a friend who thinks that 'both [men and women] were equal when created', and that 'all depends on cultivation'. The speaker, on the contrary, conjures up an irreverent picture of Apollo leading a team of 'wit-inspiring ladies', the Muses, who 'were always fond of fellows' rather than of women, a light-hearted dig at the traditional association of great poetry and poetic inspiration with men. Women's brains, Reeve says, are turned by the waters of Helicon. The few women who have attained fame in writing are exceptions, as are the few works which bear 'strong markings of the female mind'. The irony of the poem is fully evident only in the autobiographical climax:

> Dare now to ope your eyes and see
> These truths exemplified in me.
> What tho' while an infant young,
> The numbers trembled on my tongue;
> As youth advanced, I dar'd aspire,
> And trembling struck the heavenly lyre.
> What by my talents have I gained?
> By those I lov'd to be disdain'd,
> By some despis'd, by others fear'd,
> Envy'd by fools, by witlings jeer'd,
> See what success my labours crown'd,
> By birds and beasts alike disown'd.
> For what in man is most respected,
> In woman's form, shall be rejected.[6]

When the gender of the young prodigy-poet is female, failure, disdain and ridicule appear to be the rewards of talent. Reeve's comments on female writers in her preface and in 'To Mrs–', both highlight the difficulties faced by the woman of letters seeking membership of the literary sphere.

'A Good Citizen of the Republic of Letters': The Woman of Letters as Critic–Educator

> It is not of any consequence how much or how little one knows, but the use one makes of the knowledge one has acquired.—If like the industrious bee I have cull'd from various flowers my share of honey, and stored it in the common hive, I shall have performed the duties of a good citizen of the republic of letters, and I shall not have lived in vain.[7]

This is the voice of Euphrasia, one of three characters who conduct a debate about the value of fiction in Reeve's critical work, *The Progress of*

Romance (1785).[8] Euphrasia is the dominant personage in this work in dialogue form, analysing and defending the genres of the romance and the novel. Her friend and critic Hortensius has just told her that anyone who did not know her well would think, judging by her conversation, that her 'principal, if not only study, had been romances and novels', a comment with clearly pejorative overtones. Reeve's answer, with its image of the republic of letters as a hive, shows the woman of letters laying claim to full citizenship of the very public republic of letters; it also sees her as a tireless public educator, collecting and disseminating knowledge, enriching the 'common hive' with the honey she collects.

The classical-sounding names and the dialogue form of *The Progress of Romance* suggest a Socratic model. Such Socratic philosophical dialogue is, we should remember, the highest form of knowledge in western civilization and formal education in Reeve's time. Reeve thus positions herself audaciously, if implicitly, in the 'high' philosophical tradition, writing a work that dares to defend the feminized form of fiction as a kind of knowledge as much of pleasure. And, showing her fellowship with and high opinion of sister writers on education who were similarly creating new kinds of knowledge through works on education, she herself cites as a model for her work the dialogue form of *Theatre of Education* by the celebrated Stephanie de Genlis, the most distinguished popular educational writer of the day:

> The variety and contrast which naturally arise out of the dialogue, might enliven a work of rather dry deduction, and render it more entertaining to the reader, and not the less useful or instructive.—In this idea I was confirmed by the great success of . . . *Madame de Genlis*, in her excellent work called the *Theatre of Education*.[9]

Later, Genlis's books are again praised as 'deserving public honours, on the score of public utility'[10] – the pointed use of the word 'public' shows yet again that in the period in question, many women writers explicitly claimed an important position for themselves and other women in the public sphere.

The educative role of women is for Reeve perhaps *the* major public female vocation, expressing itself in fiction as much as in non-fiction. Both Euphrasia and Sophronia persistently express admiration for novelists particularly interested in education, most notably Sarah Fielding[11] and Sarah Scott, whose *Millenium Hall* (1762) is eulogized.[12] Reeve's own novels, *The School for Widows* (1791) and *Plans of Education* (1792), show Scott's influence: like Scott in *Millenium Hall*, Reeve depicts women who are victims of unhappy marriages, and who also plan ideal villages and female seminaries.

It is no accident that the detractor of the novel in *The Progress of Romance* is male, while its most vigorous defender is female. In Reeve's 'Hall of Fame', a strikingly large number of seats is occupied by mid-eighteenth-century women novelists – apart from Sarah Scott and Sarah Fielding, Frances Brooke, Frances Sheridan and the later, reformed, Eliza Haywood also figure in the list. Hortensius at one point exasperatedly says to Euphrasia, 'You are ready enough to pay due respect to writers of your own sex, but you are rather severe upon some of ours.'[13]

Later, Reeve argues that if, as Hortensius would have it, novels teach bad things, particularly to women, seen as especially fond of the genre, then it is equally true to say that the Classics, a staple and respected part of boys' education, contain even more morally dubious elements:

> Euphrasia: Pray Hortensius, is all this severity in behalf of our sex or your own?
> Hortensius: Of both.—Yet yours are most concerned in my remonstrance for they read more of these books [i.e. novels] than ours, and consequently are most hurt by them. . . .
> Euphrasia: It seems to me that you are unreasonably severe upon these books, which you suppose to be appropriated to our sex (which however is not the case) – not considering how many of worse tendency, are put into the hands of the youth of your own, without scruple. . . . They are taught the history – the mythology – the morals – of the great ancients, whom all you learned men revere.—But with these, they learn also – their idolatry – their follies – their vices – and everything that is shocking to virtuous manners.—Lucretius teaches them that *fear* first made the gods – that men grew out of the earth like trees, and that indulgence of the passions and appetites, is the truest wisdom.[14]

There is something depressing about Reeve's narrowly moralistic survey of the Classics – but Euphrasia is also being tongue-in-cheek, showing how the pejorative things often said about fiction can be applied equally well to the highest categories in contemporary categorization of knowledge. Reeve's argument is not that the Classics should be banned but that it is absurd to expect that some novels will not contain morally dubious elements. While Hortensius would, if he were a father, prevent his children from reading any work of fiction,[15] Euphrasia argues that such censorship would be pernicious, muzzling free speech:

> The objections to bad books of this species, are equally applicable to all other kinds of writing – indecent novels, indecent plays, essays, memoirs, dialogues are equally to be exploded; but it does not follow that all these kinds of writing are to be extirpated, because some are bad.—By the same kind of reasoning we might plead for the prohibition of all kinds of writing. . . . All these objections amount to no more than that bad books are bad things – but shall we therefore prohibit reading?[16]

Euphrasia and Sophronia therefore argue that as far as novel-reading by children and adolescents is concerned, parents should be vigilant but should not censor their children's reading; their best bet is to give their children books that they as parents approve of – exposure to what is good will cure any attraction to the bad.

The moral prudishness of Reeve's female critic–readers, characteristic of her other works as well, can veil the fact that for Reeve this does *not* entail a narrowing of subject-matter. 'Education' is not for her an anaemic and (therefore) feminine term excluding such subjects as philosophy or politics, or difficult issues such as adultery and illegitimacy. When the Reeve-persona Euphrasia argues that Barclay's *Argenis*, which Reeve had translated (as *The Phoenix*),[17] is a valuable work, she does so citing a critic who praises it for its 'philosophy and politics'.[18] *Argenis* (1621, trans. 1772) is a work that warns of the dangers of factionalism and praises monarchy: from early on, Reeve thus establishes herself as a writer of a conservative tendency. Reeve's novel *The School for Widows* presents us with an argumentative rake with whom one of the heroines argues about the legitimacy of concubinage. The same heroine takes charge of the education of an illegitimate daughter and a madwoman. *Plans of Education* inveighs on issues of national importance, such as schools of industry, slavery and trades for women. One is struck by the range of ideas in Reeve's fictions of education.

The Progress of Romance, however, ends with a reading list that is limited in range, a list of unexceptionable reading meant for young readers, with Reeve claiming that 'female readers' are chiefly targeted. The list for young ladies is composed chiefly of conduct books (Dr Gregory, Mrs Chapone, Moore, Fordyce), periodical essays (*Spectator, Guardian, Adventurer, Rambler, Connoisseur*), text-books (Genlis's works *Theatre of Education* and *Tales of the Castle*) and religious works (writings by Catherine Talbot, Elizabeth Rowe and Hannah More). Even in this list, we find many women intellectuals and writers, from Bluestockings Catherine Talbot and Hester Chapone to Reeve's much-admired public educator Madame de Genlis. Nonetheless, after representations of powerful female educators and fiction writers holding conversations about the value of fiction, we are left with a sop, a catalogue which apportions to the female pupil conduct books, religious works, periodical essays and only one fiction writer (Richardson). The list shows how tension-ridden the theme of female education is in a writer like Reeve, veering from polemical utterances about the public vocation and utility of the female educator, writer or critic, to more constricting images of the pliable young female pupil who must read prescriptive works.

The tensions we find in Reeve's work are, in the context of *The Progress of Romance*, deepened by the fact that the volume also contains Reeve's female-centred Oriental Tale of Charoba, queen of Egypt. Charoba succeeds in besting and killing a king who tries to compel her to marry him. The heroine of this tale thus evades marriage and rules independently. The patriarch Abraham only appears in the story to give her the blessing of female wile. This strategy of making the patriarch confer the boon of power on an independent-minded woman is very characteristic of Reeve's cunning – and I use the word cunning deliberately: in the two works I am about to analyse, too, female power is thus foregrounded, while weak or tyrannical patriarchs die or submit to the will of the female prota-gonists, foremost among whom is the female educator. Certainly, the discourse of 'proper education' is absent in Charoba, but there are distinct similarities between this tale of the powerful woman ruler struggling to escape an unwelcome marriage and Reeve's other heroines. It is just that the rhetoric is far more earnest in *The School for Widows* and *Plans of Education*.

'Virtuous Mind[s] Struggling against Misfortunes':
The School for Widows (1791)

Such earnestness is very evident in the way the 'virtue in distress' motif is re-energized by Reeve in the preface to *The School for Widows* (1791). Here, she announces that she is writing a novel which advocates strength of mind and independence in women. Denouncing the kind of false sentiment that praises helpless feminine weakness, she instead offers alternative exemplary figures through her heroines, Mrs Darnford and Mrs Strictland, the widows who go through the 'school' of adversity of the title.

> This word [i.e. 'sentimental'] . . . seems to have degenerated from its original meaning: and under this flimsy disguise, it has given rise to a great number of whining, maudlin stories . . . calculated to excite a kind of morbid sensibility . . . which have a tendency to weaken the mind, and to deprive it of those resources which Nature intended it should find within itself.
>
> Young people . . . should be encouraged to believe, that misfortunes are not invincible; that virtue will enable them to overcome all difficulties . . . that virtue is active, and gathers strength from exercise; and that indolence frustrates its own expectations.[19]

Reeve thus uses the Christian, more particularly Protestant and Miltonic, idea (expressed in 'Comus', *Areopagitica* and *Paradise Lost*, for example) that virtue *needs* to confront adversity to prove itself fully. In Reeve's novel, the kinds of adversity the widows of the title confront are markedly gendered – tyrannical or spendthrift husbands, the loss of a marriage settlement, an attempt by a rake to buy his friend's wife, and the difficulties that women face in trying to earn a living. She criticizes nearly all of the upper-class, fashionable characters she describes, ruthlessly anatomizes unhappy marriages, and gives a positive portrait of women who struggle to be financially and emotionally independent. If Reeve is adopting an anti-sensibility, anti-emotional position that marks her out as in the opposite camp to revolutionary writers such as Mary Wollstonecraft and Mary Hays, her rationalist rhetoric of 'sense' allies with the language of education to create a formidable critique of patriarchy and fashionable society.

Reeve brings in a Stoic strain in her preface as another tradition that validates her struggling, virtuous women. Instead of women being seen as passive and associated with the body, Reeve sees women first and foremost as *minds*, educating themselves through the school of adversity. 'It was a saying of Cato the Elder, "that a virtuous mind, struggling against misfortunes, was a spectacle that the gods beheld with pleasure and approbation." . . . virtue is active, and gathers strength from exercise.'[20]

At the beginning of the novel, Rachel Strictland, widowed recently, is looking for her old school friend, Frances Darnford. She finds that her friend is no longer within the pale of London middle-class society. Mrs Darnford had apparently been reduced to poverty through her now-dead spendthrift husband, to whom she had given up her marriage settlement. After being widowed, she has successively acted as governess, set up a school in the country, and is now 'engaged in a strange undertaking . . . she lives in a haunted house, and takes care of a madwoman, whose husband is gone abroad, and has left his house and his wife to the care of Mrs Darnford.'[21] Promising material for melodrama and/or a Gothic novel here – but Reeve's treatment of these dramatic plot details is throughout remarkably brisk, except when she makes her protagonists criticize their husbands. A review of *The School for Widows* in the *Monthly Review* was quick to grasp Reeve's antipathy to the husbands of her heroines and her desire to make the wives/widows exemplary characters: 'we think it [*The School for Widows*] is offered to the public under a misnomer, it being rather a SCHOOL for HUSBANDS; those introduced being represented as very naughty boys indeed, while their spouses, both as wives and widows, are strained up to the best female characters.'[22]

The portraits Reeve offers of the marriages of Mrs Strictland and Mrs Darnford are as excoriating as the critique of marriage in Wollstonecraft's *Maria, or the Wrongs of Woman* (1798). Here is Mrs Strictland speaking of her husband, for example, articulating a major lesson she has learned from her years in the school of unhappy marriage:

> I am restored to my liberty by the death of my husband; an awful and important event, but not greatly deplored by me. . . . I know not seemings; I disclaim them.
>
> After being the slave and prisoner of a tyrant for ten years, I feel as does the captive just delivered from his chains. It would be folly, it would be sinful in me to affect the part of a disconsolate widow.[23]

Married to a wealthy farmer, Mrs Strictland finds herself hemmed in by prohibitions. Mr Strictland disapproves of female friendships; nor can he understand why his wife should want to surround herself with books or to play the harpsichord. Strictland, then, feels threatened by even the conventional contemporary accoutrements of female education. The marriage goes through a crisis, with Mrs Strictland calling her husband 'more despotic than the king of France',[24] a particularly telling comment given the 1790s context.

The climax to the Strictlands' marital conflicts comes when Mrs Strictland has a miscarriage after a particularly violent quarrel. By this time, she has found a friend and ally in Mrs Gilson, the housekeeper, who has also gone to the school of adversity. For women writers such as Reeve or Elizabeth Hamilton, the domestic servant is a vital presence and ally for gentlewomen in their plans of education.

The housekeeper herself knows what it is like to have a sense of stifled vocation:

My parents were shopkeepers in this village. They sold almost every thing, and got a very good livelihood. My brothers were idle and unthrifty youths, they wanted to be of genteel professions, they made my father spend all his savings upon them. My sisters and I had what is thought a good education here in the country, we were taught to read and write, and the first rules in arithmetic. . . . My eldest sister and I kept the day-book, and in the evening, my father and I used to transfer it to other books. He understood his business well, and would have raised a fortune, but for his prodigal sons.[25]

The Gilson sisters' good country education and their skill in book-keeping cannot be used to build a future since it is the prodigal brothers who inherit the shop. The shrewd and competent Mrs Gilson advises Mrs Strictland to draw up a written contract, called 'Articles of Reconciliation', between her and her husband after the miscarriage. According to this, he is to pay his wife her allowance from her guardian punctually; she will be allowed to receive visits from persons of 'unexceptionable character', to write to all her friends and to procure books.[26] In short, she asks, at her housekeeper's urging, *contractually* for as much financial and mental independence as possible within the limits of marriage.

Once this is allowed, Mrs Strictland is somewhat happier. Their house, Woodlands, which is huge and old, had formerly assumed for her a near-Gothic dimension, as her friend Mrs Elton realizes:

You are here in a large and lonely house, and have found it gloomy and uncomfortable; and, though you are sometimes lively and pleasant upon the dark rooms and old pictures, I perceive that they have taken hold of your imagination. I will give you a recipe to make them familiar to you.[27]

This is a recipe to 'make . . . familiar' the dark spectre of the Gothic: Reeve had written a pioneering novel in the 'female Gothic' mode[28] (*The Old English Baron*, 1777). In *Plans of Education*, she sees the Gothic as disempowering for women. Mrs Strictland is not allowed to thrill tremblingly at the terrors in Woodlands – but the threat of succumbing to such gloom and terror lurks in the background, a threat which is in this novel symbolic of the melancholia and madness that patriarchy generates for women such as Mrs Strictland and Madame di Soranzo, Mrs Darnford's charge, who seeks refuge in madness after repeated sexual advances from a supposed protector. Mrs Elton is obviously very aware of the precarious line that Mrs Strictland is treading between sanity and madness. Mrs Elton and Mrs Gilson are to Mrs Strictland what Mrs Darnford will be for Madame di Soranzo: figures of female solidarity who pride themselves on their reason and briskness, and who pull their beleaguered female friends out of the chasm of madness.

Mrs Strictland remains unhappy with her marriage, however, despite the brave face she puts on. What makes the picture of the Strictlands' conjugal unhappiness so stark is the fact that Strictland (like Darnford) is no stereotypical villain; just temperamentally incompatible with his wife.

Strictland had many disagreeable qualities; but he had no vices. He was sober and temperate . . . industrious and frugal; this last degenerated into avarice, which excited him to accumulate wealth, which he never enjoyed. . . . I had a very strong and lively imagination, which is generally accompanied with a degree of enthusiasm towards its favourite objects. . . . I know that there is a little romance in my composition.[29]

We are given more instances of Mrs Strictland's imagination, her love of romance and her rebelliousness. She befriends a little boy who turns out to be Henry Marney, scion of the family who had earlier owned Woodlands. Holding her husband's 'nouveau riche' greed in contempt, Mrs Strictland's love for Henry is also an act of defiance against her husband's way of life. Once widowed and left with a considerable fortune, the 'romance' in her composition is channelized into plans for a model village (yet another literary female-founded village, like Munster Village), of which we hear in *Plans of Education*, the sequel to *The School for Widows*. In Mrs Strictland's utopian plans, too, education plays a prominent role. At first, we hear that she is trying to replicate the model in Shenstone's long poem, 'The Schoolmistress'.[30] Later, we hear that she is planning to establish a School of Industry and a manufactory in her village.[31]

Mrs Darnford's marriage has also been unhappy. She has been married to a man much weaker than she is, a man with a small income who is fatally fond of fashionable life. The accounts Mrs Darnford gives of various frustrating conversations with her husband have an element of black humour to them – the couple are so obviously incompatible, with the wife chafing at the husband's weakness, the husband in turn stung at his wife's relentless competence and good sense. When the marriage is at its happiest, their exchanges go something like this:

> He shook his head—'. . . I am afraid you are too good and too wise for me.'
>   'Few husbands pay such compliments to their wives: but I will try to deserve them by my conduct.'
>   'Oh, Fanny, you are sly; you do not think I meant you a compliment. You are a good girl, but you are too serious. Don't preach to me, for it does me no good.'[32]

Neither of them can help their characters, however; she continues to preach, he to resent her attempts. Slowly, the good humour between the two disappears completely: 'He was displeased at my remarks; he would not be so catechized; he was judge of his own conduct, and would endure no such monitor.'[33] His wife is not to 'preach' to him; she is not to presume to be his teacher, his catechist, his monitor. When we look at novels such as Frances Burney's *Cecilia* (1782) and *Camilla* (1796), with their bleak pictures of women beleaguered by misguided male monitors, Reeve's depiction of an attempted and failed role reversal seems poignant. Nor is Mrs Darnford allowed to use her competence in money matters to help him:

'I will tell you the way to be rich.' 'Pray do, and I will thank you.' 'By regularity and economy.'

'Paltry bourgeois qualities! I hate and despise them.' 'They are as necessary for gentlemen as for citizens.'

'I leave them to citizens and stewards.' 'Let me be your steward?' 'Yes, that you may check my expenses – no, thank you.'[34]

Frances values thrift and would be proud to be a 'bourgeois' steward (a very early use of the term 'bourgeois', although I shall argue later in this chapter that Reeve cannot primarily be classified as an emergent bourgeois writer), while her husband would like to be a leisured gentleman. At this point, Mrs Darnford, increasingly isolated from her husband, and drawn more and more to the role of educator and working woman, trains herself to be a teacher. While she and her husband are living in the country, she makes friends with a farmer's daughter who desires to 'improve herself in reading and writing'. She loves the company of Mrs Darnford, who becomes her 'preceptress'. The educative bond between the two cuts across classes and is also affective: 'When my husband was with Lord A–, she was my constant companion; and my vulgar taste preferred her conversation to that of those I had met in the *best company*.'[35]

Having discovered this educative vocation latent in herself, Mrs Darnford systematically and diligently trains herself to be a professional educator – in an age where there is no formal system for training teachers, Mrs Darnford acts as auto-didact, both reading and writing on education:

> I thought I perceived in myself a talent for the education of youth; and I resolved, if I should be reduced to indigence, to undertake something of this sort. . . .
>
> I read many books of this kind: I wrote remarks on them: I drew plans of seminaries of education. In short, I endeavoured to qualify myself for this employment.[36]

Darnford's financial situation worsens and he tries to make his wife give up her marriage settlement. This she refuses to do for a very long time, not until after she has left her husband. She leaves him when she realizes that her husband has been persuaded to sell her to his ostensible friend, Lord A–. Lord A–, a member of the large club of engaging rakes in eighteenth-century fiction, never offers to marry his friend's wife. Even after Mr Darnford's death, Lord A– tries to argue that concubinage is an honourable state: as a result of his views, he and his projected mistress have an amicable intellectual debate, with Lord A– citing Cato and the Old Testament to justify concubinage.[37] Mrs Darnford argues back spiritedly, but praises Lord A–'s honesty: 'I respect your sincerity, in disdaining to raise expectations you never intended to fulfil. I wish all men, that had your opinions, were as honest in this respect.'[38] What could have been the stuff of rants and faints becomes instead an intellectual and moral argument – but this composure is achieved after a long struggle on Mrs Darnford's part to earn her living with dignity.

Mrs Darnford starts her life as a working woman when she becomes a governess. Although her plan had been to start a school, she is dissuaded by her father's executor, who tells her that 'Schools are talked up, and talked down, by those who know nothing of the requisites, or the real government of them. . . . The conducting of a seminary of education is an arduous and laborious under-taking; it is not duly estimated, nor sufficiently rewarded.'[39] However, Reeve shows that while running a school may be hard, the career of a governess is thankless, undignified and humiliating. Mrs Darnford finds her students inat-tentive and deliberately insolent, while her employer regards this as a matter of course:

> I had a conversation with Lady Haughton. She was not convinced of the deficiency in the young pupils' education. She said . . . that her children were thought amiable and accomplished by as good judges as myself, and she would not suffer them to be made unhappy, in order to teach them what they had no desire to learn. I asked, 'What service I was to do them in this situation?' 'Why, I want you to sit with them when I am engaged, and when their masters attend them; and if you do not like this, Mrs Darnford, you may leave my family whenever you please.' 'It will be very easy, madam, to find a person qualified for this office; a servant may do it, but I could not be satisfied to receive a salary for doing nothing.'[40]

Here, in fictional form, is a critique of the treatment of governesses by most upper-class contemporary employers, and of the lack of weight and serious-ness given to this occupation. The Edgeworths, in *Practical Education* (1798), also argue that governesses deserve high salaries and should occupy a position of dignity in society; to describe the calling of a governess, they use the term 'profession'.[41] In Reeve, though the word 'profession' is not used, an implicit meritocratic charge is already present.

Mrs Darnford decides that the best way of using her skills is not to be found in fashionable society. Disgusted with the upper and middle classes, she moves to a town in the provinces, where she takes lodgings in the house of a car-penter's widow, Mrs Martin. With both women struggling to find some means of livelihood, they go into partnership, and open in the house 'a SCHOOL for FEMALE CHILDREN; where reading, English, writing, and all kind of needle-work, are taught in the best manner'. Mrs Darnford makes Mrs Martin's two daughters assistants in the school.

When the school proves a success, she is asked by the lax and fashionable rector of the parish to confine it to more upper-class children, and to teach French and Italian to more upper-class girls, such as the rector's daughters. This she refuses to do.[42] 'Degrees of subordination are necessary; I look upon them as such; but there are degrees of merit in every one of these that are superior to every temporary distinction. . . . Merit is not limited to any set of people, but is to be found everywhere.'[43]

We need to remember the contempt Reeve shows in *The School for*

Widows for genteel, fashionable, vain people, and a corresponding sympathy for more lower-class characters as friends and pupils for her heroine. The gentlewoman trying to earn a living, Reeve shows, cannot find a refuge when she most needs it in her own class – and she will not abandon her original friends in better days. Indeed, Mrs Darnford and the Martins grow so close that she adopts Patty, one of the Martin daughters. Patty says of Mrs Darnford that 'this dear lady has been the parent of my mind, she has given me a new set of thoughts, and even senses. I feel an affection for her that I cannot describe.'[44] This, as in the relationship between Mrs Darnford and the farmer's daughter, is the best sort of educative bond for Reeve, one which is also affective.

Mrs Darnford, in turn, describes the Martins as 'relations of my soul'.[45] Mrs Martin describes her lodger as the 'good angel' who came under her 'humble roof' and as a 'friend' who also functions as her 'oracle at home'.[46] Unlike Mr Darnford, she is grateful when her partner takes on the role of teacher: 'she condescended to instruct me after the school-hours; and oh! what delightful evenings have I spent in her company! She deserved knowledge, because she made a wise and good use of it.'[47]

It is thus through female friendships and alliances that Mrs Darnford's vocation as an educator finds the warmth and respect it deserves. Mrs Strictland, too, asks her friend to 'come and share my heart and fortune, not as a dependant, but as my *counsellor* and *instructress*, and my daughter's *governess* and friend': again, the female educator is seen as creating an affective bond of female friendship and solidarity.[48] The characters of the friends Rachel Strictland and Frances Darnford conform to the late eighteenth-century fictional model of female friends, sometimes sisters, who are complementary to each other, and are portrayed as types of sense and sensibility, of the rational and the emotional (like Jane Austen's Elinor and Marianne in *Sense and Sensibility*). There is a strong element of yearning and desire in their relationship, one of the many same-sex bonds in the novel. Women here look for education, both formal and experiential, are helped to find it by members of their own sex, and are thwarted in their attempts by weak male figures.

The school Mrs Darnford and Mrs Martin start expands into a little shop which stocks haberdashery and stationery. Mrs Darnford eventually leaves the school to the management of the carpenter's widow, when a certain Captain Maurice asks her to take charge of a mysterious, temporarily insane Italian woman, Madame di Soranzo, and of his illegitimate daughter. That is exactly the sort of challenge to appeal to Mrs Darnford – but before she goes, she advises Mrs Martin as to how she ought to make provision for her children. Mrs Gilson's fate is not to befall the Martin daughters: the eldest daughter is immediately to be given a share in the business, with the rest being left for the two younger daughters. Strikingly, however, they will forfeit all right to the business if they marry (is Mrs Darnford's own sponging and unscrupulous husband on her mind here?). The son is to be set up in business and provided for, for two years. After this, he will be on his own; if he marries, he is to buy his own house.[49] All the provisions are designed to protect single women and widows.

In her new employment, Mrs Darnford succeeds in bringing her charge out of her melancholia, in a variant of her pedagogic role. We are given an inset story of the love triangle between Captain Maurice, Antonio di Soranzo and Isabella di Soranzo. When the Italian Other makes an entrance, Reeve gives a far freer rein to melodrama – Madame di Soranzo loses her mind after relentless sexual advances from Captain Maurice, a friend of her now-dead husband. Eventually, the Captain goes abroad, leaving Mrs Darnford in charge of di Soranzo. Even though she is locked up in a room, Isabella di Soranzo slowly learns to trust her wardress and companion, who exerts herself to free her charge. Characteristically prosaic, Mrs Darnford writes to her employer, requesting him to give up all claims to Isabella: 'I had written to Captain Maurice, upon his return from the West Indies, acquainting him with our present situation; and desiring him to release Donna Isabella from all engagements to himself.'[50]

Mrs Darnford speaks almost legalistically – and sure enough, as a result of her rational efforts, di Soranzo is rescued from her Gothic prison. If one is allowed to draw a parallel, it is as if Grace Poole manages to rescue her charge, Bertha Rochester, the madwoman in the attic, from madness and confinement. The competent working woman exorcises the Gothic terrors that predatory male sexuality unleashes.

Writing to Mrs Strictland about her rich, varied and often painful experiences, Mrs Darnford argues that her encounters with adversity have given her a wider experiential education: 'What advantages have I not gained from my trials! They have taught me to know the world and myself; to separate the grain from the chaff of my acquaintance; to gain real and sincere friends, to pity and forgive my enemies.'[51]

By the end of the novel, all the widows – Mrs Darnford, Mrs Strictland, Mrs Martin, Madame di Soranzo – all of whom have encountered adversity and come out stronger from their trials, are free in their different ways. Their life-stories are woven together to produce a bold and unusual female *Bildungsroman*: in Reeve's world view, marriage is not the end of female education and development – quite the reverse. At the end of the novel, Mrs Darnford writes of the new-found freedom of Madame di Soranzo, but also of herself and the other widows, in a passage charged with symbolic overtones:

> I have ordered the double door to be opened. . . . The room is to be new white washed and painted. . . . I will have no more haunted rooms here, any more than you have at Woodlands. The virtuous have nothing to fear. *'The wicked flee when none pursueth; but the righteous are bold as a lion.'*[52]

In this passage, as indeed in the overall dynamic of the novel, Reeve foregrounds and praises an ideal of ethical but also eminently rational and competent female independence and competence, more specifically, an ideal of a successful female educator. At the same time, in the background lurks the constant threat of a Gothic vision in which patriarchy disempowers women, threatening them with madness and the terror of haunted rooms. Mary Wollstonecraft was to write of marriage bastilling her heroine Maria in *The Wrongs of Woman* – Reeve is more determinedly optimistic and stresses the ability of women to avert such confinement, or to break out of it through the help of the empowered educator. Nevertheless, the same imaginative awareness of the constant see-saw between female empowerment and disempowerment drives both *The School for Widows* and *The Wrongs of Woman*.

'A Spirit of Reformation among Us'?: *Plans of Education* (1792)

The sequel to *The School for Widows* belongs firmly to the climate of the post-French Revolution war of ideas. It is in many ways an explicitly reactionary work, deliberately seeking, in the aftermath of the French Revolution and the revolutionary threat, to reinscribe the value of a hierarchical structure of society: it polemically speaks against abolition of slavery, and against class mobility. It advocates an alternative programme of social 'reformation' at various levels, with schemes for keeping the poor employed in Schools of Industry and, at the core of the work, a plan for an unusual female community with a seminary which will primarily benefit poor but well-born young girls.

The School for Widows and *Plans of Education* exemplify the way in which categories such as gender, race and class are often disturbingly deployed in texts by conservative late eighteenth-century and early nineteenth-century women writers. Reeve, who is a sympathetic portrayer of the lives of genteel but poor women, and of women belonging to the upper ranks of the lower classes, is at the same time, in *Plans of Education*, explicitly racist and anti-abolitionist,[53] and is unenlightened even as regards her view of the poorest sections of her own society. Unlike many conservative reformers of her time, including Mrs Trimmer, whom she praises,[54] she advocates that the poorest children in Schools of Industry not be taught to read or write.[55] Such deliberate advocacy of exclusion from education and curtailment of freedom are very much part of a work which continually bears traces of a fear of change, of disorder, of rebellion. Reeve thus cannot be fitted into a neat model of the emergent bourgeois woman writer – her espousal of female paid work, cross-class alliances and professionalism in *The School for Widows* need to be read with her explicitly reactionary, pro-slavery, pro-aristocracy and pro-gentry polemics in *Plans of Education*.

Even Reeve's plan for a female seminary and community, which bears many traces of the positive view of female competence found in *The School for Widows*, shows an anxiety to strictly define and delimit women's lives and trades, and takes as its model the seventeenth-century aristocratic female community and school of St-Cyr, founded by Madame de Maintenon.

A sense of crisis pervades *Plans of Education*, a fear that things could easily fall apart unless confronted with suitable strategies. The motive of the work, writes Reeve, is 'an ardent wish of promoting the good of society, and lessening evils caused by indolent and bad members of it'.[56] There is a 'spirit of reformation' in the country, which will, Reeve hopes, be 'effectual to the whole body of the common people of this land, which does exceedingly stand in need of it'.[57] The principal spokeswoman in the work is again Frances Darnford, this time writing to Lady A–, wife of the Lord A– we had met in *The School for Widows*. The spirit of reformation has obviously touched Lord A–, now a good husband who confesses his past misdeeds to his wife. The couple and Mrs Darnford form a cordial connection, with Mrs Darnford again in the role of educator. Mrs Darnford continues to live in her unusual 'ménage' with the now sane Isabella di Soranzo, Miss Brady, Captain Maurice's illegitimate daughter, and her own adopted daughter, Patty Martin. By this time, Mrs Darnford's dreams of becoming a professional are fully realized – she, whose husband had refused to make her his unofficial steward, is now appointed the steward of Miss Brady's fortune.[58]

Mrs Darnford sharply criticizes young women being given a 'good education' beyond their station, which then leads to a lack of a suitable vocation:

> We have observed from the increase of boarding schools, and from the general stile [*sic*] of education among the middling and lower ranks of people, every degree educating their children . . . above their present circumstances, and future expectations; that a great number of young women come into the world without fortunes suitable to their educations, and . . . are exposed to all the dangers of a deserted and friendless situation . . . the unfortunate sufferers are the objects of our tenderest pity. . . . How often are they seduced by designing men! or become the victims of their own credulity and innocence. . . . Our present undertaking is partly designed to provide for these helpless, friendless, destitute young women, to take them from the dangers that surround them . . . to give them some business for their future support.[59]

The complaint about educating young girls above their station is not a new one: we have already encountered it in Mary Hamilton's *Munster Village*. But there is a further fear lurking in the passage, that highly educated but resourceless women such as these will be forced into prostitution ('seduced by designing men', 'victims of their own innocence and credulity'). Hence the urgency to find suitable paid work for such women. In this combination of an awareness of the threat of prostitution for women, sympathy for prostitutes and an urge to check prostitution by finding jobs for women, Reeve is not unusual among women writers in the 1790s.[60] She is in fact an early articulator of such views, which radi-cal writers like Mary Hays, Mary Anne Radcliffe and Anne Frances Randall also express later in the decade. Radcliffe, for example, in her *The Female Advocate*, quotes a remarkable letter from *The Morning Herald*, 17 August 1798:

> My friend and self, a few days ago, having dined with an officer at his barracks, returned home between ten and eleven: in Panton Street we were accosted by an unfortunate woman, who first solicited our charity in English; but overhearing us in our progress speak French, she renewed her suit in that language, probably thinking we might be foreigners, and therefore did not understand the nature of her first application . . . she spoke both fluently and elegantly, the

evident result of a liberal education . . . my friend . . . replied to her in Italian, and we were not a little surprised to find her not only a mistress of that language, but also well versed in Latin.[61]

The implication is that *because* this young woman is so highly educated, she cannot find a job. Reeve, though she herself had received such an advanced education, has no time, in *Plans of Education*, for this kind of 'liberal education' which leads to helplessness. Her ideal village school has a very basic curriculum:

> There are wanting among us schools of a different kind, where young people might acquire necessary and useful knowledge, without learning to ape the vanities and follies of their superiors; who, as your ladyship archly observes, used to have the privilege of enjoying them exclusively.
>
> I never knew but one school of this kind, and that sunk when its founder and pillar was removed. A young woman of low birth and education, raised a school in a country village, upon a very plain and simple plan; she had a good understanding and many useful qualifications.[62]

This young woman teaches her pupils housework, needlework and reading. When she marries the squire, however, she becomes a 'Lady of the Last Edition', a wonderful term that, in the context of the passage, sums up how intimately education, books and women educators had become linked in the late eighteenth century. A prey to the latest fads in educational theory, she ruins her school.

Reeve urges that serious attention be paid to the fact that many young women are and will, in the foreseeable future, remain single – yet society does not try to make provision for such women. Instead, 'old maids' are made the butt of ridicule in literature and life. Her argument is similar to Elizabeth Hamilton's, as we shall see.

> In Protestant countries, though no vows are made, no confinement is exacted; yet nearly as many females are as much condemned to a state of celibacy, as if they were shut up in a convent.[63]
>
> Those who believe themselves possessed of wit, use it to turn them [i.e. old maids] to contempt and ridicule; not because they are unworthy, but because they are unfortunate. . . . The Aunt Deborahs, and Mrs Malaprops, are the standing jest of the modern writers.[64]

For such women, a Protestant convent of sorts is the answer.[65] Reeve, in creating such a fictional female retreat, follows in the footsteps of Mary Astell in her work, *A Serious Proposal to the Ladies, for the Advancement of Their True and Greatest Interest* (1694). While Astell advocates a highly intellectual, almost contemplative, education, Reeve's plan is designed to provide a useful education geared towards training women for paid work. Here is Reeve's rationale for her planned community:

Though Protestants in general have a rooted aversion to the name of a convent, it is certain that there are many benefits arising from these institutions, as well as inconveniences and abuses; particularly to such women as are forsaken by their relatives, and deserted by the world. . . . There are many women of small fortunes, with cultivated minds, and enlarged hearts, that would chuse to retire from the bustle of the world, and devote their time and talents to the benefit of others, rather than sink into *ennui*, which always attends indolence. These might found an asylum for themselves, and a seminary of education for others.[66]

One is inevitably reminded at this point of some other women with 'cultivated minds, and enlarged hearts' who had founded an 'asylum for them-selves, and a seminary of education for others', in the pages of Sarah Scott's *Millenium Hall* (1762) (Euphrasia and Sophronia, we remember, had praised the book in *The Progress of Romance*). Like Reeve in *The School for Widows*, Scott places single women and widows at the centre of her novel, and anatomizes women's often painful experience of marriage. Though Reeve does not mention Astell or Scott in *Plans*, one gets a sense of her place in a female literary tradition of works on female education.

Reeve proposes that 'ladies in the first year of their widowhood', 'ladies, whose husbands are sent abroad in public offices', 'single ladies, who have not settled their plan of life' and 'ladies of more advanced age . . . who wish to retire from the world',[67] should enter into a voluntary engagement for three years in the first instance, to be renewed or revoked at the end of that period. The structure of the seminary would be a Sisterhood, with a Council, comprising twelve members. The Council would meet weekly and govern the community. The head would be a Superior. Each member of the Sisterhood would have a particular office: there would be, in addition to the Superior, a Treasurer, a Superintendent of the Household, a Governess, a Sub-governess, a Housekeeper, an Intendant of the garden, an Intendant of the cellar, an Intendant of all the 'works done in the community, particularly those made and sold for the benefit of the poor young women in it', a Secretary, an Accountant, and an Intendant of the dairy and poultry.[68] The conception of the Council is a combination of the secular and the religious: we have the Superior and the twelve members of the Council, the number bringing to mind the twelve apostles. At the same time, the offices are practical and administrative, a committee through which the Sisterhood will administer every aspect of their undertaking.

The community would be more or less self-sufficient, with its own lands, its own poultry and its own dairy. The female seminary that it would house would take both fee-paying and charity pupils. The latter will consist of 'a certain number of young girls, the daughters of clergymen, officers in the army and navy, placemen, or any profession whose parents have died in indigent circum-stances, and left them entirely destitute of any provision.'[69] It is poor daughters of professionals that are targeted, in other words, and they will in turn be educated to be working women: to be assistant teachers, milliners, mantua-makers, clearstarchers, lace-makers, stay-makers, embroiderers, plain workers, spinners, knitters, or florists.[70] They would spend part of their time using the skills they are being trained in, and what they make will be sold. The profits would be used for the charity pupils, to set them up in business or as their marriage portion.[71] These pupils are to be called 'Assistants' to the Sisterhood, even their name signalling their status as nascent working women. Indeed, Reeve's emphasis on training poor young women for paid work in such clear and unequivocal terms is unprecedented. In *Millenium Hall*, young girls from neighbouring villages are educated only to be servants or wives, while in Lady Mary Hamilton's *Munster Village*, although the female pupils in the village are given a useful education, there are no specifications as to what is to be taught and how this will be useful.

Reeve, an indigent clergyman's daughter, comes from the same social order that she seeks to privilege and train in her ideal female seminary. Unlike Wollstonecraft in *Vindication of the Rights of Woman*, or Mary Hays in *Appeal to the Men of Great Britain in Behalf of Women*, however, Reeve gives no hint that she would like to expand the range of occupations open to women. The occupations Reeve lists, with the exception of teaching, are menial. Such trades as lace-making, knitting and spinning, Maxine Berg has argued, were important parts of the eighteenth-century traditional industrial economy, and mostly employed women, but were becoming marginal in the factory system that had begun to evolve.[72] Reeve thus, in a sense, de-classes her gentlewomen, rather seeking to make them part of a competent, though by this time *residual*, work force. This again allows us to see that her 'Plan of Education' cannot be accommodated easily into an emergent bourgeois order and its world-view.

Reeve, putting governessing in the same category as clear-starching or mantua-making, certainly cannot be accused of snobbery – nor, as she, like other 1790s writers on female paid trades knows, can she afford to be, given the small number of such trades open to women. The restricted choice of trades for women brings women from various social groupings into the same work place: in Frances Burney's *The Wanderer* (1814), the down-and-out heroine Juliet Granville finds that when she works in a milliner's shop, she becomes a 'work-woman' or a 'shop-woman' (both Burney's terms), like any other 'Miss Biddy', 'Miss Jenny', 'Miss Polly' or 'Miss Betsey' – other social groupings become irrelevant.[73]

Reeve joins radical writers such as Mary Hays and Mary Anne Radcliffe in her indignation about men usurping professions traditionally followed by women, such as mantua-making and stay-making: 'There are very few trades for women; the men have usurped two-thirds of those that used to belong to them; the remainder are over-stocked, and there are few resources for them.'[74] In this respect, her argument is similar to that of Mary Hays in *Appeal to the Men of Great Britain in Behalf of Women* (1798):

> women of the higher ranks, over whom one should suppose delicacy and refinement, if not real modesty, would have more influence, admit without scruple – men hair-dressers – men milliners – men mantua-makers. Nay worse

than all these – I blush to write it – men stay-makers. . . . Why are not men made ashamed of monopolizing trades, in which if the more helpless sex were early instructed, and made thereby to taste the sweets of honest industry, might save some millions of valuable subjects to the commonwealth of virtue.[75]

Hays, like Reeve, argues that male monopolization of occupations suitable to women is a way of forcing women into prostitution, depriving them of their status as 'subjects' of the 'commonwealth of virtue'. While Hays shows her pro-revolution credentials by animadverting against the upper ranks of society (as Reeve too had done in *The School for Widows*), Reeve instead seeks to make the training of working women an integral part of a conservative plan of education where the higher classes will not mind their daughters going to the same school as poor gentlewomen who will become working women. Reeve's conception is of course an ideality; reality, according to her own account in *The School for Widows*, was likely to be the casual insolence of Lady Haughton or her daughters towards the dignified governess, Mrs Darnford. But as Reeve argues, a spirit of reformation is in the air – and while pro-French Revolution and anti-French Revolution women alike, in their discussions of female education, are approaching the same problem – how to make provision for increasing numbers of single and resourceless gentlewomen – their answers differ according to the position they see themselves as taking in the post-French Revolution political polarization. Reeve consciously returns to a seventeenth-century French aristocratic ideal for the basic model of her own planned seminary. She also argues that such female educational enterprise holds the key to national progress.

'To Found, to Protect, Maintain and Preside over Seminaries of Education . . . Confers More Real Glory than that of Conquerors and Warriors': Madame de Maintenon and the Ideal of the Aristocratic Educator

In Letter XVIII in *Plans of Education*, Mrs Darnford argues that one of the prime duties of a nation's élite is to encourage and create educational institutions:

> If the manners of a nation depend on the education of its youth, and if the prosperity of a nation depends on its virtue, surely it must be the duty of those who assume the title of parents of their people, and take to themselves at least a fourth part of their property to secure to them the remainder, to found, to protect, maintain, and preside over seminaries of education; this office confers more real glory than that of conquerors and warriors, destroyers of mankind.[76]

Manners, virtue and education are foregrounded in this passage as the best way to secure national health and prosperity. In a sense, the public character of the nation is traced back to what might be thought of as the private question of education. One gets a sense of gendering in this passage, with war or conquest being aligned with the masculine, and virtue and education with the feminine. Such gendering continues in the rest of the letter, in which Louis XIV is viewed as a jaded and wearied king, tired of war and corruption, a king who is redeemed by his 'undoubted wife' Madame de Maintenon, who assumes the role of benevolent educator and redeems the corrupt aristocracy.

Reeve sees Maintenon as having been 'educated in the school of adversity',[77] like the widows in her 1791 novel. Such experience of adversity makes Maintenon sensitive to the plight of poor young girls. First at Maintenon, then at St-Cyr, she establishes charity schools for young girls. According to Reeve, at St-Cyr, in the composition of the pupils 'the ranks were confounded; some were the daughters of the noblesse, others of tradesmen and merchants, but all poor and friendless.'[78] However, by all accounts, Maintenon educated only daughters of the 'noblesse': to qualify for entry to St-Cyr, a girl had to have at least a certain fraction of noble blood (the king himself decided whether a potential incumbent had the required fraction of noble blood, after being advised by the Judge of Genealogies).[79] For Reeve, herself a member of the gentry but not of the aristocracy, it is important that Maintenon should be seen to have educated not just the nobility but a wider grouping of gentlewomen.

If we go back to Reeve's conception of a female community and seminary, we shall find that it is influenced strongly by St-Cyr. Reeve's charity pupils were to be 'daughters of clergymen, officers in the army and navy, placemen, or any profession whose parents have died in indigent circumstances, and left them entirely destitute of any provision'.[80] The Letters Patent of St-Cyr granted by Louis XIV seek to educate young women of noble birth whose fathers have died in service, or whose families have exhausted their resources.[81] The wording is similar in both cases.[82] Like St-Cyr, Reeve's community has a Superior and other Sisters in charge of teaching and administration.[83] As in St-Cyr, so in Reeve's community both teachers and pupils are bound by vows.

Why does Reeve choose and so admire St-Cyr and Madame de Maintenon? One answer is that she sees in Maintenon's concern for poor young noblewomen, a model for her own anxiety about the fate of well-born and poor young Englishwomen. But more than this, Madame de Maintenon, through her benevolent plans of education, partially atones for the wrongs of an aristocracy which is in danger of losing sight of its responsibilities, embodied in the figure of Louis XIV.

> The enemies of kings speak of them only as tyrants. Mr Paine has spoken of Louis XIV, as a mere player, 'acting the stage tricks and pageantry of royalty'; but let us view him in another light, educated in the lap of indolence and luxury, idolized by his people, flattered by his courtiers. . . . Then view him humbled by a succession of misfortunes . . . penitent for his crimes . . . and at last becoming the father of his people, the object of their respect and veneration. Once when Madame de Maintenon was speaking to him of the good effects of the education at St-Cyr, he answered, 'O that I could give to God as many souls as my bad example has snatched from him!'[84]

According to this view, Louis XIV becomes aware that he has not acted as the true father of his nation and repents, realizing also that what Madame de Maintenon had persuaded him to encourage at St-Cyr represents his true duties. The woman educator becomes the main symbol of the redemption of a corrupt aristocracy. Reeve's notion of education is thus arguably both female-centred and highly political. The vocation of the woman educator extends to encompass an entire nation, and is seen to be the main way to effect the 'spirit of reformation' that Reeve feels is alive in her own country, as it had been a century earlier in France.

In Reeve's 'reformed' society, however, slaves are not to be emancipated, one of the reasons being a fear of miscegenation.[85] The hierarchies would be strictly maintained, with seven graded social orders of free men, each with its sumptuary laws. This gradation comes from another seventeenth-century French educational work, *Telemachus* (1699), by François de Fénelon, Maintenon's contemporary and yet another critic of the excesses and corruptions of Louis XIV's court.[86] In Reeve's plan, the children of paupers would be rounded up and set to work in Houses of Industry. Chillingly, they 'are not to be taught to read or write; being rescued from extreme poverty, they are to be hewers of wood and drawers of water, and to be thankful for their deliverance.'[87]

Exorcising Spectres of Patriarchy, Haunted by Spectres of Racism

The theme of education/cultivation and the figure of the female educator, we have seen, are crucial in Clara Reeve's writing. We have traced her awareness of the obstacles that women face in the public sphere to her earliest publication, *Original Poems*. Reeve, we have seen, is able to create strong, articulate, intellectual female educator-figures in her works, whether in a critical work such as *The Progress of Romance*, or in a novel such as *The School for Widows*, or in a novel-cum-educational treatise such as *Plans of Education*. In *The Progress of Romance*, we have found Reeve presenting an ideal of the woman of letters as public educator, and paying tribute to the mid-eighteenth-century generation of women novelists, many of them (Sarah Scott, Sarah Fielding, Madame de Genlis) deeply interested in education.

Reeve is a sophisticated writer. *The School for Widows* deserves to be considered as an important female-authored *Bildungsroman*, with its bold charting of the education and development of multiple female protagonists, many of whom have to face grim marriages and who then find fulfilling vocations outside marriage. In *The School for Widows*, the rational and sympathetic female educator's positive role is defined against a lurking Gothic vision of haunted houses, prison and madness, a vision associated with patriarchal oppression in marriage and sexuality.

Such sophistication is equally present in *Plans of Education*, which is a very *radical* conservative work, especially in its desire to find a dignified socio-economic space for poor gentlewomen. Its scheme of extensive vocational training is novel, not found in earlier eighteenth-century English writing on female education. Reeve deliberately goes back to seventeenth-century France, to

Madame de Maintenon and her seminary at St-Cyr, for a vision of female benevolence and pedagogy. In Reeve's feminocentric vision, it is someone like Maintenon who, with her commitment to education, strengthens the national good
and redeems the excesses and corruptions of the rest of the aristocracy, especially
the king: the father of the nation assumes his true role late in life only because of
his association with the female educator.

Reeve's writing is symptomatic of the gradual change in British women's
writing from the 1770s to the 1790s. Originally a writer belonging to the late
Bluestocking era, Reeve's polished poetry, prose and criticism of the 1770s and
1780s espouse women writers' public roles as educators, as well as the value of
fiction, in particular female-authored fiction. In the 1790s, Reeve emerges as a
radical conservative writer, the extremes of her viewpoint becoming foregrounded.

Reeve's work shows that the educational strand in women's writing can
function in all kinds of genres and sub-genres, and can be manipulated as a
dynamic, even shaping strand in literary criticism, fiction and political writing.
Without this discursive node, Reeve's female figures would not have half the
dignity that they do, for it is the belief in improvement through education that
forms the basis for the development of Reeve's women characters. Especially in
Plans of Education, however, such possibilities of improvement or development
are denied to women, men and children outside the classes that Reeve knows
and empathizes with. Unlike the Gothic spectre of patriarchy which is exorcised
in *The School for Widows*, *Plans of Education* remains haunted by all those
Reeve excludes from the strength and light of the female educator.

Notes and References

1 Sir Walter Scott, *Lives of the Novelists* ([1821–24] London: Oxford University Press, 1906), p. 197.

2 Miriam Leranbaum, '"Mistresses of Orthodoxy": Education in the Lives and Writings of Late Eighteenth-Century English Women Writers', *Proceedings of the American Philosophical Society*, 121 (1977), pp. 281–301.

3 J. Jean Hecht, *The Domestic Servant Class in Eighteenth-Century England* (London: Routledge and Kegan Paul, 1956), p. 18.

4 In addition to *The School for Widows*, Reeve's *The Two Mentors: A Modern Story* (London: Dilly, 1783) treats with sympathy the plight of Sukey Jones, daughter of domestic servants, who is pressurized into prostitution. The hero of the novel rescues her and helps her set up as a shopkeeper.

5 Clara Reeve, *Original Poems on Several Occasions* (London: T. and J.W. Pasham, 1769), p. xi.

6 Ibid., pp. 10–11.

7 Clara Reeve, *The Progress of Romance and the History of Charoba, Queen of Egypt*, 2 vols (Colchester: Keymer; London: Robinson, 1785; reprinted in 1 vol., New York: The Facsimile Text Society, 1930), Vol. II, p. 98.

8 Laura Runge analyses *The Progress of Romance* in her *Gender and Language in British Literary Criticism* (Cambridge: Cambridge University Press, 1997), pp. 155–63. Disappointingly, she fails to take on board Reeve's foregrounding of the public, civic-minded role of the educator–writer: she draws what seems to me to be patently false conclusions, such as that 'Reeve's critical purview is constrained to a domestic purpose and vocabulary' (p. 163).

9 Reeve, *The Progress of Romance*, Vol. I, p. vii.

[10] Ibid., Vol. II, p. 99.
[11] Ibid., Vol. I, p. 142.
[12] Ibid., Vol. II, p. 34.
[13] Ibid., Vol. I, p. 143.
[14] Ibid., Vol. II, pp. 80–82.
[15] Ibid., Vol. II, p. 85.
[16] Ibid., Vol. II, p. 97.
[17] *The Phoenix; or, the History of Polyarchus and Argenis*, translated from the Latin by a Lady, 4 vols (London: Bell and Etherington, 1772).
[18] Reeve, *The Progress of Romance*, Vol. I, p. 80.
[19] Clara Reeve, *The School for Widows* (Dublin: Wogan and others, 1791), Vol. I, pp. v–vi.
[20] Ibid., Vol. I, pp. v–vi.
[21] Ibid., Vol. I, p. 10.
[22] Review of *The School for Widows*, *Monthly Review*, 1791, Vol. V, p. 466.
[23] Reeve, *The School for Widows*, Vol. I, p. 8.
[24] Ibid., Vol. I, p. 281.
[25] Ibid., Vol. I, pp. 294–95.
[26] Ibid., Vol. I, pp. 301–03.
[27] Ibid., Vol. II, p. 5.
[28] *The Old English Baron* itself domesticates and familiarizes the Gothic. See, for example, Ruth Perry's discussion of the novel: 'Women in Families: the Great Disinheritance', in *Women and Literature in Britain 1700–1800*, edited by Vivien Jones (Cambridge: Cambridge University Press, 2000), pp. 111–31, esp. pp. 115–18.
[29] Reeve, *The School for Widows*, Vol. II, p. 14.
[30] Clara Reeve, *Plans of Education* (London: Hookham and Carpenter, 1792; rpt, New York: Garland Publishing, 1974), p. 128.
[31] Ibid., p. 216.
[32] Reeve, *The School for Widows*, Vol. I, p. 47.
[33] Ibid., Vol. I, p. 45.
[34] Ibid., Vol. I, p. 49.
[35] Ibid., Vol. I, pp. 60–61.
[36] Ibid., Vol. I, p. 109.
[37] Ibid., Vol. I, p. 203.
[38] Ibid., Vol. I, p. 209.
[39] Ibid., Vol. I, p. 173.
[40] Ibid., Vol. 1, p. 198.
[41] 'A profession we call it, for it should be considered as such, as an honourable profession, which gentlewomen might follow without losing any degree of the estimation in which she is held by what is called *the world*.' Maria and R.L. Edgeworth, *Practical Education*, 3 vols (2nd edn, London: Joseph Johnson, 1801; rpt, Poole and New York: Woodstock Books, 1996), Vol. III, p. 47.
[42] Reeve, *The School for Widows*, Vol. I, pp. 25–26.
[43] Ibid., Vol. I, p. 236.
[44] Ibid., Vol. I, p. 31.
[45] Ibid., Vol. I, pp. 31–32.
[46] Ibid., Vol. I, p. 22.
[47] Ibid., Vol. I, pp. 17–18.
[48] Ibid., Vol. I, p. 38.
[49] Ibid., Vol. I, pp. 36–37.
[50] Ibid., Vol. II, p. 271.
[51] Ibid., Vol. I, p. 40.
[52] Ibid., Vol. II, pp. 289–90.
[53] Reeve, *Plans of Education*, pp. 76–82, 89–92.
[54] Ibid., pp. 100–01.
[55] Ibid., p. 87.
[56] Ibid., p. vi.

57 Ibid., p. vii.

58 Ibid., p. 10.

59 Ibid., pp. 137–39.

60 See Vivien Jones, 'Placing Jemima: Women Writers of the 1790s and the Eighteenth-Century Prostitution Narrative', *Women's Writing*, 4:2 (1997), pp. 201–20.

61 Mary Anne Radcliffe, *The Female Advocate; or an Attempt to Recover the Rights of Women from Male Usurpation*, in *The Radicals: Revolutionary Women*, edited by Marie Mulvey Roberts and Tamae Mizuta, with an introduction by Marie Mulvey Roberts (London: Vernor and Hood, 1799; rpt, London: Routledge/Thoemmes Press, 1994), p. 113.

62 Reeve, *Plans of Education*, pp. 116–17.

63 Ibid., p. 121.

64 Ibid., pp. 122–23.

65 For the recurrence of this idea in post-Reformation English writing, principally in the context of the advancement of women's education, see Bridget Hill, 'A Refuge from Men: The Idea of a Protestant Nunnery', *Past and Present*, 117 (1987), pp. 107–30. There is no mention of Reeve in this article, however.

66 Reeve, *Plans of Education*, pp. 126–27.

67 Ibid., p. 152.

68 Ibid., pp. 142–44.

69 Ibid., p. 145.

70 Ibid., pp. 146–48.

72 Maxine Berg, *The Age of Manufactures 1700–1820: Industry, Innovation and Work in Britain* (London and New York: Routledge, 1994), p. 140.

73 Frances Burney, *The Wanderer*, edited by Margaret Anne Doody, Robert L. Mack and Peter Sabor, with an introduction by Margaret Anne Doody (Oxford and New York: Oxford University Press, 1991), pp. 426–31.

74 Reeve, *Plans of Education*, pp. 119–20.

75 Mary Hays, *Appeal to the Men of Great Britain in Behalf of Women*, in *The Radicals: Revolutionary Women*, edited by Marie Mulvey Roberts and Tamae Mizuta, introduced by Marie Mulvey Roberts (London: Joseph Johnson, 1798; rpt, London: Routledge/Thoemmes Press, 1994), pp. 200–01.

76 Reeve, *Plans of Education*, p. 198.

77 Ibid., p. 199.

78 Ibid., p. 200.

79 Jacques Prévot, *La Première Institutrice de France, Madame de Maintenon* (Paris: Editions Belin, 1981), p. 27.

80 Reeve, *Plans of Education*, p. 144.

81 '. . . parce que nous avons estimé qu'il n'était pas moins juste et moins utile de pourvoir a l'education des demoiselles d'extraction noble, surtout pour celles dont les pères, étant mort dans le service, ou s'étant épuisés par les dépenses . . . se trouveraient hors d'état de leur donner les secours nécessaires.' ['. . . because we thought it no less just and useful to provide for the education of young girls of noble birth, especially for those whose fathers, having died in service, or having been depleted by expenses . . . found themselves unable to make suitable provision for their daughters.'] Quoted in Prévot, *La Première Institutrice de France*, p. 24.

82 In *Millenium Hall*, too, the majority of the female pupils in the school were 'daughters of persons in office, or other life-incomes, who, by their parent's deaths, were left destitute of provision'. Sarah Scott, *Millenium Hall*, edited by Gary Kelly (Peterborough: Broadview Press, 1997), p. 160.

83 Prévot, *La Première Institutrice de France*, p. 28.

84 Reeve, *Plans of Education*, pp. 205–06.

85 Ibid., p. 90.

86 François de Fénelon, *Telemachus, Son of Ulysses*, edited and translated by Patrick Riley (Cambridge: Cambridge University Press, 1994), pp. 162–63. Fénelon, significantly, also describes an eighth order, comprising slaves.

87 Reeve, *Plans of Education*, p. 87.

CHAPTER THREE
'A sister adept in this art of free-masonry': Elizabeth Hamilton

Has biography no higher object than to collate facts and dates, and chronicle events? Should it not rather trace the progress of character, as developed in those habits and principles which operate universally on the happiness . . . of mankind? The history of the individual, to be complete, must include the history of his mind.

    The name of Mrs Elizabeth Hamilton has been long endeared to an intelligent class of readers . . . who . . . are prompted to enquire, not only by what gradations and by what efforts she advanced to distinction, but how far cultivation contributed to the development of her talents, in what degree her happiness was augmented by literary pursuits.[1]

Thus begins the biography and selected personal writings of Elizabeth Hamilton, novelist, educationist and philosopher. Written by Elizabeth Benger, herself a poet, novelist and author of a poem celebratory of great women, 'The Female Geniad' (1791), the biography analyses Hamilton's character, education and mind in a quasi-philosophical way, showing the operation of universal principles on the shaping of the individual; at the same time, fittingly enough in a pioneering biography of one woman writer by another, the work is particularly sensitive to the difficulties and achievements of the *female* mind. This dual charge is encapsulated in the passage I have quoted, where the generic masculine used in the first paragraph gives way in the second to the feminine gender. This duality is characteristic of Hamilton as well. Hamilton was, in her day, a highly respected writer among both men and women belonging to moderate intellectual, religious and political formations: no whiff of scandal attached to her, as it did to Jacobin, revolutionary women writers such as Mary Hays or Mary Wollstonecraft. Hamilton was close to the *Edinburgh Review* circle, at that time at the forefront of British intellectual life. Admired by Dugald Stewart and the Edgeworths, among others, she was a celebrated early psychologist, recognized as an expert on the 'science of the mind' and on education, and was part of a Scottish Common Sense philosophical tradition.

    Hamilton's writing shows an abiding concern with the special difficulties, needs and aspirations of women's education, cutting across classes and nationalities.[2] As Benger vividly shapes the development of Hamilton's life and mind, Hamilton too tried throughout her life to combine philosophical and everyday language in order to present accounts of female education and development. The operation of the individual female mind, the forces that shape it from outside and its own internal principles form the core of Hamilton's work. She wrote, like Clara Reeve, in an adventurous variety of genres – an Oriental tale (*Translations of the Letters of a Hindoo Rajah*, 1796), an anti-Jacobin novel (*Memoirs of Modern Philosophers*, 1800), a regional or cottage tale (The *Cottagers of Glenburnie*, 1808), historical and philosophical biography (*Memoirs of the Life of Agrippina*, 1804), philosophical essays aimed at a general audience (*A Series of Popular Essays, Illustrative of Principles Essentially Connected with the Improvement of the Understanding, the Imagination and the Heart*, 1813), a conduct book (*Letters Addressed to the Daughter of a Nobleman on the Formation of the Religious and Moral Principles*, 1806) and works on education (*Letters on Education*, 1801; *Hints Addressed to the Patrons and Directors of Public Schools*, 1815). Like Reeve, but with a greater range and play of styles and thought, Hamilton used the educational strand of writing creatively, to both analyse female experience and synthesize flexible principles and precepts for women.

'Hardihood and Enterprise': Elizabeth's Education

Benger tells us that Hamilton composed an autobiographical fragment which 'affords . . . an apt illustration of her firm, decided character',[3] a firmness Benger is at pains to praise throughout her biography. Hamilton was brought up by her aunt and uncle after the death of her father. Her aunt's literary talents, together with her marriage to a man who was of peasant stock, appear to have influenced Hamilton in her choice of vocation and in her scorn for exaggerated notions of gentility. Equally, her mother, we hear, 'like the mother of Sir William Jones . . . considered a good education as the noblest patrimony.'[4]

All her life, Hamilton would praise the robustness, spirit of independence and diligence that a Scottish rural education offered. Brought up near Stirling, Elizabeth 'spent two years, not in learning tasks, but in receiving more instructive lessons from nature'. Such lessons, Benger tells us, were unusual and conventionally unfeminine ones of 'hardihood and enterprise', learnt (with a playmate who was a boy) while 'fording burns in summer, or sliding over their frozen surface in winter'.[5] Not fond at all of dolls,[6] (contra Rousseau's prescriptions in *Emile* for dolls as an integral part of a feminine education, a scheme Hamilton was to condemn in *Memoirs of Modern Philosophers*), Elizabeth was a bookish tomboy, with an early admiration for heroic and warrior culture: she admired the Scottish national hero William 'Braveheart' Wallace, Shakespeare's History plays, and Achilles and Hector,[7] all this before the age of eight! She went to a coeducational school until the age of nine,[8] and commended this Scottish practice of early co-education heartily in her later works. In *Translation of the Letters of a Hindoo Rajah*, Sheermaal observes that in Scotland, until recently,

> it was . . . customary for the mothers of families to employ themselves in the
> education of their children. . . . Beneath a mother's eye, the young females were
> then sent to certain places of instruction, called day schools, accompanied by
> their brothers; a practice which would inevitably lay the foundation of a degree
> of fraternal affection.[9]

Hamilton sees such 'fraternal affection' between boys and girls as healthy: it
prevents the growth of a 'reserved and austere demeanour' between men and
women, and also excites in the 'minds of the young females' 'such a wish to
excel . . . as was altogether incompatible with the preservation of ignorance'.[10]

Elizabeth's aunt taught her 'to be self-dependent; and, consequently,
taught me to value myself upon nothing that did not strictly belong to myself,
nor upon anything that did, which was in its nature perishable.'[11] This stress on
self-dependency and self-direction is very similar to Mary Brunton's presentation
of her heroines in *Self-Control* (1810–11) and *Discipline* (1814). At the same
time, the aunt was wise enough not to try to control Elizabeth's 'ardent temper',
which was not required to bow down to 'authority' but to 'reason' – a shift
away from external prescription to a faculty of the mind.[12]

All this sounds idyllic: a free and happy childhood with few restricting
precepts of femininity. As Elizabeth grows older and becomes an ardent reader,
however, her aunt warns her of the dangers of unfeminine display of knowledge:

> She perused many books by stealth. Mrs Marshall, on discovering what had
> been her private occupation, expressed neither praise nor blame, but quietly
> advised her to avoid any display of superior knowledge, by which she might be
> subjected to the imputation of pedantry. This admonition produced the desired
> effect, since, as she herself informs us, she once hid a volume of Lord Kaimes
> [*sic*] . . . under a chair, lest she should be detected in a study which prejudice
> and ignorance might pronounce unfeminine.[13]

Note the negotiation of propriety that is going on in this passage. Benger's
words 'ignorance', 'prejudice' and '*imputation* of pedantry' argue against this
repressive attitude to female learning. Hamilton herself, when she wrote about
having to hide Lord Kames's *Elements of Criticism* (guiltily hiding a learned
work because she is a woman, in the same way that one might hide a scandalous
novel!), makes such repression a target of her attacks on existing norms of female
education:

> Do I not well remember hiding Kaimes' [*sic*] *Elements of Criticism*, under the
> corner of an easy chair, whenever I heard the approach of a footstep, well
> knowing the ridicule to which I should have been exposed, had I been detected
> in the act of looking into such a book? . . . I could not have been satisfied, if, in
> a book on education, I had not . . . endeavoured to enforce the necessity of culti-
> vating the reasoning faculty, and to explain the advantages arising from the
> capability of taking general and extensive views.[14]

Elizabeth's brother Charles played a large role in the development of her 'capacity to take general and extensive views'. The sense of discovery and adventure we find in Hamilton's novel about India, *Translation of the Letters of a Hindoo Rajah*, was inspired by Charles's experiences in India. Benger goes so far as to see his relationship with Elizabeth as semi-paternal: Charles Hamilton, she says, gave Elizabeth a 'second education', and was to her a 'paternal monitor'.[15] This casts the brother–educator as the instructing, authoritative father, Elizabeth as the receptive daughter–sister–pupil. Patriarchal and family relationships, far from being threatened, are bolstered by this sort of educative bond. Elizabeth's relationship with her brother was by no means uncomplicated, however, as this excerpt from a letter, a reply to Charles's suggestion that she should join him in India to find a suitable husband, suggests:

> The thousand delicacies that form a barrier to every woman possessed of true female feelings, I could never have attempted to overleap; nor would even the certainty of *getting a husband* weigh so deeply with me, as you gentlemen may perhaps imagine; nor am I sure I should be quite so *saleable* as you might partially suppose: I believe the pert adventures would have the advantage of me: some antiquated notions of refinement might stand in my way, such as that there were some other requisites besides fortune essential to happiness.[16]

Hamilton uses the language of refined femininity – 'thousand natural delicacies', 'true female feelings', 'refinement' – to criticize her brother's desire to marry her off. She, as a woman, distinguishes herself from a cynical breed of 'gentlemen' (her brother included), and refuses to conform to a model of 'saleable' femininity. Her refusal to voyage to India as a commodified bride has affinities with Jane Austen's criticism, in 'Catharine, or the Bower', of Miss Wynne being similarly forced to voyage to India in order to catch a husband.

Benger, despite highlighting Charles's monitorial role in Elizabeth's development, is at pains to point out Elizabeth's intellectual independence of her brother:

> Nature often lavishes on women talents unprofitable to society and to their possessor; compared with men, they are but gleaners in those fields of literature and science which yield such ample treasures; and the operations even of genius must be impeded or circumscribed by imperfect knowledge and partial experience. . . . It was not, however, that Miss Hamilton borrowed from her brother's mind, but that he taught her to explore her own latent talent and hitherto unappropriated treasures.[17]

Education is here, as so often in this period, described through the metaphor of agricultural cultivation. Elizabeth does not, like many other women, merely glean the remnants of others' harvests in the fields of literature and science, hampered as these women are by an inadequate education, formal and experiential ('imperfect knowledge and partial experience'). Derivativeness is one of the many difficulties of literary women that Benger, and Hamilton, are aware of – other such problems that Benger brings up in the biography, problems that she sees

Hamilton confronting successfully, include those of publishing under one's own name and the scarcity of encouragement and patronage.

'Unprotected Females' and the 'Adventurous Course of Writing'

Translation of the Letters of a Hindoo Rajah, Hamilton's first book-length work, was published in her name, and *Memoirs of Modern Philosophers*, though first published anonymously, was later acknowledged, since Elizabeth's view was that 'I would not on any account publish anonymously any thing which I should either be ashamed or afraid to own'[18] – a bold statement, with none of the diffidence that had become an accepted topos for the woman writer. Nonetheless, Benger says that at the time of publication of *Hindoo Rajah*, Hamilton 'was sensible that the woman, who has once been brought before the public, can never be restored to the security of a private station'.[19] Hamilton, who bridges the public and the private all the time in her writing, is thus very aware of the insecure public status of the woman writer. Once established in a literary career, she is as aware of her responsibility to encourage other women:

> It has been remarked, that women are seldom disposed to encourage the development of literary talent in their own sex. . . . Miss Hamilton never appeared to exult more in her own success, than when it invested her with the privilege of lending support to some unprotected female, about to enter on the same adventurous course.[20]

Note the words 'adventurous course' and 'unprotected female', which suggest a vulnerable but feisty woman traveller or explorer; 'unprotected female' also carries the charge of the proper woman who becomes prey to improper advances, with a sexual overtone. Hamilton's support, what would now be called female mentoring, is seen to give protection to such risk-taking women. Hamilton certainly felt that women, if they did aspire to wisdom, did better than most men:

> the more I see and know of the world, I am the more convinced, that whenever our sex step over the pale of folly (which, unhappily, is a *feat* that by far the greatest number never attempt), they ascend the steeps of wisdom and virtue more readily than the other. They are less encumbered by the load of selfishness; and, if they carry enough of ballast to prevent being blown into the gulf of *sentiment*, they mount much higher than their stronger associates.[21]

The metaphors of mobility are remarkably bold here. Wise and virtuous women have to take risks to step beyond an established boundary – in an image from ballooning, they are seen to be less encumbered than men by the weight of selfishness and, provided they can avoid the 'gulf of sentiment' (Hamilton is firmly rationalist and anti-sentimental here, as elsewhere in her work), they reach higher regions of the air than many men. These metaphors alert us to the dynamic, far-ranging and adventurous nature of Hamilton's views on female education.

Also remarkable is Hamilton's view that selfishness is a prime obstacle to education, and that it is a characteristic masculine self-ideal. She saw the foremost enemy to a proper education to be 'the opposition of the selfish propensities to the cultivation of benevolence and the attainment of felicity',[22] and we shall see how much Hamilton has to say about the gendered nature of selfishness.

'Antique Maidens' with 'Ardent Minds':
Vindicating Unusual Girls in the Early Writing

Benger's selection from Hamilton's early writing, both published and unpublished, shows us a Hamilton interested in describing intelligent, benevolent female characters. Hamilton was fascinated by the life of Arabella Stuart, about whom she collected much information and round whom she based a historical novel – an embryo of her later interest in historical biography. Her own love and longing for her sister, whom she was separated from, appears in her novel: 'Two sisters . . . supplant the heroine in the reader's affections . . . the two sisters have been separated from infancy, one of them instructed with Arabella in Protestant principles, the other educated by her father in the tenets of the Romish Church.'[23]

Even in this early work, Hamilton tries to go beyond sectarian differences – the different religious educations that the two sisters receive do not impede the love and friendship that grow between them once they meet. Hamilton makes the two sisters encounter Shakespeare, who declaims a eulogy on female friendship and presents them with a copy of *As You Like It*, seen by Hamilton as his tribute to the subject![24]

We also notice in the juvenilia, Hamilton's awareness of the social pressures besetting girls who are perceived as not quite 'normal': too learned, too socially uneasy, too indifferent to their common destiny of marriage. Hamilton sees herself as one such figure; in an early poem published in the *Lounger*,[25] she proleptically describes herself in old age as 'an antique maiden much decayed', a 'cheerful, pleased old maid' who refuses to wear the 'fashion'd livery' of what she described to her brother as 'saleable', marriageable womanhood. Throughout her oeuvre Hamilton, who remained single, vindicated old maids, as did Clara Reeve, another old maid.

In another essay published in the *Lounger* on 17 December 1785, Hamilton tries to explode that powerful contemporary ideological monolith, the notion that one should educate women so that they can be companions for their husbands.

> Many ladies may be led to the attainment of mental accomplishments, in hopes of recommending themselves to the notice of the other sex; who, from their superior education, and more solid judgment, would, one might presume, be more guided by the dictates of good sense, than led by the blind caprices of fashion. But, methinks, Sir, it would not be altogether fair to mislead your inexperienced female readers with such fallacious hopes. Tell them as much as you please of the internal rewards that belong to virtue: that . . . to enlighten their understandings with some degree of knowledge, will prove to them an inexhaustible source of delight in the lonely hours of solitude, and procure veneration and respect to their declining years. But on the fine fellows who, in their

days, deign to mingle in the female world, such accomplishments will have as much influence, as the harmonious compositions of Handel on . . . deaf people.[26]

The recognition that female education is not primarily a matter of social, marriage-directed calculations but that it brings with it '*internal* rewards' (emphasis mine) is striking, with similarities to Mary Astell's praise of the contemplative, intellectual ideal for women in *A Serious Proposal to the Ladies*. As important is the point that the solitary hours of women and their old age require internal resources – the gentlewoman's leisure and privacy are given importance in this view of education. And there is a sense of a distinctly 'female world' in which women live.

In another essay, part of an unpublished periodical project called the 'Breakfast Table', Hamilton seeks to present an unusually fervent, intelligent 'good girl' who is unappreciated in the usual round of empty drawing-room chat. The speaker in the essay is the father of two daughters, Josephine and Agnes. Josephine, the elder, is praised universally as a model young girl, 'extolled as a miracle of good sense by all her mother's visitors', exhibiting a 'quiescent gentleness of . . . temper and manners, which leads her to assume the appearance of a *profound* deference for the sentiments and opinions of those who address themselves to her in conversation.'[27] Quiescence, gentleness, an appearance of deference to others' opinions – Josephine shows all the marks of a socially acceptable 'good girl'. The father's voice, though obviously fond of Josephine, is much more anxious to vindicate the much-misunderstood younger Agnes.

> Agnes is not such a universal favourite as her elder sister. It is only where she is thoroughly known that she is entirely beloved: and she is only to be known by such as are possessed of qualities in some degree congenial with her own. Her whole soul glows with the fire of genius . . . her ardent mind expands to the reception of every new idea; her sensibility vibrates to the emotions of all who suffer or complain. But in the common business of life Agnes takes no interest. In the chit chat, which in common characters supplies the place of conversation, she bears no part.[28]

Agnes is thus both creative and receptive, both intellectual and emotional. Agnes's mind 'expands' (yet another metaphor of movement) to every new idea. She fails to participate in a salacious drawing-room conversation about the bankruptcy and death of a certain 'Mr Squanderfield'. What most people do not know, says the father, is that Agnes has taken over the responsibility of seeing to it that Squanderfield's destitute and orphaned daughters are provided for. Agnes's combination of a near-precocious intelligence, sympathy for others, her discomfort with the triviality of the established social round, and her ability to act as a responsible, benevolent member of society is characteristic of Hamilton's *weltanschauung*. In particular, Hamilton saw philanthropy as one of the most important vocations available to educated women. In Charlotte Percy, too, Hamilton's semi-autobiographical persona in *Translation of the Letters of a Hindoo Rajah*, we meet a grown-up version of Agnes, a benevolent female author bearing the marks of melancholy.

Hamilton's 'Black Baby': Female Education in
Translation of the Letters of a Hindoo Rajah (1796)

Translation of the Letters of a Hindoo Rajah (1796), an Oriental tale which Hamilton described as her 'black baby',[29] is her earliest and in many ways most adept fictional treatment of female education, anticipating many of the later theoretical discussions. As scholars such as B. Rajan have observed,[30] its adoption of the perspective of Indians, more particularly of Hindus, makes it a particularly fascinating work. The principal influence on Hamilton's view of India was her brother Charles, who spent many years in India, wrote a *History of the Rohilla Wars* and a translation of the *Hedaya*, a compilation of Islamic laws, and who died in 1792. Even with this influence, however, *Hindoo Rajah* is, as Hamilton herself attests in the preface, a bold work for a woman. Hamilton begins with a preliminary dissertation on Hindus, which summarizes current scholarship, especially the researches of William Jones, on India. She sees her literary journey beyond Europe as an attempt to widen the horizons of female learning:

> It may be censured . . . as a presumptuous effort to wander out of that narrow and contracted path, which they have allotted to the female mind. . . . From her earliest instructors she imbibed the idea, that toward a strict performance of the several duties of life, Ignorance was neither a necessary nor a useful auxiliary, but on the contrary, that she ought to view every idea as an acquisition, and to seize, with avidity, every proper opportunity for making the acquirement.[31]

Yet another bold set of metaphors here: female learning greedily seizes and acquires new ideas. It is fitting, in this context of this metaphor of greed, that *Hindoo Rajah* should support the British colonial project in India, not just in its trading and commercial activities but in its nascent attempts at warfare and active assumption of political power. Charles Hamilton was a protégé and partisan of Warren Hastings, and Hamilton's work unabashedly supports Hastings's wars and his belief that the British, and not the current Muslim rulers, were the right people to take control of India. In Hamilton's construction of India, the Hindus, a mild and peaceable people with a storehouse of ancient learning, are rescued from the predatory and corrupt rule of Mohammedan rulers by the British, who also carry with them the enlightened message of Christianity. Hamilton has no doubt that Hinduism is in many ways unenlightened, although it bears traces of monotheism. Hindu women are seen as receiving no education. *Sati*, a common practice, is said to be the only way in which Hindu women can reach heaven. Brahmin pundits are shown to be intent on preserving their power effectively to keep the Hindus in a state of benighted ignorance. Hamilton's sympathy with the nascent British imperialist project in India shows yet again, as in Reeve's case, that categories such as gender, race and class work in tension with each other in these late eighteenth-century and early nineteenth-century conservative women writers.

Although Hamilton is clearly fascinated by India, her major aim in using the Oriental tale, like other writers before her, is to expose the follies of her own civilization, and this she does with skill. The framework she chooses is as follows. In the course of the Rohilla Wars (around 1774), Zaarmilla, an Indian princeling, nurses to life a British soldier called Captain Percy, obviously loosely based on Charles Hamilton. Zaarmilla is bewitched by the accounts Percy gives of Christianity and of Britain, especially by his accounts of their superior treatment of women and the attention given to their education. This perspective is rudely undercut, however, by his friend Maandaara. Highly sceptical about the enlightened west, the latter enlists the help of the brahmin pundit Sheermaal, who offers page after page of satirical remarks about Britain, the result of a former trip to that country. A final synthesis is achieved when the naïve Zaarmilla himself goes on a visit to Britain, and sees the negative and the positive aspects of British society first-hand. Zaarmilla is astonished and delighted to hear from Percy that

> Christian women . . . may enjoy heaven without the company of their husbands! Throughout the Christian Shaster,[32] they are exalted to perfect equality with man. . . . Where women are destined to be under no control but that of reason, under no restraint save the abiding consciousness of the searching eye of Omnipotence, what vast importance must their education appear, in the eyes of the enlightened. According [sic], we find that seminaries of female instruction, called boarding-schools, are in England universally established; where . . . the improvement of the understanding is as successfully attended to . . . and . . . as fully attained . . . as by their brothers at the university.[33]

Belief in the value of women's cultivation of reason and in the empowering nature of Christianity for women are recurrent themes in Hamilton's writing. In this 1796 work, Hamilton is trying to counter the sweeping criticism made by Godwinian philosophy of 'things as they are'. She wishes to show that Christianity, and the entire set of duties and practices it buttresses and supports, does grant women equality and freedom – while the abuses that the Jacobins point out are the result of corruptions of this system. I have been arguing that the dialectic between restraint and freedom in female education is one that my chosen writers confront again and again in their writing: there is a deeply utopian charge to Hamilton's association of Christianity and female freedom. In *Memoirs of Modern Philosophers*, Hamilton argues that long before her radical contemporaries, the Gospel of Christ preached against a discriminatory attitude to women. Jesus Christ was 'the first philosopher who placed the female character in a respectable point of view. Women, we learn from the gospels, frequently composed a great part of his audience: but to them no particular precepts were addressed, no sexual virtues recommended.'[34]

Zaarmilla discovers from Sheermaal's accounts of 'boarding-school bibbies'[35] with their monkey tricks, that the ideality and the reality of education in England are vastly different. One senses Hamilton's bitterness at women's educational deprivation behind Sheermaal's equation of female boarding schools with the universities that their brothers attend, given her comments on the superficial, irregular training in accomplishments that she sees boarding schools providing. In *Letters on Education* (1801), Hamilton, like Maria and Richard Edgeworth in *Practical Education* (1798), indicts this sort of education.

> If school discipline can do little towards ameliorating the temper and disposition with regard to boys; I am afraid that with girls it can do still less. . . . With the objects to which their attention is directed, the reasoning faculties have no concern. In the routine of accomplishments to which they are destined, no one power of the mind is called into exercise, except the memory . . . so multiform, so perpetually changing are the objects of their attention, that it is impossible the mind should ever be long fixed to acquire habits of regularity or arrangement. The education of dancing-dogs, and tumbling monkeys [*sic*] is in this respect preferable to theirs, as they seldom are troubled with learning more than one accomplishment at a time.[36]

Hamilton is precise in the terms she uses in this passage. In boarding schools the female mind, in particular the faculty of attention, is directed to objects which do not require the use of reason. As a result, the mind becomes inactive. Only memory, a secondary, inferior power of the mind, is used in acquiring accomplishments, and to make matters worse, women are taught to acquire lots of accomplishments without 'regularity or arrangement', or even concentration in depth on any one of these activities. The comment that dancing dogs and tumbling monkeys are better educated than women makes the point that like these performing animals, women perform accomplishments not for themselves but for the amusement of others.

Hamilton argues, like Reeve, that an inevitable result of this sort of false education is that women do not acquire the mental or social resources to earn their own living. Sheermaal observes:

> women do actually sometimes carry on certain branches of trade; but to infer from this, that they are generally esteemed capable of business, or receive such an education as to enable them, if left destitute of fortune, to enter into it, would be doing them great injustice. No, in that country, as well as in this, all men allow that there is nothing so amiable in a woman as the *helplessness of mental imbecility*.[37]

This passage is very similar in tenor to Mary Wollstonecraft's arguments in *A Vindication of the Rights of Woman* (1792), and to a famous passage in Jane Austen's *Northanger Abbey* (discussed in the last chapter) where imbecility is said to be a major desideratum in women wishing to catch husbands. The social acceptability of 'mental imbecility' in women has damaging results in all spheres of life, including the inability of fortuneless young women to provide for themselves. As we saw in the context of Reeve's writing, this issue of the plight of fortuneless young women unable to find suitable trades preoccupied many 1790s writers. Like Mary Hays, Mary Anne Radcliffe and Anne Frances Randall, and other radical writers, Hamilton criticizes women being forced out of the few trades open to them: 'The females who belong to the caste of *people of style*, are particularly zealous in reprobating the exertions of female industry, and are careful to employ *men* only in all these branches in which fortuneless women have attempted to procure subsistence.'[38]

In *Hindoo Rajah*, Hamilton is already a firm believer in vocations for women, whether in undertaking the education of others, or supervising estates, or writing. The exemplar of these ideals is Lady Grey, a widow who supervises her estates efficiently, and educates her children as well as a niece. In the schematic structure so characteristic of eighteenth-century educational fiction, Lady Grey has a sister, Miss Ardent, a learned lady and an admirer of sceptical schemes of philosophy. Hamilton, however, complicates the dyadic schema by adding a third character, their brother Sir Caprice Ardent, easily the most contemptible of the three; it is characteristic of him that at the end of the novel he should change his adherence from one extreme, Godwinian philosophy, to another, Methodism!

Miss Ardent is described as characterized by 'vanity' and an 'affectation of original sentiment and intrepid singularity of conduct',[39] by which she loses sight of her own 'naturally gentle and benevolent character'. Yet, the philosopher Dr Severan, Zaarmilla's guide in his travels across England, is quick to point out that learned ladies are no more or less ridiculous than male pedants:

> And did your highness never see a male pedant? . . . Did you never behold a man destitute of early education . . . who had by some chance, acquired a knowledge of books; and did he not appear as proud of his superior information, as ridiculously vain . . . as any learned lady that ever lived?[40]

Miss Ardent, in fact, has many good traits in her, and is an adept and acute satirist of fashionable society. The triadic schema is extended to the next generation, to three daughters of Sir Caprice – Julia, Olivia and Caroline – educated by Sir Caprice, Miss Ardent and Lady Grey respectively. Again, it is Julia, in Sir Caprice's charge, who fares the worst in Hamilton's hands. Julia is shown to possess false gentility, a term that is associated by Hamilton with the empty round of fashionable accomplishments culminating in parents prostituting their daughters in the name of gentility, an act Sheermaal compares to sacrifices made to the goddess Kali.[41]

In an emblematic episode where the three girls have to cope with an accident that befalls an old man in their country-house, Julia faints and has hysterics. It is Olivia who is undaunted by the sight of the old man's blood and nurses him, while Lady Grey's pupil, Caroline, rushes for help. Olivia and Caroline are seen as complementary to each other, as Agnes and Josephine were.

'The Light of the Mind is Important for the Performance of Every Duty':
Memoirs of Modern Philosophers (1800)

Even in *Memoirs of Modern Philosophers*, Hamilton's most conservative work (attacking such Jacobin writers as Godwin and Mary Hays), the female mind is set at a premium. Here, Harriet, the exemplary heroine, '[having] performed every domestic task, and having completely regulated the family economy for the day, was quietly seated at her work with her aunt and her sister, listening to Hume's *History of England*, as it was read to them by a little orphan girl she had herself instructed.'[42]

Harriet uses her 'enlightened intellect, and calm and steady judgment' not just for study but also in her household work, and has enough time 'for the cultivation of her understanding, and the fulfilment of every social as well as every domestic duty'. Harriet exemplifies the rational, dignified Christian woman who recognizes that domestic work is also done with the mind:

> Nor will she who is the mother of a family, consider its humblest duties as mean, or void of dignity and importance. The light of the mind is important for the performance of every duty; and great is the mistake of those who think ignorance the ground of innocence and virtue.[43]

On the other hand, Julia Delmond, who is seduced by a corrupt Jacobin figure, becomes pregnant and dies, has a mother who gives her a minimal, old-fashioned, 'feminine' education. Thus, Mrs Delmond 'had before her father's return ... taken the trouble to teach her her sampler, and had besides endeavoured to initiate her into the mysteries of cross-stitch, chain-stitch, and gobble-stitch',[44] activities which do not suit 'the genius of the little romp' Julia, 'who did not much relish the confinement necessary for these employments'. Such a traditionally feminine activity as sewing is thus seen as an inadequate curriculum for girls, while Julia's vigorous energy, the implicit message goes, should have been directed to more challenging intellectual exercise. Mrs Delmond also makes her daughter learn by heart portions of the church catechism and the same psalms she had learnt as a child, so that Julia's religious education is purely mechanical, making her easy prey for her father's scepticism and the enticement of novels.

In a reversal of the usual pattern of corrupting, novel-reading females, Hamilton makes Julia's father, Captain Delmond, the main source of her problems: filled with exaggerated notions of romantic honour associated with what Hamilton sees as the uselessness of soldierly values and war, Captain Delmond passes on his love of fiction and lack of respect for religion to his daughter.

The pointing up of the inadequacy of Julia's education, in contrast to the intellectual rigour of Harriet, complements Hamilton's sympathy for Wollstonecraft's advocacy of a better female education in *Vindication of the Rights of Woman*. Hamilton is squarely on Wollstonecraft's side as far as the latter's denunciation of Rousseau's scheme for female education (found in his *Emile*, 1762) is concerned. In a discussion of Rousseau's novel *La Nouvelle Héloise* in *Memoirs*, where Hamilton criticizes its sexual morality, Dr Orwell says of Julie Wolmar's conduct:

> of Rousseau's system of female education, I think that the circumstances you allude to might very naturally be the result. A creature instructed in no duty but the art of pleasing, and taught that the sole end of her creation was to attract the attention of the men, could not be expected to tread very firmly in the paths of virtue.[45]

Rousseau's ideal female pupil Sophie, we remember, was moulded to become a subservient companion to Emile, and was taught to privilege beauty, coquetry and domesticity over the development of the intellectual faculties. By Hamilton's reasoning, Julie, in Rousseau's *La Nouvelle Héloise*, shows the consequences of such an education – her lapse from chastity is the result of Rousseau's privileging of 'sexual virtues', by which women are seen as governed both by the desires of men and by a preoccupation with their own physicality.

Nonetheless, Hamilton blames Wollstonecraft for taking her arguments too far:

> The inconsistency and folly of his system . . . was, perhaps, never better exposed than in the very ingenious publication which takes the Rights of Women [*sic*] for its title. Pity that the very sensible authoress has permitted her zeal to hurry her into expressions which have raised a prejudice against the whole. To superficial readers it appears to be her intention to unsex women entirely.[46]

Hamilton certainly does not believe in 'unsexing' women entirely. She does not believe, as Wollstonecraft did, in sexual freedom for women – *or for men, for that matter*; like Mary Brunton, Hamilton will not tolerate a sexual double standard for men and women. Nor does she jettison the ideal of the domestic woman, who is for her a vital and publicly useful member of society.

For Hamilton, a major problem with Rousseau or the Jacobin writer Mary Hays (author of *Memoirs of Emma Courtney*, 1796, which *Memoirs of Modern Philosophers* parodies) is that they encourage young girls to imagine themselves as heroines of fiction, and that too of amatory fiction, with disastrous consequences; equally, such views ignore ordinary girls, their needs and vocations, which may not necessarily be love or marriage. Martha Goodwin asks 'what Rousseau would have done with all the ordinary girls, for it is plain his system is adapted only for *beauties*, and should any of these poor beauties fail in getting husbands, GOD help them, poor things! they would make very miserable old maids.'[47]

In *Hindoo Rajah*, too, Hamilton criticizes novels for purveying fantasies of marriage that have little to do with reality, and for their criticism of old maids. From the novels Zaarmilla reads on his voyage to India, he learns that

> marriage in Europe is never contracted but from the most pure and disinterested

motives. Every young woman who is handsome and accomplished, however humble her birth, or small her fortune, is there certain of attracting the love and admiration of numbers of the highest ranks of the community.[48]

The same novels portray old maids as 'a sort of venomous animal, so wicked in its temper and so mischievous in its disposition, that one is surprised that its very existence should be tolerated in civilized society'.[49] Hamilton, like Reeve, thus comes down hard on the marginalization of unmarried women by society, a marginalization that is actively fostered by the prevailing system of education. If we think of her *Lounger* essay criticizing the idea that women should be educated primarily to provide companionship to their husbands, or her conception of Charlotte Percy as an unmarried young woman with a talent for authorship, or her criticism of novels that assume all women to be beautiful heroines of amatory fiction, we realize that Hamilton seeks throughout her oeuvre to argue for a female education that does not privilege marriage.

In *Popular Essays*, Hamilton was to make the same point theoretically. She criticizes the way women are taught to engross their imagination with fantasies of matrimony, leading to a waste of intellectual and moral energy.[50] In *Memoirs of Modern Philosophers*, as a contrast, Hamilton creates an exemplary 'old maid', Mrs Fielding, Henry Sydney's father's first love, who remains single, and retires into the country where she lives with farmers and composes treatises on female education.[51] Her life shows how much use can be made of the intellectual faculties when they are not concentrated exclusively on marriage.

Nor is Mrs Fielding the only exemplary old maid in the novel – another example is Harriet Orwell's aunt Martha Goodwin, who, before she dies, writes to Harriet urging her to suppress her love for Henry Sydney. Hamilton, one might say, downplays, even condemns, the value of affect in all her writing, particularly when it comes to romantic love between men and women. She sees such love as inextricably intertwined with wrongful imagination and fantasy, and as part of the misguided system of current female education. Figures such as Mrs Fielding and Mrs Goodwin offer alternatives – with their benevolent dedication to the good of society.

Nor is melodrama allowed to obtrude into such women's lives. Henry's father, after being separated from Mrs Fielding, later marries. When Mrs Fielding discovers this, she and Mrs Sydney, far from being hostile to each other, become friends, and the former becomes a dear friend of the family as well as Henry's well-wisher; eventually, it is Mrs Fielding's help that allows Harriet and him to marry. So Harriet, having steeled herself and subdued her love for Henry, on the advice of one 'old maid', finds that she gets him after all, through the help of another 'old maid'. One can see how firmly Hamilton is reshaping the conventional courtship plot, and giving a major role to exemplary, educative single women.

Education and the Mind

After *Memoirs of Modern Philosophers*, Hamilton was to spend much of her time writing works on education, rather like Mrs Fielding. Hamilton's writing formulates general principles of education, without paying too much attention to such particulars as exactly what curriculum is to be followed. *Popular Essays* advocates the study of the mind as a foundational element in the pursuit of education.

> [p]erhaps not one of a thousand connects with the idea of education . . . any notion of the general improvement of the faculties of the human mind . . . that education is not pronounced *good* . . . in proportion as it has tended to exercise and invigorate all the faculties of the soul, and all the affections of the heart, but as it has imposed upon the memory a certain number of facts, and of words descriptive of the ideas or opinions of the wise and the learned, and produced a facility in the performance of certain external acts. . . . Justly may we call that a good education which tends to develop and bring into action those faculties that are most essentially requisite in conducting the ordinary business of life, and at the same time gives . . . a direction to the active principles of our nature. . . . A good education may, according to this definition, be the privilege of a peasant as well as of a prince.[52]

I do not think one can overemphasize how synthetic and democratic Hamilton's view of education is. Teaching the pupil to internalize and act on principles, developing the faculty of attention as an aid to making the powers of perception active, developing the benevolent affections, and moving away from any conception of education that prizes external accomplishments or rote-learning are hallmarks of Hamilton's views.

Again and again, she shows the ways in which the prevalent system of education does not live up to these ideals, and the ways in which it is particularly inadequate for women. In her essay on attention, she targets women in particular for the lack of development of that faculty. While she notices the perceptual passivity that poor girls suffer from (of which we hear more in *The Cottagers of Glenburnie*), she also criticizes middle-class women's education, which teaches them to pay too much attention to items such as dress.

> Among the vain, frivolous, and uncultivated of my own sex, attention is chiefly directed to dress. The perception with regard to every change of fashion, and every minute particular in the form, colour, and arrangement of personal ornament and decorations, will, in such persons, be found astonishingly acute. . . . But let us not imagine that, if the attention has been thus engrossed, the perceptions with regard to other objects will be found equally lively.[53]

As a remedy to such ill-directed attention, Hamilton advocates the cultivation of the powers of *independent* reasoning in women:

Even where great pains and care is [*sic*] bestowed on the cultivation of the female mind, it is seldom these are calculated to enable the object of them to exert her own reason in the discovery of truth. Our chief aim is to enable our pupil, not to examine, but repeat our arguments, and to rest satisfied with our conclusions.[54]

Hamilton is making an important point here. You may spend time and effort in cultivating your daughter's mind, but unless you teach her the all-important principle that she can, of her own volition, exert her own reason, you miss the main point of education, which gives an individual agency. (We have seen that in Mary Hamilton's *Letters from the Duchess de Crui*, Lady Filmer is very aware that her pupil Lady Harriet must be taught to think independently.)

In *Letters Addressed to the Daughter of a Nobleman on the Formation of the Religious and Moral Principles*, Hamilton, through 'The Story of the Tame Pigeon', criticizes a female education that does *not* teach active cultivation of reasoning and of principles.

> [Lady N] had been an amiable daughter, a good wife, and a fond mother – but she had been neither one or other from principle. . . . For the sweetness with which she accommodated herself to the inclinations of her parents, and her husband, Lady N had obtained much applause . . . but it was in her the offspring of indolence and timidity. . . . Having been successfully guided by the wisdom of judicious parents, and of a sensible husband, Lady N had always appeared to act with uncommon prudence; but when left solely dependent upon her own judgement, she found that she had been very imprudent in never having given herself the habit of exerting it.[55]

Pliability, sweetness of temper and obedience – Lady N passively practises all these 'feminine' virtues, producing disastrous consequences once she is left a widow, in charge of a large estate. She puts herself into the power of a dishonest woman called Mrs Pegg, who makes all her decisions for her. An orphan boy, Tom, suffers wrongful dismissal because of Lady N's refusal to exert her own judgement.

If Lady N, a noblewoman, is a negative exemplum, a positive one is Bell, a young peasant girl who helps to bring up the young nobleman Albert, in another story in the work – Hamilton's conduct book presents its precepts through such vivid short pieces of fiction. Bell is a young nursery attendant 'ignorant of the wisdom of the schools, but . . . well acquainted with the precepts of the gospel'.[56] 'By others,' says Albert,

> I was taught *to say* there was a God, from her I first learned to make inferences from the important truth. But for her I make no doubt I should to the present day have had my mind clouded by a thousand vulgar prejudices and superstitions which would have taken too strong a hold of my imagination to have been eradicated.[57]

Albert's governess, on the other hand, teaches him accomplishments mechanically:

> I had been taught to read English by my sister's governess, who went over the routine of lessons, exactly as the horse which you see in yonder farmyard, goes round in turning the threshing-mill. . . . In fact Mrs Middleditch did all that could with justice be expected. She had served an apprenticeship to certain accomplishments and by teaching them was to gain her bread.[58]

Implicit in the passage is Hamilton's disapproval of any view of education as a quasi-mechanical trade, to learn which one serves an 'apprenticeship', like a journeyman. Bell, the young peasant girl, on the other hand, has true 'wisdom', which is not mechanical.

In another essay in *Popular Essays*, 'On the Propensity to Magnify the Idea of Self', Hamilton argues that women have suffered from a patriarchal desire to magnify the idea of the masculine self.

> Perhaps we might . . . find reason to conclude, that even in Christian and civilized nations, the propensity to magnify the idea of self has had a similar operation. The same propensity which incited the barbarian to resolve into his will other wills, and to connect with his life the lives of all his bosom slaves, may be observed to have operated in the spirit of almost all our ancient laws, as far as they concern the sex. From these it is evident, that women have, by the legislators of Europe, been generally contemplated, as having no other existence than that which they derived from being identified with their husbands, fathers, brothers, or kinsmen. . . . For ages an heiress was considered in no other light than as a sort of promissory note. . . . The sentiments and associations to which such laws and usages gave strength and permanence, may . . . be found . . . still to retain an influence. . . . Hence arises that jealousy with which men may sometimes be observed to regard the advancement of the other sex in knowledge, which they have considered as their own appropriate privilege, and with which they have been accustomed to connect the idea of self.[59]

Hamilton imputes the legal and political disabilities of women and slaves to an inner faculty of the masculine self, the desire for self-aggrandizement, benefiting one group of human beings over another. According to laws and traditions, a woman has no autonomy, no self, but is subsumed into the self of the man (as the legal principle of coverture in marriage demonstrates). Even an 'heiress', who notionally will own property herself one day, is a mere 'promissory note', a token who is exchanged between men in the patriarchal economy. From law to education, Hamilton sees women in danger of remaining subsumed under the privileges of a powerful masculine self-ideal.

Thus Hamilton finds, in the context of her own *Letters on Education*, that men underestimate or denigrate women's capacity for knowledge, so that they underestimate the intelligence of the female reader:

> I was . . . much disheartened on finding that all my male friends, on reading the

three last letters, declared, that they believed them to be above the comprehension of all, except a learned female reader. Glad am I, however, to find that their apprehensions were groundless. All the ladies of my acquaintance have read them with satisfaction; and I have received letters, even from young ladies, upon the subject, which show not only that they understood, but were capable of weighing, with accuracy, every argument addressed.[60]

Fiction, Biography and Philosophy

After *Letters on Education*, Hamilton embarked on an ambitious scheme to integrate her views on the mind, education and character, into an unusual kind of biographical writing that would combine historical and philosophical interest. As she put it: 'To cherish in young minds a habit of reflection, and to lead to a philosophical application of history and biography, is another end which I propose.'[61] The principal aim was, as ever, to give 'an illustration of the principles of the human mind'.[62]

> Instead of the regions of fiction, I should wish to have recourse to the records of authentic history; and by the analysation of some distinguished characters, show the consequences of the regulation of the passions, and the operation of the various faculties. . . . Induced . . . to confine my biographical sketches to characters whose actions have necessarily been exposed to public view, I intend commencing with my own sex, and have thoughts . . . of giving the lives of the two Agrippinas, widow and daughter of Germanicus.[63]

The deliberate decision to choose a woman connected with a public role, rather than a man (such as Germanicus, Agrippina's husband), throws much light on Hamilton's views.[64] She tries (overcoming her childhood admiration of macho warriors!) throughout her work to speak against a conventional kind of heroism, usually found aligned with the masculine, associated with war and the magnifying of self. Her indictment of war and chivalric values in *Memoirs of Modern Philosophers* is an example of such views. She denigrates warrior-heroes in a letter to Miss J–B–, dated 1809:

> a hero – that is to say, a pest to society. His delight in the deep play of war and desolation must arise from excitements in which the selfish principle is most predominant. The stake for which he throws is the power of identifying with self millions of human beings, and of extending this idea over lands and seas. . . . We must not be so sanguine as to expect to convert heroes into reasonable creatures; but I think that many young minds may be benefited by representing them in their proper colours.[65]

Again, that indictment of the masculine magnifying of self, which produces disastrous results. Hamilton's Agrippina, while she is a good soldier's wife, suffers from the martial ambitions and political intrigue of Tiberius's Rome. In Hamilton's projected series of biographies, Agrippina's companion was to be Princess Palatine, daughter to James I, 'a partner . . . to Agrippina of her own sex, and one who, like her, had experienced vicissitudes of fortune'[66] – as in the writings of Mary Hamilton, Clara Reeve and Mary Brunton, we find here an eagerness to focus on the development of the female self through adversity.

Hamilton, although she wrote three important pieces of fiction, was sceptical about the value and epistemological status of fiction. In *Hindoo Rajah*, we remember, novels were criticized for the fantasies of marriage that they create and for their contempt for old maids. There, too, Hamilton had satirized the vogue of calling novels 'true histories'. In *Memoirs of Modern Philosophers*, Bridgetina's head is turned by her refusing to read anything but 'novels and metaphysics'. Julia Delmond's soldier–father, we saw, is himself addicted to romances, and educates his daughter to love fiction and religious scepticism. Hamilton thus concurs with the legions of writers who condemned novels and novel-reading. Part of her opposition is explicable by her moderate, anti-Jacobin Christianity; another part of it by her hostility to the association between fantasies of love and marriage and fiction, something which she, as a woman who had chosen not to marry, clearly had strong feelings about.

But to notice only this is to miss the point – that Hamilton makes all these criticisms of the novel *in fiction*, showing her belief that it is possible to challenge and attempt to reform the fictional ideology that she criticizes. There is no doubt that Hamilton did believe (unlike Austen) in the superiority of bio-graphy, history and philosophy to fiction; yet, again and again in her career, she returns to fiction. *Agrippina* was meant to be a work on the philosophy of the mind, a biography and a historical work rolled into one – and Hamilton sought to distinguish it clearly from fiction. But *Agrippina* has the quality of a historical novel as much as of biography, with its accounts of the bloody intrigues in Tiberius's court. Hamilton wished to write other biographies of a similar nature, among them one of Locke and the one about Princess Palatine. None of the others eventuated, but Hamilton *did*, significantly, manage to write another piece of *fiction*, *The Cottagers of Glenburnie*. The role of fiction as a site of contestation, particularly for women writers, is played out throughout Hamilton's career.

Women and the Science of the Mind
While Hamilton acknowledges that such women as Agrippina (connected closely as they were with politics and public life) witnessed far more of public affairs than most women of her own time and class, she also thinks that women living in a domestic setting have a particularly good opportunity for acquiring a knowledge of human character, the kind of knowledge that enables Hamilton to write her biography.

> I am well convinced that they must ever be content with a very narrow and
> superficial knowledge of human character, who do not study it at the seasons
> when it is to be seen in undress; or rather in the nakedness in which it sometimes
> appears in the domestic scene. The men who boast a knowledge of the world,
> know mankind only as they appear in one or two particular habits, and these

assumed ones. . . . Women have more frequent opportunities for doing so than men have; but women seldom generalize: their attention is solely occupied with little particulars . . . but where they are more capable, they have much in their power, as I am convinced that a single week spent *tête-à-tête* with a person, in their own house, gives a more thorough insight into the mind and disposition than would in years be obtained in the common intercourse of society.[67]

Hamilton thus makes the domestic sphere a locus where the most ambitious and general philosophical knowledge is attainable for women. In a striking metaphor, humanity is seen to be 'naked' in the home, while in 'the world' it 'assumes' veiling, disguising garb. To make female philosophers of 'capable' women emerges as a main aim of Hamilton's plan for female education.

Hamilton's model of the mind is more or less that of the then highly influential Scottish Common Sense school of philosophy. Common Sense philosophy criticized Humeian scepticism and Berkeleian idealism alike. Instead, it argued that the mind and matter are two different sorts of substance, each governed by distinct processes. The task of philosophy is not to engage in metaphysical speculation, but rather to engage in empirical description of reality. Common Sense philosophy was moderate to conservative in its leanings and took a positive view of Christianity. As far as women are concerned, this model, with its Empiricist emphasis on the importance of early association and habit, together with a 'common sense' belief in the inner processes of the mind and an Enlightenment meliorism that attacks prejudices, is by no means unfruitful or unproductive. A recent commentator has also argued that the Common Sense philosopher Dugald Stewart had a tendency to 'marginalize politics. . . . Civic virtue is dramatically de-politicized, 'privatized', and made a matter of pedagogy.'[68] Stewart also, says Haakonssen, believed that 'the future was becoming a present force and producing its own realization. This was due especially to the spread of education.'[69] It is obvious why Hamilton found the Common Sense intellectual formation congenial, with its feminized, privatized, moderate, optimistic thrust, and its belief that one should take the best from the past but not hesitate to attack outmoded prejudices, such as sexism in education.

Of all the prejudices inimical to the establishment of a sense of justice, practical and universal, I take the early distinction that is made between the sexes, from which boys acquire ideas of an inherent superiority, grafted on pride, and supported by selfishness, to be the most fatal, and therefore the most important.[70]

Nor is Hamilton's model of the mind aridly rational, as this delightful passage from a letter written in 1801 shows:

I perfectly agree with you in considering castles [in the air] as more useful edifices than they are usually allowed to be. It is only plodding matter of fact dullness that cannot comprehend their use. I do not scruple to confess to you, as I find you are a sister adept in this art of free-masonry, that I owe to it three-quarters of my sense, and half my virtue. It is by giving free scope to the imagination, that one becomes thoroughly acquainted with the real dispositions of one's own heart: it is by comparing the ardent efforts of exalted virtue, formed by the fancy, with what conscience tells us we have performed, that we are instigated to improvement; and by tracing the combinations of which our castles have been composed, we acquire a knowledge of our own commands, as at once enlightens the understanding and betters the heart.[71]

'A sister adept in this art of free-masonry': this phrase is an apt epigram for Hamilton's educational project. The solid, substantial connotation of masonry, working as it does with stone, is balanced by the daring and freedom which can build castles *in the air*. There is also an implicit sense of a secret society or sisterhood engaged in such construction. Equally, the intimate relationship between the inner conscience and its realization through work is subtly conceptualized here, with castles in the air providing the ideal of virtue that the conscience must will into performance.

Women and the Education of the Lower Classes: *The Cottagers of Glenburnie* (1808) and *Hints Addressed to the Patrons and Directors of Public Schools* (1815)

In Hamilton's discussions of the education of the lower classes, she stresses repeatedly the need for women from all classes to busy themselves in this work of free-masonry: imaginative, sympathetic women can reform the mechanical, stultifying prevalent system of education, and can make the system function more efficiently and humanely.

In *The Cottagers of Glenburnie: A Tale for the Farmer's Ingle-nook* (1808), it is the education of the Scottish peasantry that is the focus. Generically, the work is fascinating: it is a 'national tale',[72] a 'cottage' or regional tale, and a reformist tale. Hamilton's 'Dedication' is worth quoting:

> A warm attachment to the country of our ancestors naturally produces a lively interest in all that concerns its happiness and prosperity; but though in this attachment few of the children of Caledonia are deficient, widely different are the views taken of the manner in which it ought to be displayed.
>
> In the opinion of vulgar minds, it ought to produce a blind and indiscriminating partiality for national modes, manners and customs. . . . Nor is it to readers of this description alone that . . . my cottage tale . . . will appear erroneous or absurd.[73]
>
> The politician, who measures the interests of his country by her preponderance in the state of empire, regards all consideration for individual happiness as a weakness; and by the man who thinks riches and happiness are synonymous, all that does not directly tend to increase the influx of wealth, is held in contempt.[74]

Hamilton is scathing about all those who 'dictate to the opinion of numbers', considering 'the great mass of people' as 'so many teeth in the wheels of a piece of machinery': a dig at political economy.[75] The work thus chimes with Stewart's feminized Common Sense views, and, distancing itself from politics and the pursuit of wealth, is highly feminocentric, representing national interests in a microcosm in a village rather than computing national prosperity. At the centre of the tale is a female educator, Mrs Mason (that image of the teacher as mason again, as well as calling to mind Wollstonecraft's good teacher Mrs Mason, the narrator in *Original Stories from Real Life*), who reforms and renovates the village of Glenburnie. *Cottagers*, then, like *Millenium Hall*, *Munster Village* and *Plans of Education*, belongs to the line of eighteenth-century female-authored works guided by a utopian impulse, works which have at their centre the figure of the powerful female educator–reformer.

 Cottagers is primarily a work written for and about the Scottish rural classes. It is set in 1788, i.e. before the turbulence of the French Revolution. Throughout her oeuvre, Hamilton took an idealized view of Scottish rural life. The austere dignity of the peasants, the universal access to education, the regular and intensive instruction in Christianity, the schoolmaster's close bonding with the community he served, the industry shown even by children – all these are elements that Hamilton had extolled earlier in her work, notably in the account Henry Sydney gives of his Scottish travels in *Memoirs of Modern Philosophers*. Hamilton, unlike Adam Smith, saw industrialization, by and large, as an evil. Instead, she eulogized rural, agricultural Scotland. This is Henry Sydney speaking about the relative merits of agriculture and industry, for example:

> 'How much better, have I said to myself, how much more usefully would these poor wretches have been employed, had the men been engaged to cultivate some of the many thousand acres of waste land. . . . And the women – how had they been preserved from vice and misery in the bosom of domestic industry!' 'I am afraid,' said Dr Orwell, 'that few converts will be made to your opinion. There is something so fascinating in the idea of wealth, that it can never be deemed too dear a purchase. The ostentatious display of the riches acquired in any branch of commerce or manufacture presses on the sense, and inflames the imagination.'[76]

Though Hamilton valorizes rural, feudal Scotland, she is also democratic: *Cottagers* argues that 'the pleasures of the heart, and of the understanding, as well as those of the senses, were intended by Providence to be in some degree enjoyed by all; and, therefore, that in the pleasures of the heart and the understanding all are entitled to participate.' This democratizing charge is further extended by the fact that both the middling and the lower classes feature in the work. We are told the story of Mr Stewart and his two daughters, of whom Bell foolishly and vainly prides herself on her 'gentility', and is appalled to discover she has married a shoemaker's son. Mrs Mason admonishes her, asking her rather to respect an honest tradesman's son – and Bell learns to lose her false pride in birth.

 We first encounter Mrs Mason when she visits the Stewart family in Gowanbrae. Bell Stewart is shocked to discover that the visitor has come 'riding double' on a horse. 'I thought she had been a lady', says Bell scornfully, and later, castigating her sister Mary for her friendliness towards Mrs Mason, she says: 'I don't know what you call improper, if you think it proper to keep company with a servant, and to make as much fuss about her too as if she were a lady.'[77]

Mrs Mason had indeed started life as a servant, then had risen to be a governess. Her life-story is told to Mary Stewart, whose mother was a cousin to the Lady Longlands in whose employ Mrs Mason had been. In many ways Mrs Mason's story is one of depressing, tractable industry. Her mother, her earliest instructress, dies when she is ten. Knitting stockings, Betty Mason comes to the notice of the castle and is employed as a servant in the great house. Her story there is one of trials and afflictions, under the petty tyranny and caprices of Lady Longlands and her maid, Mrs Jackson. Hamilton manages to convey with vividness the drudgery as well as the (very) small pleasures of a servant's life. While Betty works with Lady Longlands on chair covers, 'I . . . sat all the day in her dressing-room, and had nothing to complain of except hunger; but of my being hungry my lady never thought, though she must have known that I often fasted nine, and sometimes ten hours at a time.'[78]

On the contrary, when she is working at much harder physical work with Molly the housemaid, she is much happier:

> As there were many polished grates to scour, and a vast number of rooms to keep clean, we had a great deal to do; but it was made easy by regularity and method; so that in winter we had time to sit down to our needles in the evening, and in summer generally contrived to get a walk as far as the dairy.[79]

Her real trial comes when she refuses to tell a lie to protect the young Lord Lintop, heir to the estate, who had thrown a ball of lace that Betty had been working on, into the fire. When his dishonest nurse lies, blaming the accident on Betty, the latter is threatened with dismissal, only to be saved by Lord Lintop's father, who dismisses the dishonest servant and takes Betty to be his wife's serving-maid. The 'good–bad' didactic pairing is very present in such parts of the plot, with no excuses made for the bad nurse Jenny. At the same time, even in the narration of this incident, the cross-class alliance between Betty Mason and Miss Osburne, the later Mrs Stewart, is emphasized – the latter, a poor gentlewoman like Reeve's heroines, is as much if not more oppressed than Betty, dependent as she is on her arrogant aunt as a poor relation.

During her tenure as lady's maid, Betty makes further progress in learning through the help of Miss Maldon, an aunt of Lady Longlands, yet another exemplary spinster 'who lived with her, and who had a great deal of good sense, and, with a sober and religious turn of mind, was at the same time so lively and cheerful, that her company was liked by young and old.'[80]

After years of service, Mrs Mason comes to Glenburnie to discover that she is, 'for the first time in her life, completely her own mistress'; but, 'she was already sensible, that the idea of a life, completely independent of the will of others, is merely visionary, and that, in all situations, some portion of one's own will must necessarily be sacrificed.'[81] She busies herself with the engaging, if often inefficient and indolent, cottagers of Glenburnie. Mrs Mason's scheme for reforming the village is not particularly imaginative; instead of allowing the villagers not to be 'fashed', i.e. not bothering about troublesome things, she advocates industry and attention to detail. In doing so, however, she follows a cherished educational idea Hamilton propagated elsewhere: the importance of attention in any work that one undertakes, beginning from perception. In arguing against the cheerful indolence of the Glenburnie cottagers, Hamilton is undoubtedly using an idiom of improvement which in a sense devalues any imaginative dimension of the traditional way of life in the village she describes. Tractability, cleanliness and industry are the virtues Hamilton enjoins for the model subjects she proposes – the women are taught to become ideal servants and wives. At the same time, however, Hamilton seeks to address issues of gender inequality squarely, and seeks also to make good use of traditions of the peasantry she had eulogized throughout her oeuvre – the church school, coeducation for children, and a sense of fraternal bonding between men and women. Education is for Mason more than rote-learning, or even mere docility.

> 'But when folks gi' their bairns the best education in their power, what mair can they do?' 'In answer to your question,' replied Mrs Mason, 'I will put one to you. Suppose you had a field which produced only briers and thorns, what method would you take to bring it into heart? . . . And after you had opened the soil by plowing, and enriched it by the proper manure, you would sow good seed in it, and expect, by the blessing of heaven, to reap, in harvest, the reward of your labours.'[82]

Again, we find Hamilton's stress on the importance of the careful educational development of the individual, who, like a field, must receive proper cultivation – one needs to plough, to fertilize and to sow good seed before one can expect a harvest. Hamilton argues that Scotland is already far more fortunate than many other countries in the field of education, since here, even the lowest classes and women as well as men receive this sustained care through their education in the parochial schools. Nonetheless, Hamilton argues in her *Hints Addressed to the Patrons and Directors of Public Schools* (1815), girl students, even in Scotland, tend to be more backward than their male counterparts.[83]

The school at Glenburnie has both male and female pupils, though it appears that they have at least some separate classes. The girls, unlike the boys, spend a large amount of their time spinning indoors. Where Adam Smith saw the spinning undertaken by Scottish peasant women as unremunerative,[84] Hamilton, in *Memoirs of Modern Philosophers*, had presented this activity as integral to a harmonious, industrious family economy. There, Henry Sydney had offered a sentimentalized picture of two little girls busily spinning away in their cottage while their mother made oatcakes.

By the time she wrote *Cottagers*, however, Hamilton came to see that spinning could easily become mechanical drudgery. Mrs Mason decides that the reason the girls in the village school are lagging behind the boys is that their 'education was neglected', not in the matter of schooling, but because

> while the boys, by being constantly employed either in observing the operations that were going on without doors . . . had their attention exercised, and their observation called forth, the girls, till able to spin, were without object or occupation. After the first week, the labour of the wheel became mechanical, and required no exertion of the mental faculties. The mind . . . remained inert, and the power of perception, from being so long dormant, became at length extinct. . . . It was her [Mrs Mason's] first care to endeavour to rouse the sleeping faculties. To effect this, she not only contrived varieties of occupation, but made all the girls examine and sit in judgment on the work that was done . . . whether at the needle or book, she rendered their tasks easy and cheerful, by the pleasantness of her manners, which were always kind and affectionate.[85]

The girls' minds remain inert, their faculties lie sleeping, their judgement is not cultivated – these are all complaints Hamilton makes about more upper-class girls' education too. She thus perceives that gender discrimination in education is universal. At the same time, she recognizes that affection and kindness play key roles in the educative process, as Mrs Mason's demeanour towards her pupils demonstrates.

With all her stress on the need for improvement in Glenburnie, Hamilton shows a deep faith in the Scottish countryside and the Scottish peasantry, seen to have a wonderful potential for turning out sturdy, industrious, well-educated men and women. In contrast to this, Hamilton feels that the charity schools of her day, particularly those for girls, are much worse than Glenburnie even in its unreformed state. Her *Hints Addressed to the Patrons and Directors of Public Schools* recognizes the imaginativeness of what was then a very new trend in educational theory – the Swiss educationist Johann Heinrich Pestalozzi's gradual, child-centred educational methods, which involved observing closely the pupil's mental processes and attempting to teach concepts by breaking them down into very simple components.[86] Pestalozzi, like Hamilton, 'recognized the importance of training the whole personality of a child – his hands and his powers of observation as well as his reasoning'.[87]

Hamilton's work also criticizes the bad management of charity schools, and advocates a greater and more active involvement of women in the management of such schools. Research on philanthropy in the late eighteenth century has argued that in this period, it was indeed women who undertook most of the actual philanthropic work, while men formulated the policies and were seen as being 'in charge'.[88] Hamilton argues that the diffidence often displayed by women in the management of schools is damaging.

> Is it in these enlightened times to be supposed, that women of good sense and good education are so incompetent to judge or to act, that the choice and application of proper means for the education of their sex cannot properly be

> committed to them? But the ladies will have it so. They are anxious to be
> disburthened of the weight of responsibility . . . the benefits which would
> otherwise arise from the active exertions of the patronesses are liable to be
> circumscribed, by the timidity which imposes a restraint on the expression of
> sentiment and the freedom of action.[89]

Such women are like Lady N, anxious not to exercise their own judgement
and initiative. The female pupils of such schools also, consequently, do not learn
initiative and leadership: Hamilton notes that, when applying the monitorial
system (in which pupils acted as sub-teachers or monitors, and took on part of the
responsibility of teaching and class management) in girls' schools, very often
monitors had to be brought in from boys' schools because of 'the operation of
previous circumstances, which had been more favourable to the exercise of the
faculties in one sex than in the other' – i.e. few girls had been taught to take on
responsibility and leadership.[90]

Hamilton is indignant at the bad education that female charity pupils
receive. She blames the over-correct administration of these schools, which
encourages mere imitation in the pupils.[91] Again, education has become mechanical, monotonous, inert, imitative and purely external rote-learning. No wonder
that the pupils churned out by such charity schools fare far worse in later life
than the daughters of peasants.

> Both [charity school pupils and peasant girls] have experienced the blessings of
> protection; but on quitting the roofs under which they have respectively been
> educated, while the simple cottager carries with her the endearing recollections
> of parental tenderness, and the assurance of being still an object of interest in
> those she loves, the élève of charity bears with her . . . no hope of dwelling in the
> memory of those she leaves behind. . . . Feeling as if alone in the world, she arms
> herself with obstinate indifference to a destiny, in which, whether good or evil,
> she believes that none will sympathize.[92]

Charity pupils lack, among other things, an integral part of a good education – the cultivation of affective ties. Hamilton therefore proposes that charity
pupils should 'be made to stand to each other in those endearing relations from
which all the charities in life are ordained to emanate', with the elder girls acting
as 'sisters' to each other and 'mothers' to the younger ones.[93] Such cultivation of
'endearing relations' will not only enrich them emotionally, but will also have
the practical advantage of 'training girls for becoming expert and judicious in
the management and early education of infants of a superior class'.[94] This combination of concern for the development of the full personality, including its affective
aspect, and a desire to find dignified paid vocations for lower-class girls is symptomatic of Hamilton's practical but humane vision of female education, which cuts
across ranks and seeks to synthesize the development of inner faculties with the
fulfilment of the female mind in everyday life.

A Writer Robed in the Livery of Respectability,
A Sister Adept in Free-masonry

Hamilton was a Scottish writer, a Common Sense philosopher, a novelist, a satirist, an educator and a philanthropist. She was also a woman, which she never allowed her readers to forget. She was conservative and believed in class hierarchies, in benevolent landlords and landladies, in subordinate but independent-minded peasants, and the virtues of rural existence. She was an admirer of Warren Hastings and William Jones, and supported the nascent British imperialist project. Disjunctions and tensions abound in her work. But she was *not*, I have shown, merely or primarily either an anti-revolutionary writer or a bourgeois hegemonic writer.

Hamilton was indeed a woman of letters, and, as Austen termed her, a 'respectable' writer.[95] But she believed in the virtues of a broadly organized, not too disciplinary field of knowledge, in which fiction, educational tracts, conduct books and works on philosophy, all made their contribution to learning. Hamilton sought to show that numerous other women, who were not public women of letters as she was, women who spent their lives primarily in the domestic sphere, could become some of the best practitioners of a supposedly abstruse 'discipline' such as philosophy – gentlewomen, the exemplary amateurs, are also potentially some of the best 'men of letters', their gender affording them the flexibility to move between various domains of experience and knowledge, and in particular making them what we would today call excellent psychologists, well-versed in Hamilton's 'science of the mind'. Philanthropy, authorship, philosophy, spinning, domestic service, marriage – all are possible vocations for women, and all require the cultivation of the mind.

Hamilton cuts across classes in her thoughts about women's education – she is as attentive to the needs of charity school girls or Scottish peasant girls as she is to those of wealthier women. Her bias is clearly towards educated gentlewomen, but recurrently in her work we find the figure of the peasant–educator, most notably Betty Mason, who airs some of Hamilton's most cherished views on education. Her educational thought may seem too rationalist and too limited in its class contours – this is, however, unjust to her espousal of a bold, creative reason which must work in tandem with the affections and imagination, as well as to her sympathetic, uncondescending attitude to the education of lower-class girls.

Hamilton's achievement as an educational thinker and writer, particularly on female education, is enormous, and has not been given due acknowledgment. Not only does she use rigorous philosophical language to analyse the faculties and operations of the human mind, she also uses the same language skilfully to show how much women are discriminated against in their education. She integrates, too, philosophy and fiction – despite her distrust of many elements in the fiction of her day, Hamilton returns repeatedly in her oeuvre to writing fiction which does not indulge in the sort of delusional fanstasy she deplores.

Again and again, Hamilton highlights the many lacks in the prevailing systems of female education – the perceptual faculties of women are not developed, encouraging lazy passivity; their attention is directed, by the process of purported education, to superficial accomplishments, dress and marriage; they are taught to be quiescent, gentle and unthinking, leading to disastrous consequences; their selves are subsumed under an overweening, masculine self-ideal of false heroism and warmongering which is threatened by female education. Such generalizations are vivified in Hamilton's fiction. Harriet listening to Hume's *History of England* read aloud by an orphan girl she has educated, or the servant-turned-teacher Mrs Mason asking a villager to plough, fertilize, sow good seed, and only then expect the harvest of a good education – such vignettes occur again and again in Hamilton's fiction.

Hamilton uses metaphors of education conveying a sense of freedom and mobility: education enables women to rise, like balloons, to regions high in the air, or allows them to build castles in the air with other women joined in a secret sisterhood of free-masonry. Elizabeth Hamilton's multiple achievement – writing in a confident, intellectually rigorous, philosophical mode on male and female education, writing simultaneously as a woman writer advocating women's education, and writing successful fictions of female education cutting across genres – is an immensely distinguished one, placing her in the ranks of Mary Wollstonecraft and Maria Edgeworth.[96]

Perhaps more than any writer of her day, Hamilton showed that it was possible to be an independent woman of letters, unassociated with a religious denomination, politically moderate, respectable and intellectually adventurous. For someone who had chosen in her teens to construct herself as an 'antique maiden' who refuses to wear the 'fashion'd livery' of femininity, this was a notable achievement, particularly as Hamilton foregrounded in her writing the role and potential of other women like her who refuse to wear this livery, from the teenager Agnes sitting uncomfortably in a drawing room to the disabled teacher Betty Mason. The 'livery' of respectability was one that readers and critics of her day were happy to clothe Hamilton in, but, while she acceded to the construction of this impeccably respectable persona, she never ceased to see female education as an adventurous journey undertaken by self-aware and self-dependent women.

Notes and References

[1] Miss [Elizabeth] Benger, *Memoirs of the Late Mrs Elizabeth Hamilton, with a Selection from Her Correspondence and Other Unpublished Writings*, 2 vols (London: Longman, Hurst, Rees, Orme and Brown, 1818), pp. 1–3.

[2] There are sections on Elizabeth Hamilton in Ann H. Jones, *Ideas and Innovations: Best Sellers of Jane Austen's Age* (New York: AMS Press, 1986), pp. 19–48, and in Gary Kelly, *Women, Writing, and Revolution, 1790–1827* (Oxford: Clarendon Press, 1993), pp. 126–61, 265–304. While Kelly's discussion is detailed and valuable, it virtually ignores the early writing, is not attentive to the very personal charge in Hamilton's work, and suffers from its prioritization of the categories of middle-class cultural revolution and the French Revolution, to the detriment of Hamilton's more pervasive concern with gender, independent of other political considerations. More

akin to the spirit of the present chapter is Janice Farrar Thaddeus's brief but illuminating essay, 'Elizabeth Hamilton's Domestic Politics', *Studies in Eighteenth-Century Culture*, 23 (1994), pp. 265–84.

3 Benger, *Memoirs of the Late Mrs Elizabeth Hamilton*, Vol. I, p. 3.

4 Ibid., Vol. I, p. 26.

5 Ibid., Vol. I, pp. 32–33.

6 This representation of the happy, free education of a tomboy has similarities with a passage in Wollstonecraft's *Vindication of the Rights of Woman*, in which she is refuting Rousseau: '. . . I will venture to affirm, that a girl, whose spirits have not been damped by inactivity, or innocence tainted by false shame, will always be a romp, and the doll will never excite attention unless confinement allows her no alternative.' Mary Wollstonecraft, *A Vindication of the Rights of Woman*, edited by Carol H. Poston (New York and London: W.W. Norton and Co., 1988), p. 43. Austen's description of Catherine Morland's education in *Northanger Abbey* is also similar.

7 Benger, *Memoirs of the Late Mrs Elizabeth Hamilton*, Vol. I, p. 35.

8 Ibid., Vol. I, p. 36.

9 Elizabeth Hamilton, *Translation of the Letters of a Hindoo Rajah*, 2 vols (Dublin: H. Colbert, 1797), Vol. I, pp. 95–96.

10 Ibid., Vol. I, p. 96.

11 Benger, *Memoirs of the Late Mrs Elizabeth Hamilton*, Vol. I, p. 43.

12 Ibid., Vol. I, p. 45.

13 Ibid., Vol. I, p. 50.

14 Ibid., Vol. II, pp. 31–32.

15 Ibid., Vol. I, p. 47.

16 Ibid., Vol. I, p. 93.

17 Ibid., Vol. I, p. 109.

18 Ibid., Vol. I, p. 131.

19 Ibid., Vol. I, p. 128.

20 Ibid., Vol. I, p. 138.

21 Ibid., Vol. I, pp. 148–49.

22 Ibid., Vol. I, p. 183.

23 Ibid., Vol. I, p. 53.

24 Ibid., Vol. I, p. 60.

25 Ibid., Vol. I, p. 95.

26 Ibid., Vol. I, pp. 278–79.

27 Ibid., Vol. I, pp. 347–48.

28 Ibid., Vol. I, p. 349.

29 Ibid., Vol. I, p. 126.

30 B. Rajan, 'Feminizing the Feminine: Early Women Writers on India', in Alan Richardson and Sonia Hofkosh, eds, *Romanticism, Race, and Imperial Culture, 1780–1834* (Bloomington and Indianapolis: Indiana University Press, 1996), pp. 149–72.

31 Hamilton, *Translation of the Letters of a Hindoo Rajah*, Vol. I, p. xxiii.

32 i.e. Scriptures.

33 Hamilton, *Translation of the Letters of a Hindoo Rajah*, Vol. I, pp. 21–22.

34 Elizabeth Hamilton, *Memoirs of Modern Philosophers*, 3 vols (London: Robinson, 1800; rpt, London: Routledge/Thoemmes Press, 1992), Vol. I, pp. 199–200.

35 'Bibby', i.e. 'bibi': Hindustani term for a woman.

36 Elizabeth Hamilton, *Letters on Education* (Dublin: Colbert and Kelly, 1801), pp. 150–51.

37 Hamilton, *Translation of the Letters of a Hindoo Rajah*, Vol. I, p. 93.

38 Ibid., Vol. I, p. 94.

39 Ibid., Vol. II, p. 72.

40 Ibid., Vol. II, p. 73.

41 Ibid., Vol. I, pp. 97–99.

42 Hamilton, *Memoirs of Modern Philosophers*, Vol. I, pp. 107–08.

43 Ibid., Vol. I, p. 201.

44 Ibid., Vol. I, p. 148.

[45] Ibid., Vol. I, p. 194.

[46] Ibid., Vol. I, p. 196.

[47] Ibid., Vol. I, p. 195.

[48] Hamilton, *Translation of the Letters of a Hindoo Rajah*, Vol. II, p. 18.

[49] Ibid., Vol. II, p. 19.

[50] Elizabeth Hamilton, *A Series of Popular Essays, Illustrative of Principles Essentially Connected with the Improvement of the Understanding, the Imagination, and the Heart*, 2 vols (Edinburgh: Manners and Miller; London: Longman et al., 1813), Vol. I, pp. 170–71.

[51] Hamilton, *Memoirs of Modern Philosophers*, Vol. II, p. 334.

[52] Hamilton, *Popular Essays*, Vol. I, pp. 34–36.

[53] Ibid., Vol. I, p. 80.

[54] Ibid., Vol. I, p. 149.

[55] Elizabeth Hamilton, *Letters Addressed to the Daughter of a Nobleman on the Formation of the Religious and Moral Principles*, with an introduction by Gina Luria, 2 vols (London: Cadell and Davies, 1806; rpt, New York: Garland Books, 1974), Vol. II, pp. 127–29.

[56] Ibid., Vol. II, p. 163.

[57] Ibid., Vol. II, pp. 163–64.

[58] Ibid., Vol. II, pp. 167–68.

[59] Hamilton, *Popular Essays*, Vol. I, pp. 303–04.

[60] Benger, *Memoirs of the Late Mrs Elizabeth Hamilton*, Vol. II, pp. 32–33.

[61] Ibid., Vol. II, p. 48.

[62] Ibid., Vol. II, p. 47.

[63] Ibid., Vol. II, pp. 41–43.

[64] Elizabeth Hamilton, *Memoirs of the Life of Agrippina, the Wife of Germanicus* (London: G. and J. Robinson, 1804). On *Memoirs of Agrippina*, see Jane Rendall, 'Writing History for Women: Elizabeth Hamilton and the *Memoirs of Agrippina*', in Clarissa Campbell Orr, ed., *Wollstonecraft's Daughters: Womanhood in England and France 1780–1920* (Manchester: Manchester University Press, 1996), pp. 79–93.

[65] Benger, *Memoirs of the Late Mrs Elizabeth Hamilton*, Vol. II, p. 108.

[66] Ibid., Vol. II, p. 59.

[67] Ibid., Vol. I, pp. 251–52, journal entry, June 1808.

[68] *The Collected Works of Dugald Stewart*, edited by Sir William Hamilton, with an introduction by Knud Haakonssen, 11 vols (Edinburgh: Thomas Constable and Co, 1854–60; Bristol: Thoemmes Press, 1994), Vol. I, p. xii.

[69] Ibid., p. xi.

[70] Hamilton, *Letters on Education*, p. 173.

[71] Benger, *Memoirs of the Late Mrs Elizabeth Hamilton*, Vol. I, pp. 139–40.

[72] Sir Walter Scott acknowledged his debt to *The Cottagers of Glenburnie* in the 'Postscript' to *Waverley*. Hamilton's feminized 'cottage tale' thus becomes a forebear of Scott's large-scale national historical novel. On 'national tales' by women writers (notably Edgeworth and Lady Morgan) and their eclipsing by Scott's model of the historical novel, see Ina Ferris, *The Achievement of Literary Authority: Gender, History, and the Waverley Novels* (Ithaca and London: Cornell University Press, 1991), pp. 105–33.

[73] Elizabeth Hamilton, *The Cottagers of Glenburnie* (3rd edn, Edinburgh: Manners and Miller, 1808), pp. viii–ix.

[74] Ibid., p. ix.

[75] Ibid., p. ix.

[76] Hamilton, *Memoirs of Modern Philosophers*, Vol. I, p. 244.

[77] Hamilton, *Cottagers of Glenburnie*, pp. 5–6.

[78] Ibid., p. 35.

[79] Ibid., pp. 38–39.

[80] Ibid., p. 75.

[81] Ibid., p. 177.

[82] Ibid., p. 183.

[83] Elizabeth Hamilton, *Hints Addressed to the Patrons and Directors of Schools; Principally Intended to Shew, that the Benefits Derived from the New Modes of Teaching May Be Increased by a Partial Adoption of the Plan of Pestalozzi*, introduced by Jeffrey Stern (London: Longman, Hurst, Rees, Orme and Brown, 1815; rpt, Bristol: Thoemmes Press and Taipei: Unifacmanu Trading Company, 1994), p. 3, pp. 20–21.

[84] For a discussion of Smith's views on this subject, see Kathryn Sutherland, 'Adam Smith's Master Narrative: Women and the *Wealth of Nations*', in *Adam Smith's Wealth of Nations: New Interdisciplinary Essays*, edited by Stephen Copley and Kathryn Sutherland (Texts in Culture, Manchester and New York: Manchester University Press, 1995), pp. 97–121, p. 100.

[85] Hamilton, *Cottagers of Glenburnie*, pp. 388–89.

[86] On Pestalozzi's educational method, see Michael Heafford, *Pestalozzi: His Thought and Its Relevance Today* (London: Methuen, 1967).

[87] Josephine Kamm, *Hope Deferred: Girls' Education in English History* (London: Methuen and Co., 1965), p. 128.

[88] F.K. Prochaska, 'Women in English Philanthropy 1790–1830', *International Review of Social History*, 19 (1974), pp. 426–45.

[89] Hamilton, *Hints*, pp. 74–75.

[90] Ibid., p. 81.

[91] Ibid., p. 137.

[92] Ibid., pp. 161–62.

[93] Ibid., p. 173.

[94] Ibid., p. 175.

[95] Letter to Cassandra Austen, 6–7 November 1813, in *Jane Austen's Letters*, collected and edited by Deirdre le Faye (Oxford and New York: Oxford University Press, 1997), p. 252.

[96] Maria Edgeworth, who knew Elizabeth Hamilton personally, paid tribute to her role as pioneering female author on the human mind, in an obituary published in the *Gentleman's Magazine*. Edgeworth, 'Character and Writings of Elizabeth Hamilton', *Gentleman's Magazine*, 86 (July–December 1816), p. 623.

CHAPTER FOUR

'The courage to rise superior to the silly customs of the world': Mary Brunton

After the death of Mary Brunton in 1818, her husband, Rev. Alexander Brunton, published a posthumous memoir and a selection from the journals and letters of his wife.[1] Published along with Mary Brunton's unfinished tale 'Emmeline', the memoir presents Brunton primarily as a woman of letters (like Elizabeth Benger's memoirs of Elizabeth Hamilton, published in the preceding year), even as it presents her respectability, propriety and domestic happiness as integral parts of this persona: the biography 'exhibit[s] the history of her [Brunton's] mind, and her habits of composition'.[2] Brunton's two completed novels (*Self-Control*, 1810–11 and *Discipline*, 1814) also describe the history of two young women, the growth of their minds, their education, formal and experiential, and their search for happiness. Although Brunton's own life was rather less adventurous than those of her heroines – Laura Montreville and Ellen Percy – her husband's representation of her education and her own description of her heroines' education, both bear marks of contemporary assumptions about female selfhood.

Alexander is quite critical of Mary's early education, which was 'not conducted on any regular plan'.[3] With a father most often away from home, Mary was educated largely by her mother, represented as an insufficiently domestic woman, trained rather in the 'accomplishments which adorn a court, than those which are useful in a domestic life'.[4] Nevertheless, he concedes that the mother's 'original though desultory conversation' must have stimulated her daughter's mind. She taught her daughter music, French and Italian, and a habit of translating from these languages, a skill to which Alexander attributes his wife's 'great facility and correctness' in composition. Mary is thus portrayed as an accomplished, intelligent and original child, but also as a lonely one who was largely left to her own devices, peopling her daydreams with figures drawn from her reading in poetry and fiction. Alexander's construction of his wife has resemblances to his wife's heroines, particularly in the presentation of ambivalent authority-figures, and in its admiration of female inwardness and originality.

Mary, rather like Laura in *Self-Control* (1810–11), soon learnt to take on domestic responsibilities in her father's household in Orkney, but such tasks left her, 'from her sixteenth to her twentieth year', with 'very little leisure for self-improvement'.[5] Alexander sees her marriage as a turning point in his wife's life. She acquired a more systematic education, partly supervised by him. Mary's reading 'received rather a more methodical direction'[6] from Alexander, and in the evenings he read out to her 'books chiefly of criticism and Belles Lettres'.[7] So great was the husband's influence that Mary 'contracted', Alexander tells us with more than a trace of smugness, 'far more than enough, the habit of speaking as a pupil'.[8]

It was at Bolton in her husband's parsonage that she learned to love Thomas Reid's works on the philosophy of the human mind.[9] Brunton sees some of his wife's ambitious intellectual pursuits, such as her attempts at learning mathematics, as only partly successful: happy when 'the address to the intellect was direct and pure', she lost interest when oblique methods of proof such as reductio ad absurdum were in question.[10] Brunton is thus shown to have lacked not the intellectual *rigour* but the *application* necessary for scientific education. In this, Alexander's representation of his wife is different from that of Laura (in *Self-Control*), who perseveres in her study of mathematics. Alexander is also at pains to tell us that Brunton was not a specialist – as indeed women were not encouraged to be. Thus, Brunton's reading did not 'lead [. . .] to marked proficiency in any one branch of study'.[11]

Alexander describes a striking trait of her mind, 'that habit of observing the varieties and beauties of nature'.[12] This was a trait that Brunton again shared with her heroines, along with other heroines of the time, such as Fanny Price, born in the same year as Ellen Percy. Education, of herself and of others, became an integral part of Brunton's self. She supervised the religious education of two wards of her husband, and in doing so, she re-examined her own principles; like Elizabeth Hamilton, 'in her own mind, and in the minds of her pupils, she was anxious to make religion an active principle'.[13]

What is found in the memoirs and Brunton's letters, and not in *Self-Control* and *Discipline*, is the charting of Brunton's change from 'an active and prudent young housewife' to a literary lady.[14] It is in Edinburgh that Brunton is seen as slowly acquiring the confidence to examine others' opinions and to defend her own. As she mixed in a wider circle, some of them literary people, she even engaged in 'little friendly controversies' with wit and confidence.[15] But the biggest single factor in her development was a female friendship formed in Edinburgh with Mrs Izett. For the six years that the two women lived in the same city, they 'read together – worked together – and talked over, with confidential freedom, their opinions, from minuter points to the most important ones'.[16] Even after Mrs Izett moved away from the capital, the friends maintained 'the only close and confidential correspondence, beyond the bounds of her own family, in which Mary ever engaged'.[17]

Alexander gives two reasons for the composition of *Self-Control*, in neither of which Brunton's own writing is the main impetus. Firstly, she wrote to fill up the many blank hours when Mrs Izett was busy with other things. Secondly, when she asked a literary friend whether he would publish a work by her husband, he told her that he would also like to publish a work by *her*. These accounts show the woman writer beginning her labours accidentally or hesitantly, not with a burning sense of vocation. Despite this hesitancy, however, Alexander's account makes clear that Brunton had independent views about her own work: obviously not as much of a docile pupil of her husband's as he thought, Brunton, even when she had her writing read by Alexander, would quite often reject his suggestions for improving *Self-Control*.[18]

All this time, as a letter dated 30 August 1810 makes clear, Brunton was suffering the usual anxieties of the woman writer who puts herself on display in the public sphere through her writing. Once *Self-Control* is in press, she writes:

> I would rather, as you well know, glide through the world unknown, than have (I will not call it *enjoy*) fame, however brilliant. To be pointed at – to be noticed and commented upon – to be suspected of literary airs – to be shunned, as literary women are, by the more unpretending of my own sex; and abhorred, as literary women often are, by the more pretending of the other! – My dear, I would sooner exhibit as a rope-dancer.[19]

Brunton's remark that she would 'sooner exhibit as a rope-dancer' throws into relief an acute problem facing contemporary women: the relationship between the private and the public spheres, as well as that between the literary public sphere and the public sphere of the performing arts. In her fiction, and in her letters,[20] Brunton disapproves of women singing, dancing and otherwise performing publicly as an occupation; on the other hand, such activities as painting or writing, where the female artist does not display herself directly, earn her approval. This point of view is very common in Brunton's contemporary women writers, from Maria Edgeworth to Jane Austen or Hannah More. I shall call it 'anti-Corinnism', given that Madame de Staël's novel *Corinne* (1807) crystallized the debate in its championing of the heroine Corinne, *improvisatrice* and performer, and prompted implicitly anti-Corinne fictions, among them Hannah More's *Coelebs in Search of a Wife* (1808) and Maria Edgeworth's 'Vivian' (1812).

Yet Brunton's analogy between the woman author and the rope-dancer, as well as her descriptions in *Self-Control* of Laura's travails as a painter (when, in her attempts to sell her paintings, Laura, rather than her paintings, becomes the commodity) suggest that the literary and the performing public spheres are not in fact distinct from each other. For literary women as much as for rope-dancers, fame is always in danger of engendering ostracism[21] – the more 'unpretending' of their own sex avoid them, and the more 'pretending' men avoid them.

Alongside such anxieties, Brunton had more technical ones about the craft of fiction. In a letter to the *grande dame* of contemporary Scottish letters, Joanna Baillie (the dedicatee of *Self-Control*), Mary explains what an inexperienced author she is:

> Till I began *Self-Control*, I had never in my life written anything but a letter or a recipe, excepting a few hundreds of vile rhymes, from which I desisted by the time I had gained the wisdom of fifteen years; therefore I was so ignorant of

the art on which I was entering, that I formed scarcely any plan for my tale. I merely intended to shew the power of the religious principle in bestowing self-command; and to bear testimony against a maxim as immoral as indelicate, that a reformed rake makes the best husband. For the rest, I was guided by the fancy of the hour.[22]

Letters and recipes, accepted products of the housewife's pen, gave way to fiction. But what guided Brunton's characterization was her religious and moral purpose. In the letter to Baillie, Brunton is firm and precise about the truths she seeks to inculcate: female self-command is for her, as for the other writers I examine in this book, a vital principle, nurtured by her heroines' Christianity.

That Brunton was gradually overcoming her anxieties about authorship is clear from another letter, dated 4 October 1810, in which the tone is very different, almost elated:

> you must not expect to hear from me for three months to come! Ay! stare if you please – but do not presume to challenge mine award – for, know, that I am one of the republic of letters. People are always great upon their new dignities; and truly mine are new enough. This is the first day of them; this day the first page of fair print was presented to my eyes, and they are to be feasted with four sheets a-week, for three or four months to come.[23]

Even with its tinge of irony, the pleasure in this passage at the newly acquired membership of the republic of letters is pervasive, heightened by the striking image of 'feasting' upon the printed proofs of her novel. Now, the very thought of the 'failure' of *Self-Control* makes her 'flesh creep'. She feels part of the community of writers: she 'cannot express . . . what a fellow feeling' she has 'with the poor wretches, whose works fall dead from the press'.[24]

Published anonymously, *Self-Control* soon begins to invite speculation as to the author. When it is rumoured that Brunton is the author, 'all the excellencies of the book are attributed to Mr B, while I am left to answer for all its defects.'[25] Mary is irritated at this, but is as irritated at a lady, MS, 'who, exasperated by hearing her own sex deprived of any little credit it might have done them, averred, in the heat of her indignation, that "to her *certain knowledge* Mr B had never written a word of it"'.[26] Brunton is as unhappy as MS that her authorship should be ascribed to her husband, but wants 'to creep a little closer into my shell; and shrink, if possible, a little more from the public eye'.[27] And yet, even this discomfort fades, as in a letter dated 19 April 1811, she describes herself as 'composedly' hearing both praise and censure[28] with an equanimity rather like that of her heroine Laura in *Self-Control*.

'Decently Kerchiefed, like our Grandmothers': Laura and *Self-Control* (1810–11)

In a letter dated 10 April 1810, Brunton describes Laura as 'so decently kerchiefed, like our grandmothers, that to dress her is a work of time and pains'.[29]

Laura is a serious and fervent heroine, as this comment and the epigraph to the novel suggests:

> His warfare is within. – There unfatigued
> His fervent spirit labours. – There he fights,
> And there obtains fresh triumphs o'er himself.
> And never-withering wreaths, compared with which
> The laurels that a Caesar reaps are weeds.[30]

The lines come from Book VI (The Winter Walk at Noon) of William Cowper's *The Task* (1785): Cowper was Brunton's favourite poet, and Alexander had encouraged her to write on him.[31] Cowper describes a feminized poet-persona, the Christian who has chosen a rural, contemplative life. Like women, his 'sphere' is 'humble', 'shining' with his 'fair example'. Like women, too, he has no power but 'small influence', his tasks mainly charitable and nurturing, 'soothing sorrow', 'quenching strife' and 'aiding helpless indigence'. While he must spurn the 'self-approving haughty world', gendered female ('with her whistling silks'), for Laura the epitome of the threat of worldliness is formed by the very masculine Colonel Hargrave, the 'reformed rake' who never reforms. Another obviously influential text for *Self-Control* is Richardson's *Clarissa*, where the heroine, assailed by Lovelace, the arch unreformed rake, is as inward-looking and meditative a 'fervent spirit' as Laura. Elements of the Protestant tradition of self-examination and spiritual autobiography are thus strongly present in *Self-Control*, as they are in *Clarissa*.

Brunton's interest in the inner self of the Christian woman was augmented by her interest in such writers of the Scottish Enlightenment as Thomas Reid and Joanna Baillie. *Self-Control*, as we have seen, was dedicated to Joanna Baillie, author of *Plays on the Passions* (1798). Brunton claims that while she may fall short in points of artistic excellence, 'In purity of intention I yield not even to JOANNA BAILLIE'.[32] Her novel, she claims, has an affinity with *Plays on the Passions* in its 'portraitures of the progress and of the consequences of passion', with passion as the 'rebel' which only religion can subdue. In her own 'Introductory Discourse' to *Plays on the Passions* (1798), Baillie shows this combined interest in psychology and religious morality. Her interest is similar to Elizabeth Hamilton's in the study of human character.

> From that strong sympathy which most creatures, but the human above all, feel for others of their kind, nothing has become so much an object of man's curiosity as man himself. . . . Every person . . . not deficient in intellect, is more or less occupied in tracing, amongst the individuals he converses with, the varieties which constitute the characters of men. . . . From this constant employment of their minds most people, I believe, without being conscious of it, have stored up in idea . . . strong marked varieties of human character.[33]

While such 'sympathetic curiosity' (an important Scottish Enlightenment term) drives Baillie to show the 'progress' of passions like love and hatred with a moral design that is unobtrusively present, Brunton foregrounds the virtues which her heroines must practise and acquire in order to subdue their passions, epitomized in Laura's love for Hargrave. Modern readers may forget Brunton's boldness in showing that Laura loves Hargrave, even if she must from principle repulse him. Many contemporary readers were critical of this. As Brunton noted, 'It is alleged that no virtuous woman could continue to love a man who makes such a début as Hargrave. All I say is, that I wish all the affections of virtuous persons were so *very* obedient to reason.'[34]

Laura's love for Hargrave is one of the 'traces of human imperfection' in her character that Brunton alludes to in the dedication. Brunton is aware of the mixture of psychological realism and moral–religious idealism in her representation of her first heroine. Laura, she says, even with her imperfections, is an ideal character, 'unnatural' to some extent; the author does not 'ascribe any of the virtues of Laura to nature, and, least of all, the one whose office is to regulate and control nature'.[35] Where does Laura's self-command come from then? Brunton gestures towards the operation of divine grace in human nature, that which refines and improves upon the fallen state of humanity.

Laura's education shows the way in which the spiritual manifests itself in the secular, everyday world. Her parents, her first preceptors, are weak figures. Her father, disillusioned in his hopes for happiness, at first wishes Laura to be neither beautiful nor intelligent because such qualities will only cause her suffering. Faced with her loveliness and the 'uncommon acuteness of her understanding',[36] however, he becomes a doting father. Throughout the book, we see Montreville as a well-meaning but weak man, whose spirits, as well as his material comforts, are kept up and looked after by his daughter. Laura's mother is no less unsatisfactory. Born in an aristocratic family (like Brunton's own mother), Lady Harriet is discontented at her quiet married life. Determined to turn Laura into her own idea of a paragon, 'a model of yielding softness' and 'a pensive beauty', she finds instead that her daughter has 'inexhaustible' spirits, and a 'reasonable' and 'reasoning' temperament. Through Laura, Brunton shows that spiritedness and rationality, on the one hand, and firmness or self-control, on the other, are not opposed pairs of attributes. Equally, Mrs Montreville, who wishes for pliable softness in her daughter, is herself subject to fits of 'ungoverned anger'.[37]

Laura's most influential teacher is her mother's friend Mrs Douglas, from whom she learns to be an active Christian. Brunton has mixed feelings towards the idea, 'the fashion of the age', which accounts for 'every striking feature of a character from education or external circumstance'.[38] As a Christian, she clearly believes that there is more to character than can be explained from environment and habit alone. Nevertheless, she does trace the awakening of Laura's religious spirit to her enthusiastic reading of stories about 'self-devoting patriots and martyrs', and the important lesson Mrs Douglas teaches her in the course of one such reading. Laura, 'her little form erect with noble daring', invites martyrdom if she is prosecuted, only to be told that self-denial does not begin at the stake: the 'cross' has to be taken up daily, whenever something pleasurable or valuable to the self is given up for the sake of duty.[39] Self-denial is thus, for Brunton (as selfless activity is for Elizabeth Hamilton), an eminently *active* virtue requiring courage ('erect with noble daring') and not a matter of passive suffering.

Such self-denial is undeniably a key component in Laura's 'self-control', although it is not the only one. Her initial decision to repulse Hargrave, one which she has to invoke repeatedly in the face of constant pressure from him and from her father, is at first an act of denial of her love. Paradoxically, it soon turns into self-assertion and the assertion of principles. Laura refuses to accept the sexual double standard: when Montreville tries to persuade her that Hargrave may reform after marriage, Laura asks if he would have agreed to his *son* marrying a woman who had lost her chastity?

> 'Tell me then, were Colonel Hargrave your son, and were I what I cannot name, could any passion excuse, any circumstances induce you to sanction the connexion for which you now plead?'
> 'My dear love,' said Montreville, 'the cases are widely different. The world's opinion affixes just disgrace to the vices in your sex, which in ours it views with more indulgent eyes.' 'But I,' returned Laura, 'when I took upon me the honoured name of Christian, by that very act became bound that the opinion of the world should not regulate my principles, nor its customs guide my practice. Perhaps even the worst of my sex might plead that the voice of a tempter lured them to perdition; but what tongue can speak the vileness of that tempter!'[40]

Laura's modesty, her inability to 'name' the unchaste woman, is strikingly balanced by her espousal of the 'honoured name' of Christian – refusing to categorize the 'fallen woman' as a prostitute, she is articulate in affirming her Christianity and in naming the 'vileness' of the male tempter who instigates the woman's loss of chastity.

One may ask whether Laura's self-control leads to a constant diminution of her sense of self: is she always abnegating her self, or does self-control, paradoxically, become a positive principle of selfhood? As the passage I have quoted demonstrates, I would argue that the second of these alternatives is the truer one, with 'self-control' increasing Laura's articulacy, autonomy and firmness of principles. Laura combines an experiential education with a continuous process of inner development (what Brunton in *Discipline* calls an 'education for eternity'), resulting in a compelling picture of powerful Protestant womanhood.[41]

Laura's assertion of principle in the arena of sexuality is only one manifestation of her remarkably self-willed, self-contained, self-possessed persona. Her self-command comes through to the reader as effortless when, during Warren's attempted abduction, her calm disdain of that gentleman's designs leaves him dumbfounded: 'Laura now rose from her seat, and, seizing the reins with a force that made the horses rear, she coolly chose that moment to spring from the curricle . . . leaving her inammorato [*sic*] in the utmost astonishment at her self-possession, as well as rage at her disdainful treatment.'[42]

Laura's self-possession is particularly evident in her dealings with her aunt's caprice and tyranny. When her aunt accuses de Courcy of having fathered an illegitimate child, Laura immediately sets off to Norwood, the de Courcy house, to ask whether this is indeed the case. No signs here of blushing maiden modesty: Laura is quite clear that she has a right to know about the character of her suitor.

Laura does not confide in anyone about Hargrave's proposal to make her his mistress. She refuses to tell her father on the grounds that he might be provoked into a duel with Hargrave. But Laura's individualism is not explicable simply by practical considerations. It is a principle she lives by, so that even Mrs Douglas does not know all that has happened in her life. Her refusal later to confide in her aunt provokes incivility and tyranny. No authority-figure is allowed to help or hinder Laura in her endeavour to maintain self-control.

Nor does Laura have less of a battle to fight within herself: rejecting Hargrave is hard for her, and the conflict within her is evident to Mrs Douglas:

> She soon noticed that an expression, as of sudden torture, would sometimes contract, for a moment, the polished forehead of Laura; that it was now succeeded by the smothered sigh, the compressed lip, the hasty motion that spoke of strong mental effort, now subsided into the languor of deep unconquered melancholy.[43]

'Strong mental effort', 'unconquered melancholy': Laura is obviously deeply disturbed and has to draw on all the resources within her, especially her religion, to recover:

> Shall I refuse to find pleasure in any duties but such as are of my own selection: Because the gratification of one passion – one misplaced passion, is refused, has this world no more to offer? this fair world, which its great Creator has stamped with his power, and stored by his bounty, and ennobled by making it the temple of his worshippers, the avenue to heaven! Shall I find no balm in the consolations of friendship, the endearments of parental love – no joy in the sweets of benevolence, the stores of knowledge, the miracles of grace![44]

Christianity then offers Laura a means of broadening her vision, of seeing the world as a large place filled with friendship, knowledge, grace and activity, away from the claustrophobia of love. Laura is a reflective heroine, whose education advances as much by her meditations as by more conventional means. Yet, such educative, reflective moments are to be constantly threatened in the book, as they are after the preceding passage by Hargrave's importunate demands.

Laura is also, like her creator, attuned to nature, which she often reads allegorically, as on her voyage from Scotland to England:

> [T]o her, the majestic Forth, as it widened into an estuary, seemed itself a 'world of waters'. But when on one side the land receded from the view, when the great deep lay before her, Laura looked upon it for a moment, and, shuddering, turned away. 'It is too mournful', she said to her father – 'were there but one

spot, however small, however dimly described, which fancy might people with beings like ourselves, I could look with pleasure on the gulf between – but here there is no resting place. Thus dismal, thus overpowering, methinks eternity would have appeared, had not a haven of rest been made known to us.'[45]

Her feeling for nature, vivified by religion, is shown as very different from that of the affectedly sentimental July Dawkins, the daughter of Laura's landlady, who longs 'to have been permitted to mingle my sighs with the mountain breezes'.[46] July is a novel-reading heroine who superficially changes her self according to the works she reads: one moment timid and infantile, another moment she is wonderfully wise:

> After reading Evelina, she sat with her mouth extended in a perpetual smile, and was . . . very timid. . . . When Camilla was the model for the day, she became insufferably rattling, infantine, and thoughtless. After perusing the Gossip's story, she, in imitation of the rational Louisa, suddenly waxed very wise – spoke in sentences – despised romances – sewed shifts – and read sermons. But, in the midst of this fit, she, in an evil hour, opened a volume of the Nouvelle Eloise. . . . The shifts were left unfinished, the sermons thrown aside, and Miss Julia returned with renewed *impetus* to the sentimental.[47]

Brunton, then, indirectly accuses Burney of creating heroines who are timid, childish and thoughtless. In showing the effects of July reading the conservative writer Jane West's *A Gossip's Story* (1797), Brunton also recognizes the paradoxical power of fiction to preach against itself – yet, the 'despiser of romances' sloughs off her new-found character the moment a new work captures her imagination. Novels, Brunton thus says, can contribute to readers losing a sense of stable selfhood. Nevertheless, deepening the paradox, Laura too reads and enjoys fiction, her favourite hero being Jane Porter's Thaddeus of Warsaw in the novel of the same name (1803), who was partly based on the real-life Polish patriot Tadeusz Kosciuszko.[48]

July's ineptness as reader/viewer also expresses itself when she mistakes Laura's painting of Leonidas taking leave of his wife for one of Tom Jones; this prompts an inevitable discussion of Henry Fielding's novel, with Laura and her father ranged against it. While July praises Tom Jones's 'warmth of heart and generosity', Laura finds that in him these qualities

> do not appear to me of that kind which qualify a man for adorning domestic life. His seems a constitutional warmth, which in his case . . . is the concomitant of a warm temper – a temper as little favourable to gentleness in those who command, as to submission in those who obey. If by generosity you mean the cheerful relinquishing of something which we really value, it is an abuse of the term to apply it to the profusion with which your favourite squanders his money.[49]

Brunton's heroine quite clearly does have this gentleness and this selfless generosity; equally clear is Brunton's preference for a set of feminine qualities over more 'masculine' ones such as 'constitutional warmth'. And the arena where Tom Jones's value is judged is the domestic, private sphere, in Brunton's novels the preferred domain of the heroes as well as the heroines.

That an excessive taste for fiction can corrupt domestic virtues in men and women is clear from Brunton's account of Hargrave. A far more sinister hero than Tom Jones (although with a similar set of sexual values), the Lovelace-like Hargrave is shown to be vitiated by indolence and novel-reading[50] (his ruin begins when he reads one of Smollett's picaresque novels): yet another example (as in Elizabeth Hamilton's *Memoirs of Modern Philosophers*) of a *man* corrupted by fiction.

While Hargrave's mother mistakenly takes his 'turn for reading' as positive, the exemplary mother of Montague de Courcy is a more rigorous and perceptive educator. Maternal educators, Brunton thus argues, play crucial shaping roles in men's lives. Mrs de Courcy manages to persuade an extravagant husband to curtail his expenditure, and after his death, acts as sole guardian to her children. She does not send her son to a public school, preferring instead domestic instruction under a clergyman who lives nearby. Every Sunday she instructs her children in Christianity: 'The peculiar precepts of Christianity she taught him to apply to his actions, by applying them herself; and the praise that is so often lavished upon acts of boldness, dexterity, and spirit, she conscientiously reserved for acts of candour, humility, and self-denial.'[51]

Montague is thus a fit partner for Laura, the same lessons inculcated in each. His preferred life, too, is a domestic one, his pursuits classical studies, chemistry and drawing. Montague gains Laura's friendship by involving her in such intellectual pursuits: he reads to her, borrows books from her, brings medals to show her, undertakes joint chemical experiments with her and teaches her mathematics.[52] Respect for Laura's mind and her self-command is crucial in de Courcy's eventual success in marrying her.

Laura meets de Courcy when she decides that to help her father she is going to earn money by selling her paintings.[53] A visitor at Mrs Douglas's sees one of Laura's pictures and, unaware who the painter is, remarks: 'If this be, as I suppose, the work of a young artist, I shall not be surprised that he one day rise to both fame and fortune.'[54] Fired by enthusiasm, Laura fails to realize how crucial the word 'he' is, and takes artistic success to be a goal achievable by women as well as by men. She determines to accompany her father to London and help him by selling her paintings. Brunton describes with indulgence the enthusiasm with which Laura looks forward to her commercial success as a painter – in a startling metaphor, a woman looking forward to earning a living is compared to a man looking forward to marriage, in a reversal of gender roles: 'Never did youthful bridegroom look forward to his nuptial hour with more ardour, than did Laura to that which was to begin the realization of her prospects of wealth and independence.'[55]

At the first shop Laura goes to, she learns that there is much difference between a female consumer and a female producer of art. The first dealer, seeing an 'elegant' lady, thinks she has come to make an addition to her 'cabinet': the moment he hears that she is not a wealthy buyer but a painter herself, his tone changes to condescension, and her gender enters into the conversation – he will look at the picture 'to oblige so pretty a lady', as if she, and not her picture, is on sale.[56] Laura, on her part, is indifferent to praise for her beauty, and responds to a florid compliment from a roué calmly, admitting without happiness that her 'features' are indeed 'uncommonly regular'[57] – but when her paintings are sold she is genuinely happy because she feels she is 'USEFUL'.

Laura's father objects to her selling her paintings.

> Captain Montreville saw in his daughter's well-earned treasure only the wages of degrading toil. 'It is hard, very hard,' said he with a deep sigh, 'that you, my lovely child, should be dependent on your daily labour for your support.' 'Oh call it not hard, my dear father', cried Laura. 'Thanks, a thousand thanks to your kind foresight, which, in teaching me this blessed art, secured to me the only real independence, by making me independent of all but my own exertions.'[58]

Where Laura sees in a positive light female independence in earning a living, part of her ethic of dignified individualism, her father sees her 'degraded into an artist', a prey to 'the caprice of the public', no longer the gentlewoman who depends on father or husband for support. Laura's hopes of being a successful painter are of course doomed: her paintings are bought by her future suitor, Montague de Courcy, who sees her before he sees her paintings. Brunton is wry about his quick appreciation of Laura's 'genius', aided by his earlier admiration of her beauty:

> De Courcy again turned to the picture, which he had before examined, and on this second inspection, was so fortunate as to discover that it bore the stamp of great genius – an opinion in which, we believe, he would have been joined by any man of four-and-twenty who had seen the artist. 'So,' thought he, 'this lovely creature's genius is equal to her beauty, and her worth perhaps surpasses both; for she has the courage to rise superior to the silly customs of the world, and can dare to be useful to herself and to others. I knew by the noble arching of her forehead, that she was above all vulgar prejudice.'[59]

Montague can applaud Laura for daring to earn her living, rising 'above all vulgar prejudice' and 'the silly customs of the world' which frown on women earning their bread, but ironically can do so, Brunton hints, at least partly because he has been attracted by her beauty. Brunton may be unable to move out of novelistic conventions about beautiful heroines whose talents form a kind of adjunct to their beauty, but she is able to take a sharply sceptical look at them.

Katrin Burlin has analysed[60] a later episode involving Laura's painting, 'The Choice of Hercules', in which both the heroine's father and Montague misinterpret her motives in painting de Courcy as Hercules and herself as Virtue. As

Burlin points out, 'thinking marriage the only respectable profession for Laura, her father regards her painting room as a place of potential amorous intrigue rather than of artistic performance'.[61] Both he and Montreville mistakenly think that in choosing to paint herself and de Courcy in her picture, she intends to express her love for the latter.

After her father's death, Laura's ethic of usefulness and industry does not permit her to live with her friend Mrs Douglas, who, even though she would welcome Laura, has far too small an income to support a dependant. Laura considers becoming a governess: 'she was an utter novice in the manufacture of all those elegant nothings, which are so serviceable to fine ladies in their warfare against time . . . the seclusion of her native village had doomed her to ignorance of the art of dancing. . . . Her knowledge of music, too, was severely limited.'[62]

In her lack of accomplishments Laura is unlike Ellen in *Discipline* or Juliet Granville in Frances Burney's *The Wanderer*. Laura has perforce to live with her aunt, with whom her trials are severe. Lady Pelham adroitly strips Laura of the little money she has, pleading an urgent need for a loan; she is also incensed because Laura refuses to confide in her about her two suitors. As a marker of the moral and intellectual difference between the two women, Brunton shows them starting the study of mathematics simultaneously. While Lady Pelham abandons it at the first signs of difficulty, Laura perseveres (unlike her creator, if Rev. Mr Brunton is to be believed!).

> Lady Pelham . . . was convinced that 'of all studies that of mathematics must be the most delightful . . .'. She obliged Laura to join her in this new pursuit. Upon the study of this science, so little in favour with a sex who reserve cultivation for faculties where it is least wanting, Laura entered with a pleasure that surprised herself, and she persevered in it with an industry that astonished her teacher. Lady Pelham was, for a little while, the companion of her labours; but, at the first difficulty, she took offence at the unaccommodating thing, which shewed no more indulgence to female than to royal indolence. – Forthwith she was fired with a strong aversion to philosophers in bibs, and a horror at *she*-pedants.[63]

Brunton's attitude towards Lady Pelham's attitude to study is sardonic: the same woman who is at first enthusiastic about mathematics is later vociferous in turning round and condemning female pretensions to knowledge. The terms she uses, 'philosophers in bibs' and '*she*-pedants', are stock terms of ridicule for learned women. Brunton's criticism of Lady Pelham's attitude to female learning and her comment that women in general 'reserve cultivation for faculties where it is least wanting' indict the superficiality and lack of rigour present in the general run of female education.

'Loose, Floating, Easy Robes, that Will Slip on in a Minute':[64] *Discipline* (1814)

Ellen Percy, heroine of Brunton's second novel *Discipline*, was conceived of as a more true-to-life picture than Laura: Brunton described her second 'brat'[65] as 'too common-place a person' for the 'falls of Niagara' (referring to a passage in *Self-Control* where Laura escapes her abductor by canoeing down the Niagara falls!).[66] Brunton also consciously made *Discipline* a more comic novel.[67] Paradoxically enough, this lighter novel, begun at the end of 1812, was written, Rev. Mr. Brunton tells us, 'more slowly and with more labour' than the earlier work, with Brunton occupying herself in 'female work' such as 'sewing or knotting' in the intervals of writing – a noteworthy association of female writing with other more traditional kinds of female occupations. As a result, the novel is better worked out than its predecessor. Nonetheless, Brunton avowed a primarily Christian purpose for this novel too.

> [T]he great purpose of the book is to procure admission for the religion of a
> sound mind and of the Bible, where it cannot find access in any other form.
> . . . I am quite sure I might make twice as much of my labour, if I could bring
> myself to present to the public an easy flexible sort of virtue – possessing no
> strong support, and being, indeed, too light to need any – instead of the old-
> fashioned erect morality, which 'falls not, because it is founded on a rock'.[68]

Ellen has a long way to go before she can walk erect and find a secure footing on this rock. Related in her voice, the work presents her as a wayward girl whose early education is deficient, to say the least:

> [F]rom the earliest period of my recollection, I furnished an instance at least, if
> not a proof, of the corruption of human kind; being proud, petulant, and
> rebellious. Some will probably think the growth of such propensities no more
> unaccountable than that of briars and thorns; being prepared, from their own
> experience and observation, to expect that both should spring without any
> particular culture. But whoever is dissatisfied with this compendious deduction,
> may trace my faults to certain faults in my early education.[69]

One can trace here, as in *Self-Control*, the ambivalence in Brunton about whether human character is produced more by innate characteristics or more by environment, more by nature or nurture. Certainly, her parents are shown to bear a share in the development of Ellen's character: her mother, a 'gentle being' who 'bore my wayward humour with an angel's patience', 'exercised a control too gentle over a spirit which needed to be reined by a firmer hand than hers'.[70] When servants report Ellen's pert sallies of wit in a politic spirit of flattery, Mrs Percy is unable to reproach her daughter; when she, in turn, reports these to her husband, he is pleased with his daughter. In this household, with its nominally clear structure of authority (the servants at the bottom, the mother in the middle and the father at the top), Ellen succeeds in subverting the structure: she, a child and a girl, queens it over the household.

> I was the dictatrix of my playfellows, the tyrant of the servants, and the idolized
> despot of both my parents. . . . Nothing could be unimportant which opposed
> my sovereign will. That will became every day more imperious; so that, however

it governed others, I was myself still more its slave, knowing no rest or peace but in its gratification.[71]

Ellen, then, is a girl and a child with an ungoverned will which loves to govern others. That her gender makes this unruliness and imperiousness particularly troublesome is made clear by the following comment of her father's: 'It is a confounded pity she is a girl. If she had been of the right sort, she might have got into Parliament, and made a figure with the best of them. But now what use is her sense of?'[72]

In a man, then, such verbal skill and fire might have been channelized into the vocation of politics, a vocation denied to women. Her mother's answer to her husband's regret is to hope that Ellen's 'sense' will aid the achievement of her 'happiness' – denied access to a public vocation or profession, happiness, that most elusive and ambitious of goals, is what Ellen must look for. Ellen's father manages to deconstruct even this yearning: Ellen's 'happiness' is to be synonymous with her patrimony, 'two hundred thousand pounds', which she will 'never know the trouble of earning' (ironic in the light of Ellen's later struggles to eke out a living).[73] In the early part of the novel, Brunton shows that Mr Percy's wealth, as well as his constant harping on it, seriously damages Ellen.

Ellen's parents are thus both in their own ways unsuccessful as parental educators, so that the mature Ellen asks whether her waywardness is to be ascribed entirely to her parents' lax discipline.

> She [i.e. Ellen's mother] continued unconsciously to foster in me that spirit of pride, which may indeed admit the transient admiration of excellence, or even the passing fervours of gratitude, but which is manifestly opposite to vital piety – to that piety which consists in a surrender of self-will, of self-righteousness, of self in every form, to the Divine justice, holiness, and sovereignty. It was, perhaps, for training us to this temper, of such difficult, yet such indispensable attainment, that the discipline of parental authority was intended. I have long seen reason to repent the folly which deprived me of the advantages of this useful apprenticeship, but this conviction has been the fruit of discipline far more painful.[74]

I am struck by the mixed feeling in this passage towards Ellen's mother's failure in exercising parental authority. There is more than a hint of indulgence towards the mother's attitude, as well as a sense of hesitancy about the efficacy of parental discipline in teaching this ideal, self-denying sort of piety. Only 'perhaps' was parental discipline instituted as a 'training' or 'apprenticeship' for the ideal; it is quite clear that in itself such discipline cannot produce true self-denial. In this Christian, female-centred *Bildungsroman*, Ellen has to undergo an experiential education which, at one and the same time, forces her to assert her self – travel unaccompanied, struggle with poverty, try to earn her living by making toys and governessing – and teaches her to abnegate aspects of her self, such as vanity and moral vacillation. As in Amelia Opie's *Adeline Mowbray, or the Mother and Daughter* (1804), an initial state of transgression forms the basis for a novel which, in a larger sense, vindicates such transgression – to put it crudely, had they not erred in some way or the other, our heroines would not have received the painful but rich exposure to experience that is their lot.

The question is, does Ellen's journey through life force her to undergo deformation, more particularly as a woman? Certainly, her mother's dying wish is that God the 'Father' should be 'kinder' to her than her earthly parents, even if that kindness shows itself in 'chastising'.[75] Yet it is arguable that Brunton, in fact, shows how few inner resources Ellen receives from her early education (so that she has little to lose), even in terms of affiliations and solidarity, setting aside questions of principle. Whereas at journey's end Ellen finds herself in the Highlands, with strong ties of friendship binding her to women such as the upright, independent-minded peasant Cecil Graham and Ellen's future sister-in-law Charlotte Graham, in her early life Ellen is damaged by her father's pride in riches and by the competitive and manipulative version of femininity she learns at her fashionable boarding school. Brunton anatomizes the mismanagement that leads to the growth of competitiveness between Ellen and the aristocratic Lady Maria:

> I was commended, Lady Maria reproved. Had the reproof and the commen-dation extended only to our respective degrees of diligence, the equitable sentence would neither have inflamed the conceit of the one, nor the jealousy of the other; but my former champion, whose business it was to examine our profi-ciency, incautiously turned the spirit of competition into a channel not only unprofitable but mischievous, by making our different success the test of our abilities, not of our industry; and while I cast a triumphant glance upon my fair competitor, I saw her eyes fill with tears not quite 'such as angels shed'.[76]

Thus in the 'baby commonwealth'[77] of school Ellen learns that women should compete with other women. Her rivalry with Lady Maria is aided and abetted by the politicking of Juliet Arnold, a girl whose father has left most of his fortune to his son, the son in turn foisting his sister on to the boarding school. Juliet 'was educated to be married', to be adept in the art of 'manoeuvring' herself – she knows 'what to withdraw from the view, and what to prepare for exhibition';[78] she can, in fact, perform femininity.

Unlike Laura, Ellen is taught many accomplishments – French and Italian, without any taste for the literature in those languages; landscape painting, without any acquaintance with nature; fan painting and making card purses – accom-plishments that qualify her for nothing useful, except perhaps helping her in her later, brief toy-making career. Religion is confined to repeating a page of the Catechism by rote every Sunday.[79] One is reminded of Elizabeth Hamilton's indictment of female boarding-school education, where the pupils receive a super-ficial training in accomplishments, a training inferior to that of performing dogs or monkeys.

Ellen's late mother, on the other hand, is shown to have possessed an ethic of industry and useful benevolence. An old woman, Mrs Wells, proves to have been the recipient of Mrs Percy's charity, which takes the form of her teaching others useful skills such as making gowns and sewing, enabling the woman's daughters to 'earn their bread'.[80] But when Mrs Wells requests Ellen to employ her daughter as a dress-maker, and asks if the heiress could direct her in dress-making, Ellen confesses that she 'can no more direct Sally in making a gown, than in making a steam-engine'.[81] That Brunton's heroine does not have any idea of how the things she wears are made is an admission of her moral failure – Brunton's ethic of female vocation is highly functional.

All along, Ellen has two well-wishers and monitor-figures, Miss Mortimer and Maitland, who try to inculcate this ethic in her, but not till Mr Percy's death and financial ruin does Ellen respond. Part of the problem, as Miss Mortimer shrewdly diagnoses, lies in Ellen's powerful affections, her need to love and be loved, which lead her to attach herself to Juliet Arnold despite misgivings.[82] While formal education teaches useless, superficial accomplishments, Miss Mortimer attempts the education of Ellen's heart. In Maitland, Ellen's future husband, Miss Mortimer finds an ally. Like Knightley in *Emma* (1816), Maitland is a blunt, down-to-earth mentor–hero. The larger part of Ellen's experiential educa-tion, unlike Emma's however, occurs in Maitland's absence, so that Ellen emerges as by far a more independent heroine.

After her father's death and ruin, shorn of riches and prestige, for a short period Ellen is under Miss Mortimer's tutelage. She learns to enjoy reading theological works because her friend wishes her to gain a thorough and 'unfemi-nine' grounding in points of doctrine.

> [T]to what purpose should I perplex myself with these books, when you own that some of the best Christians you have ever known were persons who had never thought of reasoning upon the evidences of their faith' – 'Because, my dear,' answered Miss Mortimer, 'the exercise of your highest natural faculties upon your religion is calculated to fix it in your mind, and endear it to your affections.' . . . Through Miss Mortimer's persuasion, I steadily persevered in this line of study; and, if my understanding possesses any degree of soundness or vigour, it is to be attributed to this discipline. My education, if the word signify learning what is afterwards to be useful, was now properly beginning; and every day added something to my very slender stock of information.[83]

When Miss Mortimer's 'education for eternity'[84] culminates in her death, an example of holy dying, Ellen learns also to confront death. She is now left homeless and friendless, and the only respectable profession open to her (as to Mrs Strictland in Reeve's *The School for Widows*) is teaching.

> My own labour . . . was now become my only means of obtaining shelter or subsistence; and, foreign as the effort was to all my habits, the struggle must be made. But how was I to direct my attempts? What channel had the customs of society left open to the industry of woman? The only one which seemed within

my reach was the tuition of youth; and I felt myself less dependent when I recollected my thorough knowledge of music, and my acquaintance with other arts of idleness. When, indeed, I considered how small a part of the education of a rational and accountable being I was after all fitted to undertake, I shrunk from the awful responsibility of the charge.[85]

The tensions in the concept of education in *Discipline* are very evident in this passage. At a mundane level, Ellen needs to earn her own living and discovers, like so many other contemporary or near-contemporary writers (one thinks in particular of the host of 1790s writers we have already encountered who are eloquent on this issue, from Clara Reeve to Mary Hays and Mary Anne Radcliffe), that there is scarcely one channel 'open to the industry of woman'. Also evident is Brunton's dissatisfaction with the formal education Ellen has received, which has taught her only 'arts of idleness' instead of her mother's talent for useful work. The bleak picture Brunton gives of governessing, culminating in Ellen's incarceration in a mad-house by her vindictive female employer, reminds us of the boarding-school scenes, with yet another woman represented as manipulative and competitive towards other women. A higher ideal is represented by Ellen's desire to be fit to undertake the education of a 'rational and accountable being' – but fashionable society is shown not to want such educators.

When Ellen goes to Scotland to find that only her prospective employer's son is in residence at their house, she is certainly not seen in the light of an educator. The young law student is immediately smitten by Ellen. She overhears a conversation between the young man and a friend in which she becomes an object – 'an angel, the loveliest girl', 'her manners . . . as correct as her person is beautiful!'[86] Ellen, like Laura when she goes to sell her paintings, becomes an object of male gaze and desire. And when Ellen does succeed in finding a job in a 'respectable' family, she reaches in fact the nadir of her misfortunes (and perhaps a nadir in eighteenth-century depictions of the trials of governesses) when she is imprisoned in a mad-house. Once she is 'free' Ellen is penniless and near-destitute, her toy-making venture rendered difficult by her having to support the now sick, erstwhile sycophant–friend and betrayer, Juliet Arnold, as well as by her lack of business adroitness.

Ellen's trials as a working woman remind one of her sister–heroine Juliet Granville or 'Miss Ellis', who also appeared in 1814, in the pages of Frances Burney's *The Wanderer*: Juliet faces an even greater number of traumatic experiences in her attempts to earn a living, whether as a companion or 'toad-eater', as a seamstress or as a milliner. Laura, Ellen and Juliet, all have to come to terms with the unpleasant truth that working women are seldom valued for their work, and that they function as spectacles for the male gaze in the work place – as a milliner, for example, Juliet, rather more than the products she sells, is on display. In *Mansfield Park*, yet another novel published in 1814, Jane Austen, always more cynical about the doomed attempts of heroines to earn a living, nevertheless also manages to represent the thanklessness of being a female companion and general dogsbody – in Fanny Price's trials with her two aunts.

While Juliet, Ellen and Fanny are all absorbed into conjugal life, Ellen's case is somewhat special, given Brunton's emphasis on Glen Eredine in the Highlands, the home of the Grahams, as a near-utopian place. Right from Ellen's first encounter with Cecil Graham, whose winding sheet Ellen redeems for her, the latter is attracted to the simplicity, austerity and dignity of the Highlanders. In Charlotte Graham, presiding spirit in the Graham clan, Ellen finds a true friend and, eventually, a sister-in-law. At the end of the novel Charlotte is still unmarried: 'Some misses lately arrived from a boarding school, have begun to call my sister an old maid; yet I do not perceive that this cabalistic term has produced any ill effect on Charlotte's temper.'[87]

This is the antithesis of Juliet Arnold, the boarding-school girl whose brother refuses to make provision for her and who is educated to be married. Charlotte lives unmarried with dignity and usefulness in her own home.

While Ellen's Highland home gives her a deep sense of community, the heroine of Brunton's last, unfinished piece of fiction, *Emmeline*, becomes isolated from every form of social intercourse as a result of her divorcing her husband and remarrying. Emmeline is as attractive and sensitive a heroine as Ellen – but unlike, for example, Amelia Opie's creation Adeline, based on Mary Wollstonecraft, in *Adeline Mowbray* (1804) (another moral tale in which the author disapproves of her heroine's sexual choices), there is nothing positive that Emmeline learns from her trials, nor are there any positive female figures such as Adeline's black servant Savannah who become the heroine's allies. *Emmeline* is a stark tale which describes the heroine's gradual psychological disintegration, rather than development.

To Make a Ride Down the Niagara 'Natural, Possible and Everyday': Brunton's 'Unreal' Adventurousness

Let us go back to where we started, to Mary Brunton's slow but determined progress as an author. She, who had started to write fiction hesitantly and had doubts about the status of the novel, could, in a letter dated 15 August 1814, write this eulogy of the novel:

> Why should an epic or tragedy be supposed to hold such an exalted place in composition, while a novel is almost a nickname for a book? Does not a novel admit of as noble sentiments – as lively description – as natural character – as perfect unity of action – and a moral as irresistible as either of them? . . . I think a fiction containing a just representation of human beings and of their actions – a connected, interesting, and probable story, conducting to a useful and impressive moral lesson – might be one of the greatest efforts of human genius. Let the admirable construction of fable in Tom Jones be employed to unfold characters like Miss Edgeworth's – let it lead to a moral like Richardson's – let it be told with the eloquence of Rousseau, and with the simplicity of Goldsmith – let it be all this, and Milton need not have been ashamed of the work![88]

This is a sophisticated view of the novel, with plot, characterization, moral and rhetoric functioning harmoniously to produce a modern epic informed by a Johnsonian realism, with humanity at its centre. Brunton chooses a woman writer, Maria Edgeworth, to epitomize skill in characterization, and is manifestly proud of her vocation of novel-writing, no longer seeing the female writer's predicament as worse than a rope-dancer's.

This description of the novel occurs towards the end of Brunton's development as a writer and a woman of letters, a process her husband attempts to represent in his memoir. Brunton, we have seen, is in his work constructed in terms of many contemporary stock topoi about female education, from the unsatisfactorily domestic mother to the blossoming of the wife's mind under a husband's companionship and tutelage. Through Brunton's letters, we have traced the journey she made in her vocation as an author, slowly overcoming her anxieties about putting herself on display in the literary sphere. These personal writings describe an experiential education going beyond a formal one, almost as fascinating as those Brunton describes in her two female-centred, Christian *Bildungsromans*.

One may regret that Brunton did not depict in her fiction the education of a female author, but many of the female difficulties Laura or Ellen undergo, one is inclined to believe, would have been faced by our hypothetical scribbling heroine. Caroline Gonda has pointed out that the retiring, conservative Brunton, who compares female authorship to rope-dancing, also, paradoxically, achieves positive portrayals of women entering the 'public world of work'.[89] I have suggested that Brunton gradually moves towards a more positive view of women writing and publishing fiction. Nevertheless, I think Gonda is right in saying that Brunton did not primarily think of herself as a professional novelist – indeed, Brunton thought that not writing for money gave her a degree of moral independence. She wrote to her brother, 'I do not need to write for bread; and I would not write one volume, merely to gain the fame of Homer. A moral is therefore necessary to me.'[90] Yet, as Gonda further points out, in contrast to Brunton and her positive portrayals of women's work, Jane Austen, who freely admitted to earning money through her writing, disparaged any notion of women's paid work throughout her oeuvre.[91]

Not the retiring conservative she appears to be, Brunton is also not an aridly didactic writer who advocates repressive self-discipline. Through my narrative and argument in this chapter I have shown that, though the titles of *Self-Control* and *Discipline* appear to signal narratives of female education in which the female subject represses her subjectivity through control and discipline, in fact the pattern that Brunton gives us is far more complex, generating a dialectic between self-assertion and self-abnegation, with self-abnegation paradoxically generating self-assertion.

Structuring the development of Brunton's heroines is her Protestantism. The inadequate early education that Ellen receives from authority-figures creates a 'fortunate Fall' pattern, in which, as in Reeve's *The School for Widows*, the heroines journey through the school of adversity. The fervent inwardness of Brunton's heroines, again, owes much to her Christianity, as do her invocation of Cowper at the beginning of *Self-Control*, her repeatedly expressed Christian didactic purpose, and her obtruding of religion and moralizing into her fiction. Brunton also shows scepticism about primarily secular theories of education in which environment is seen to shape the developing subject's character. To a writer like Austen, Brunton seemed patently to lack verisimilitude and naturalness.[92] Brunton's work, then, cannot be accommodated into a model of the well-formed, realistic, secular novel privileging inwardness and organic evolution.

Brunton, as we have seen, takes a positive view of women's paid work in her fictions. But the tribulations that Brunton's heroines face as working women remain experiences they undergo *en route* to marriage. Laura's wish to become, and remain, 'independent of all but my own exertions' proves to be an unsustainable economic dream. That daughters of the house may choose to remain unmarried rather than display themselves on the marriage market is a possibility in yet another novel published in 1814, Maria Edgeworth's *Patronage*. Edgeworth does not give her heroines, also called Percy, the state that she chose in her own life – both Caroline and Rosamond are happily married off. Nevertheless, in *Patronage*, as in *Self-Control*, *Discipline* and *Mansfield Park*, the husbands of the heroines choose a life where private happiness is valued over public ambition, and where the women are valued for their intelligence, ethics and cultivation.

Instead of drawing attention, through the discourse of education, to the systematic exclusion of women from the public sphere, as Mary Hamilton did, or laying claim to the public sphere, as Mary Wollstonecraft or Mary Hays or Clara Reeve did, it is now a question, for Brunton, Austen and Edgeworth, of women presiding over a private sphere that is crucial to the happiness of men as well. This represents a diminution of possibilities and a shrinking world for women, although one can see why this happens – given the bleak anatomies that Burney or Brunton give of women trying to survive on their own and to earn their living, 'female difficulties' seem best resolved by a renewed commitment to domesticity. But as we also know, plot resolutions are hardly the crux of fiction, and the extended attention given by Brunton or Burney to the sympathetic portrayal of working women is what stands out.

Brunton's work, like that of the other writers I analyse, remains a site primarily of tensions rather than neat resolutions – tensions between self-assertion and self-abnegation, between wandering and finding a home, between the inner and the outer, between religious intent and secular plot, between naturalism of style and non-naturalism, between marriage and spaces outside marriage. Slipping between mad-house and drawing-room, between studying mathematics and theology, between earning money and presiding over the home, between achieving the end of marriage and yet not seeing marriage as the only end to women's existence: the ambulatory and ambitious nature and texture of such narratives embody the fact that they are not disciplinary narratives about pliable female pupils. As Austen acknowledged disapprovingly in her ironizing of Brunton's non-naturalism, rushing down the Niagara Falls in a canoe is an eminently work-aday enterprise for Brunton's heroines, one more stage in their attempts at self-direction amidst the risky business of life.

Notes and References

1 Alexander Brunton, 'Memoir of Mary Brunton', in Mary Brunton, *Emmeline, with Some Other Pieces, to Which Is Prefixed A Memoir of Her Life, Including Some Extracts from Her Correspondence*, with a new introduction by Caroline Franklin (Edinburgh: Manners and Miller, 1819; rpt, London: Routledge/Thoemmes Press, 1992).

2 Brunton, *Emmeline*, p. v.

3 Ibid., p. vi.

4 Ibid., p. vii.

5 Ibid., p. viii.

6 Ibid., p. ix.

7 Ibid., p. ix.

8 Ibid., p. xv.

9 Ibid., pp. ix–x.

10 Ibid., p. x.

11 Ibid., p. x.

12 Ibid., p. xi.

13 Ibid., p. xiii.

14 Ibid., p. xv.

15 Ibid., p. xvi.

16 Ibid., pp. xvi–xvii.

17 Ibid., p. xvii.

18 Ibid., p. xix.

19 Ibid., p. xxxvi.

20 'I am clear for furnishing women with such accomplishments as are absolutely incapable of being converted into matter of exhibition.' Letter to Mrs Balfour, 17 January 1818. Ibid., p. xcvi.

21 Cf. Maria Edgeworth, 'Letter from a Gentleman to His Friend Upon the Birth of a Daughter', where the letter-writer speaks of the danger of educating his friend's daughter to be a 'literary lady': 'You make her incapable of friendship with her own sex. Where is she to look for friends, for companions, for equals? Amongst men? Amongst what class of men?' In Maria Edgeworth, *Letters for Literary Ladies*, edited by Claire Connolly ([1795] London: J.M. Dent, 1994), p. 10.

22 Brunton, *Emmeline*, pp. xli–xlii.

23 Ibid., p. xxxviii.

24 Ibid., p. xxxxix.

25 Ibid., p. xlv.

26 Ibid., p. xlv.

27 Ibid., p. xlv.

28 Ibid., p. xlvii.

29 Ibid., pp. xxxi–xxxii.

30 *The Poems of William Cowper*, edited by John D. Baird and Charles Ryskamp, 3 vols (Oxford: Clarendon Press, 1995), Vol. II, pp. 260–61.

31 Brunton, *Emmeline*, p. lxxx.

32 Mary Brunton, *Self-Control: A Novel* (Edinburgh: Manners and Miller; London: Longman, Hurst, Rees, Orme and Brown, 1811). For the sake of convenience, I quote from the only available modern edition: Mary Brunton, *Self-Control*, introduced by Sara Maitland (London: Pandora, 1986), here, p. v.

33 Joanna Baillie, *A Series of Plays: In Which It Is Attempted to Delineate the Stronger Passions of the Mind*, with a new introduction by Caroline Franklin (London: Cadell and Davies 1798; rpt, London: Routledge/Thoemmes Press, 1996), pp. 2–3.

34 Brunton, *Emmeline*, p. xlix.

[35] Brunton, *Self-Control*, p. vi.
[36] Ibid., p. 3.
[37] Ibid., p. 3.
[38] Ibid., p. 4.
[39] Ibid., p. 5.
[40] Ibid., p. 176.
[41] For a positive view of Brunton's Calvinism in relation to her heroines, see Sarah W.R. Smith, 'Men, Women, and Money: The Case of Mary Brunton', in *Fetter'd or Free? British Women Novelists, 1670–1815*, edited by Mary Anne Schofield and Cecilia Macheski (Athens, Ohio: Ohio University Press, 1987), pp. 40–58.
[42] Brunton, *Self-Control*, p. 114.
[43] Ibid., p. 23.
[44] Ibid., pp. 34–35.
[45] Ibid., pp. 48–49.
[46] Ibid., pp. 53–54.
[47] Ibid., p. 64.
[48] On *Thaddeus of Warsaw* (1803), see, for example, Ann Jones, *Ideas and Innovations: Best Sellers of Jane Austen's Age* (New York: AMS Press, 1986), pp. 117–20.
[49] Brunton, *Self-Control*, pp. 65–66.
[50] Ibid., pp. 41–42.
[51] Ibid., p. 87.
[52] Ibid. p. 235.
[53] Laura's brief foray into painting has been analysed by Katrin R. Burlin, '"At the Crossroads": Sister Authors and the Sister Arts', in *Fetter'd or Free?*, pp. 60–84; Sarah W.R. Smith, 'Men, Women, and Money: The Case of Mary Brunton', in *Fetter'd or Free?*, pp. 44–45.
[54] Brunton, *Self-Control*, p. 29.
[55] Ibid., p. 63.
[56] Ibid., p. 67.
[57] Ibid., p. 71.
[58] Ibid., p. 102.
[59] Ibid., p. 77.
[60] Burlin, '"At the Cross-Roads"', in *Fetter'd or Free?*, pp. 65–68.
[61] Ibid., p. 66.
[62] Brunton, *Self-Control*, p. 205.
[63] Ibid., p. 255.
[64] Brunton, *Emmeline*, p. xxxii.
[65] Ibid., p. lxix.
[66] Ibid., p. lxx.
[67] Ibid., p. lxvii.
[68] Ibid., p. lxxviii.
[69] Mary Brunton, *Discipline* (Edinburgh: Manners and Miller, 1814). All quotations in this chapter come from the modern edition, Mary Brunton, *Discipline*, introduced by Fay Weldon (London: Pandora, 1986), here, p. 3.
[70] Ibid., p. 3.
[71] Ibid., p. 5.
[72] Ibid., p. 4.
[73] Ibid., p. 4.
[74] Ibid., p. 6.
[75] Ibid., p. 9.
[76] Ibid., p. 13.
[77] Ibid., p. 12.
[78] Ibid., p. 16.
[79] Ibid., p. 17.
[80] Ibid., p. 26.
[81] Ibid., p. 59.
[82] Ibid., p. 110.

[83] Ibid., p. 190.

[84] Ibid., p. 208.

[85] Ibid., p. 211.

[86] Ibid., p. 229.

[87] Ibid., p. 375.

[88] Brunton, *Emmeline*, p. lxxiv.

[89] Caroline Gonda, *Reading Daughters' Fictions 1709–1834: Novels and Society from Manley to Edgeworth* (Cambridge: Cambridge University Press, 1996), p. 202.

[90] Brunton, letter dated 27 October 1815, in *Emmeline*, p. lxxxiii.

[91] Gonda, *Reading Daughters' Fictions*, p. 196.

[92] 'I am looking over *Self-Control* again, and my opinion is confirmed of its' being an excellently-meant, elegantly-written Work, without anything of Nature or Probability in it. I do not know whether Laura's passage down the American river is not the most natural, possible, every-day thing she ever does.' Letter to Cassandra Austen, 11–12 October 1813? in *Jane Austen's Letters*, edited by Deirdre Le Faye (Oxford: Oxford University Press, 1997), p. 234.

CHAPTER FIVE

'To *torment* and to *instruct* might sometimes be used as synonymous words': Jane Austen's Early Writing

At any rate, however, I am pleased that you have learned to love a hyacinth. The mere habit of learning to love is the thing; and a teachableness of disposition in a young lady is a great blessing. – Has my sister a pleasant mode of instruction?[1]

This is Henry Tilney's voice in *Northanger Abbey*, using the serio-comic register that is characteristic of him. The near-absurdity of 'learning to love a hyacinth' (which Catherine says she has learnt to do from Eleanor, despite being 'naturally indifferent' about flowers) points to the many ways in which what appears to be natural, particularly in women, can so often be a product of acculturation and education, of gendering, we might say. Whether the mode of instruction is pleasant or not, it is entirely desirable that a young lady *should* make a 'habit' of being pliably teachable.

In this chapter, I examine some of the ways in which Jane Austen explores the limits of teachableness of female disposition in her early writing. Austen is the latest of the five British novelists of education whose works I analyse, even though I have chosen to focus on some of her earliest works, written between 1787 and 1799, for reasons I discuss later. Botanizing, repulsing rakes, selling paintings, planning female seminaries, escaping unhappy marriages and training women for paid work – the earlier chapters have shown the sheer range of activities and ideas that conservative women writers discuss in their fictions of female education.

Such works, I have also shown, evoke all sorts of tensions engendered by the process of female education – tensions, for example, between formal and experiential education, between teachers or teacher-like authority-figures and the pupil's own autonomy, between overt didacticism or prescriptions and more psychologized accounts of development, between differing conceptions of the goal of female education (marriage, paid work, or something beyond?). Stylistically, these works, in delineating female education, encompass diverse modes of writing, such as romance (Mary Hamilton), advice literature (Mary Hamilton, Elizabeth Hamilton, Clara Reeve), spiritual autobiography (Mary Brunton) and political polemics (Clara Reeve, Mary Hamilton).

As I have argued in my introduction, the educative and epistemological authority of fiction is discussed, negotiated and redefined in all of these female-centred fictions of education. While all the writers I examine try to come to grips with the difficult relationship between women, education and fiction (with Clara Reeve achieving a particularly remarkable vindication both of female education and of the educative power of fiction in *The Progress of Romance*), none offers a vindication both of novels and of female-centred novels of education as confident as their successor, Jane Austen. But the price for this was high, I argue.

I have chosen to focus on writings from Austen's juvenilia – 'Lady Susan' (written *c*. 1795), 'Catharine, or the Bower' (begun *c*. 1792) and *Northanger Abbey* (written *c*. 1797–99, published posthumously in 1818) – not least because they were begun in the 1790s,[2] when writers such as Reeve and Elizabeth Hamilton were penning their conservative feminist fictions of education. Austen's early works, with the exception of *Northanger Abbey* (which was sold in 1803 to a publisher, but remained unpublished till after her death), remained outside print, and were written for an audience of family and friends – even though, as Jan Fergus has argued, Austen's manuscripts were very like handwritten books, following many of the conventions of printed books.[3]

Austen's early fiction was in many ways unruly and parodic, as has been discussed by Sandra Gilbert, Susan Gubar and Margaret Anne Doody. Austen debunked what she saw as the exaggerations of epistolary fiction ('Love and Freindship [*sic*]'), advice literature ('A Collection of Letters'), or the female Gothic (*Northanger Abbey*). She also parodied (in 'Catharine, or the Bower') the public-minded, intellectual conservative women of the 1790s. Austen's juvenilia allow us to see the process by which Austen both placed herself in an existing tradition of fictions of female education and jettisoned major elements in such works.

Whereas Marilyn Butler saw Austen as a conservative in the post-1790s 'war of ideas' between liberal and conservative women writers, a more recent critic like Claudia Johnson has seen Austen as a depolemicizing, though not depoliticized, writer broadly aligned with post-French Revolution liberalism.[4] This chapter will show that Austen was indeed engaging in a highly revisionist novelistic enterprise – but that enterprise, already sophisticated in the 1790s, was one which involved eschewing the ambition and breadth of earlier fictions of female education, or even contemporary ones, by novelists passionate about female education such as Mary Hamilton, Clara Reeve, Mary Brunton and Elizabeth Hamilton.

The texture of Austen's early works, moving as they do between the foregrounded non-realism of parody and a naturalizing realistic impulse,[5] allows for a sceptical presentation of female education, in which education is seen as both produced by often misguided social and cultural norms and processes (Austen is here far more openly critical of the oppressive, restrictive elements in female development than she is in her later work), *and* as something which is internalized and made an active part of their selves by the heroines. The major achievement of Austen's early fiction is its anatomy and critique of female education as a process by which young women are controlled, monitored and surveyed.

Educative Mothers and Pliable Daughters, or Maternal Control and Surveillance: 'Lady Susan' and 'Letter the First'

Lady Susan writes of her daughter Frederica,

> She is a stupid girl, and has nothing to recommend her. . . . the grand affair of Education . . . I really wish to be attended to, while she remains with Miss Summers. I want her to play and sing with some portion of Taste . . . I was never obliged to attend to anything, and am consequently without those accomplishments which are now necessary to furnish a pretty Woman. Not that I am an advocate for the prevailing fashion of acquiring a perfect knowledge in all the Languages Arts and Sciences . . . to be mistress of French, Italian, German, Music, Singing, Drawing, &c. will gain a Woman some applause, but will not add one Lover to the list. Grace and Manner after all are of the greatest importance.[6]

Lady Susan, who can on occasion play the role of the mother beset with anxiety about her daughter's education and prospects, shows in this passage a genuine desire that her 'stupid' daughter should learn 'grace', 'manner' and accomplishments. In her acknowledgment of the 'fashion' of teaching women 'all the Languages Arts and Sciences', Lady Susan recognizes that female education has become a fashionable 'grand affair': education is vital to the commodification of women on the marriage market.

Lady Susan is an engaging villainess, but her anxiety about her daughter's education, her ability to enumerate elements in a potential curriculum of female education and her decision to make choices from among them – all these are very much features of writings on femininity in Austen's time, as even a cursory look at, say, a popular work such as Hannah More's *Coelebs in Search of a Wife* (1808) makes clear. This is also an anxiety about *controlling* female education. In *Coelebs*, the ideal father Mr Stanley regulates his daughters' education with a judicious admixture of love and authority; in Lady Susan, the two elements are disjoined. While she writes to her friend Mrs Johnson as the tyrannical mother who will brook no disobedience, to the Vernons Lady Susan performs the role of loving, anxious and cultivated mother.

That Lady Susan can perform the role of the rational, intelligent, well-educated woman and mother with skill is evident in her dealings with Reginald de Courcy. Reginald, in his phase of high-flown respect and love for Lady Susan, describes her maternal persona as follows: 'As a Mother she is unexceptionable. Her solid affection for her Child is shewn by placing her in hands, where her Education will be properly attended to; but because she has not the blind and weak partiality of most Mothers, she is accused of wanting Maternal Tenderness.'[7]

Lady Susan is not, as in some of Austen's own works such as 'Love and Freindship [*sic*]', or as in Maria Edgeworth's 'Leonora' (1806), a villainess of sensibility. 'Solid affection', 'not the blind and weak partiality of most mothers':

Reginald's construction of Lady Susan has similarities to the ideal rational mother envisaged in Wollstonecraft's *A Vindication of the Rights of Woman*. To his father, Reginald says that he enjoys in Lady Susan's company 'the conversation of a Woman of high mental powers';[8] he praises her 'excellent understanding' and her exemplary 'prudence and economy'. At the same time, de Courcy realizes and even relishes the idea that Lady Susan has some faults: like Edmund Bertram vis-à-vis Miss Crawford in *Mansfield Park*, de Courcy imputes Lady Susan's 'errors' to 'her neglected education'.[9] Edmund and Reginald both wish to reform and re-educate the fascinating, intelligent, wayward women they fall in love with.

Frederica soon poses a problem for Lady Susan, however, becoming a bone of contention between her and her sister-in-law, Mrs Vernon. Frederica engages Mrs Vernon's pity by her shyness and her 'silent dejection'.[10] The aunt finds her niece 'totally without accomplishment', yet 'by no means . . . ignorant'; fond of books, she also has an excellent disposition, and good natural abilities.[11] Mrs Vernon, then, is constructing Frederica as an antithesis to Lady Susan – the former is artless, shy, with a good disposition, unaccomplished and fond of reading, while her mother is morally corrupt and superficially accomplished. Lady Susan herself accepts this contrast, and thinks that Mrs Vernon favours Frederica because she is so unlike her mother,[12] and also because 'Mrs Vernon dearly loves to be first, and to have all the sense and all the wit of the Conversation to herself; Frederica will never eclipse her.'[13]

We do not get to hear Frederica's own voice, aptly enough, given that she is cast in the role of near-victim. Yet, she can also be surprisingly active: she runs away from school, rather than accept Sir James Martin's continuing attentions. Prevented from confiding in her aunt and uncle about the proposed match between herself and Sir James Martin, she decides instead to confide in Reginald. So repulsive does she find her suitor that she says she 'would rather work for my bread than marry him'.[14]

That is a measure of her desperation. In 'The Watsons', Emma and Elizabeth Watson, discussing the relentlessly calculating pursuit of marriage by another sister, try to decide which is worse – poverty or having to teach. Emma says,

> To be so bent on marriage – to pursue a Man merely for the sake of situation – is a sort of thing that shocks me; I cannot understand it. Poverty is a great Evil, but to a woman of Education and feeling it ought not, it cannot be the greatest – I would rather be a Teacher at a school (and I can think of nothing worse) than marry a man I did not like.[15]

'Education and feeling', then, enable women to resist the idea of marrying merely to avoid poverty. Elizabeth, however, finds teaching an unacceptable occupation. '"I would rather do any thing than be Teacher at a school" – said her sister. "*I* have been at school, Emma, and know what a life they lead; *you* never have."'[16] Emma is by far the more intelligent and 'refined' (as Elizabeth describes her) of the two sisters, but the reader feels that the good-natured Elizabeth, with greater experience, might have a point here (Austen's own unhappiness at boarding school must lurk behind a passage such as this). In another Austen novel, another Emma discovers that the beautiful, intelligent and accomplished Jane Fairfax loathes her prospective trade of governessing.

> When I am quite determined as to the time, I am not at all afraid of being long unemployed. There are places in town . . . offices for the sale – not quite of human flesh – but of human intellect. . . .
>
> I was not thinking of the slave-trade . . . governess-trade, I assure you, was all that I had in view; widely different certainly as to the guilt of those who carry it on; but as to the greater misery of the victims, I do not know where it lies.[17]

For Austen, then, the occupation of governessing, 'the sale of human intellect', is analogous to slavery, 'the sale of human flesh'. Such a view is similar, but also very dissimilar to Reeve's view in *The School for Widows*. Reeve too graphically describes the indignities that Mrs Strictland undergoes as a governess. On the other hand, for Reeve the female educator is an exemplary and exalted figure, and once Mrs Strictland sets up her own school, she finds fulfilment in teaching. For an Emma Watson, an Elizabeth or a Frederica, earning one's bread by teaching is the direst of prospects.

To return to 'Lady Susan', Frederica's entreating letter to Reginald precipitates an open conflict about her temperament and her education between the two mother-figures, Mrs Vernon and Lady Susan. The mother argues that Frederica is a stupid, unreceptive, stubborn pupil and daughter:

> Sir James is certainly under par . . . and had Frederica possessed the penetration, the abilities, which I could have wished in my daughter, or had I even known her to possess so much as she does, I should not have been anxious for the match. . . . Frederica never does justice to herself; her manners are shy and childish. She is besides afraid of me; she scarcely loves me. During her poor Father's life she was a spoilt child; the severity which it has since been necessary for me to shew, has entirely alienated her affection; neither has she any of that Brilliancy of Intellect, that Genius, or Vigour of Mind which will force itself forward.[18]

The assumptions made here about Frederica's natural abilities, her education and her capacity to love, construct her as a shy, wilful, unintelligent, unloving child and pupil. An entire complex of expectations about young women is evident. Ideally, a young lady should have vigour of mind and brilliancy of intellect, be mature and easy in company, and be a loving daughter *as well*. It is typical of Lady Susan that she should also expect genius, penetration and an ability to push herself forward: she is in many ways a performing heroine, in contrast to Mrs Vernon, who prides herself on her domesticity.

Mrs Vernon is not presented without irony, either. She sees her home though rose-coloured glasses as an idyllic space, with 'regular employments . . . Books and conversation, with Exercise, the Children, and every domestic pleasure'.[19] In many ways she is as vain about her domestic idyll as Lady Susan is about her talents as coquette. Mrs Vernon is alternately bewildered and exasperated by her sister-in-law, and more or less openly competes with her. Even though she is kind to Frederica, her niece is a pawn in the battle between the two female authority-figures in her life. Frederica's position as female pupil is thus always firmly subordinate to the conflicting whims and wishes of her mother and aunt.

In Austen's sardonic hands, Reginald is ironized even more conspicuously than his sister, coming across as a young man at once gullible, indecisive and pompous. There are significant similarities between the Frederica–Reginald relationship in 'Lady Susan' and the Fanny–Edmund relationship in *Mansfield Park*: Austen's sympathy and ascription of agency to the apparently passive young woman is present from very early in her writing, as is the resigned anatomizing of the well-intentioned, priggish mentor–hero.

After Lady Susan remarries and packs Frederica off to live semi-permanently with her aunt and uncle, Frederica is kept waiting for the somewhat depressing telos of her life, marriage with Reginald. Thus,

> Frederica was therefore fixed in the family of her Uncle and Aunt, until such time as Reginald de Courcy could be talked, flattered, and finessed into an affection for her – which, allowing leisure for the conquest of his attachment to her Mother, for his abjuring all attachments and detesting the Sex, might be reasonably looked for in the course of a Twelvemonth.[20]

This is black comedy indeed: the woman who has (as Henry Tilney in *Northanger Abbey* observes) only the prerogative of refusal in marriage waits for the man of her dreams, who has to be manipulated ('talked, flattered, and finessed') into loving her. One is confronted in 'Lady Susan' by the question: if finding a husband is all that female education is about, why not be less demanding of the female pupils concerned? In 'Lady Susan' Austen's energies are deliberately destructive. She explodes the myth of the closely bonded mother and daughter, in which the mother is an anxious, loving agent in the daughter's education, and the daughter a pliable, obedient pupil. Even the best-intentioned of maternal guardian figures, Austen shows us through Mrs Vernon, is an anodyne figure, a pattern which recurs throughout Austen's oeuvre.

Austen's loathing of the anxious maternal educator, even when she is not obviously cruel and tyrannical like Lady Susan, is as evident in another of Austen's juvenile efforts, this time 'Letter the First: From a Mother to Her Freind [*sic*]' in 'A Collection of Letters' (written *c.* 1792). We hear the voice of a mother who is looking forward with exaggerated dread and hope to her two daughters' 'coming out', their 'entrance into the world'. Many commonplaces of eighteenth-century conduct literature for mothers and daughters appear in the letter. First is the mother's awareness that her relationship with her children will change because they are now adult, and about to enter the public, social world (an idea found, for example, in Madame de Genlis's *Adelaide and Theodore*, 1782).

> My children begin now to claim all my attention in a different Manner from that in which they have been used to receive it, as they are now arrived at that age when it is necessary for them in some measure to become conversant with the World. My Augusta is 17 and her Sister scarcely a twelve month younger.[21]

The 'entrance into the world' is seen as a perilous stage in women's lives, on the threshold of adulthood, when young girls will have to socialize in the public world and negotiate a transition from one form of authority, the parental, to another, that of the husband. The 'children' will no longer be childlike – they will be young ladies, who may take false steps or step beyond the pale of propriety. Where the dangers are perceived as so large, it is not surprising that grand terms such as 'entrée into Life', 'entrance into the World' and 'entry into Public' are used to describe the coming out.

For A–F–, then, the coming out of her daughters is a solemn event, which requires advice and warnings on her part.

> 'My dear Girls, the moment is now arrived when I am to reap the rewards of all my Anxieties and Labours towards you during your Education. You are this evening to enter a World in which you will meet with many wonderfull Things; Yet let me warn you against suffering yourselves to be meanly swayed by the Follies and Vices of others, for believe me, my beloved Children, that if you do – I shall be very sorry for it.' They both assured me . . . that they were prepared to find a World full of things to amaze and shock them: but that they trusted their behaviour would never give me reason to repent the watchful Care with which I had presided over their Infancy and formed their Minds.[22]

Austen clearly feels that there is far too much ostentation in these assertions of 'watchful care' on the mother's part, too many protestations of 'Anxieties and Labours' in her attempts to 'form' her daughters' minds. This is a parody of the prescriptive tone of Madame de Genlis or Lady Sarah Pennington. Unlike Mary Hamilton and Reeve, writers of an earlier generation, Austen most definitely does not use the prescriptive register to advance her ideas on female education. She finds the mode over-anxious and over-controlling, rather like Mrs Norris in *Mansfield Park*, another authority-figure who fusses about her nieces and who is a signal failure as an educative figure. Austen is in her own way as prescriptive about female education as Hamilton or Reeve – but she presents her prescriptions indirectly through parody, irony and a representation of the inner processes of her heroines' minds.

In 'Letter the First', A–F–, at the end of their visit, is delighted 'in beholding . . . how attentively they [her daughters] observed every object they saw, how disgusted with some Things, how enchanted with others, how astonished at all! On the whole however they returned in raptures with the World, its Inhabitants, its manners.'[23] As Austen shows consummately, there is a bathetic disjunction between such ostentation of advice and reactions, on the one hand, and the mundane social activities that the young girls are inducted into, on the other:

> This very evening is fixed for their first entrée into Life, as we are to drink tea with Mrs Cope and her Daughter. . . . Tomorrow Mr Stanly's family will drink tea with us, and perhaps the Miss Phillips's will meet them. On Tuesday we shall pay Morning-Visits – On Wednesday we are to dine at Westbrook. On Thursday we have company at home. On Friday we are to be at a private concert . . . and on Saturday we expect Miss Dawson to call in the Morning – which will complete my Daughters' Introduction into Life. How they will bear so much dissipation I cannot imagine.[24]

There is poignancy beneath Austen's clear-sightedness about the fact that for the young women, this round of petty visits, mundane and even dull as it is, *is* 'the World', the very limited domain in which they will develop. Austen's ability to see the narrowness of most middle-class Englishwomen's lives goes hand in hand with a desire to represent it in a realist register, without melodrama or overt prescriptions and polemics. If this 'realism' manifests itself obviously at the level of technique, it also has to do with an underlying moral vision and ideology. Thus, Austen will not talk about female difficulties in an elevated Burneyan register; she will not represent what she sees as implausibly melodramatic versions of female seduction, assaults on female virtue or beautiful heroines struggling to earn a living. Instead, she shows in micro-detail the thousand little circumscriptions, irritations, small choices and happinesses that hem in and open out women's education.

Catharine's Bower

Catharine or Kitty Percival, the heroine of Austen's early unfinished novella 'Catharine, or the Bower', for example, lives in a humdrum, restrictive world. Having lost her parents ('as many heroines have . . . before her', Austen slyly informs us), she lives with a severe, old-fashioned aunt in a quiet village. In the course of the novella, Catharine has to encounter and negotiate the different models of female education provided by her aunt and by their fashionable visitors, the Stanleys. Catharine does, in fact, have her own alternative model of education – her sense of autonomy is symbolized in the novel by a bower which she had created herself with the help of two beloved friends, the now-absent Misses Wynne.

Mrs Percival, Kitty's aunt, is a repressive conduct book personified, a dragonish authority-figure who is obsessed with guarding her niece from importunate young men and other threats to propriety: 'a Maiden Aunt, who while she tenderly loved her, watched over her conduct with so scrutinizing a severity, as to make it very doubtful to many people, and to Catharine amongst the rest, whether she loved her or not.'[25]

Here again we find the element of surveillance, of scrutiny, which young women must face from their guardians/teachers. At the same time, we realize that Mrs Percival's severities operate in the very mundane Austenian round of events, where at worst Kitty is not allowed to go to a ball 'because an Officer was to be there', or where she may even have to dance with a partner of her aunt's introduction rather than one of her own choice. And, unlike beleaguered heroines such as Cecilia or Camilla, Kitty has a fund of good spirits and humour, so that she does not allow herself to feel over-oppressed by her aunt's anxious severity.

'Catharine' was written during in the 1790s, and it is arguable that Mrs Percival is very much a stereotype of the politically concernèd conservative woman writer of that decade. Like a Clara Reeve or a Jane West, Mrs Percival is terribly interested in politics, and discusses political issues with Mr Stanley in an 'un-feminine' way. For her, as for Reeve, education, female education particularly is crucial to the destiny and happiness of the nation.

> 'But I plainly see that every thing is going to sixes and sevens and all order will soon be at an end throughout the Kingdom.'
>
> 'Not however, Ma'am, the sooner, I hope, from any conduct of mine,' said Catharine in a tone of great humility, 'for upon my honour I have done nothing this evening that can contribute to overthrow the establishment of the kingdom.'
>
> 'You are mistaken, Child,' replied she; 'the Welfare of every Nation depends upon the virtue of it's [sic] individuals, and any one who offends in so gross a manner against decorum and propriety is certainly hastening it's ruin. You have been giving a bad example to the World.'[26]

Mrs Percival, then, grants women an important role in the welfare of the nation, but is shown to lack any breadth of vision, applying her ideas repressively to petty contexts. This is the parodically over-rigid, over-didactic state to which the conservative writers of the 1790s have been reduced to in Austen's hands. A passage such as this has led Claudia Johnson to, place Austen in the liberal, rather than the conservative camp, among late eighteenth-century and early nineteenth-century women writers on education and politics.[27] But this, I would argue, is a serious misreading of women's fiction of the period. As my chapters on Clara Reeve and Elizabeth Hamilton have argued, the sheer range of ideas and ambitions that such 'conservative' novelists interested in female education write about is absent in Austen's purged model of fiction. Seminaries to train women in paid trades, narratives about women founding schools after escaping unhappy marriages, portraits of women superintending estates – in contrast to earlier such fictions and their subject-matter, Austen's vision is narrowly unambitious.

In Austen's revisionist fiction, the concerns that a figure such as Mrs Percival has about the public sphere translates into a petty over-anxiety and authoritarianism in the private sphere, so that education becomes a form of control exercised unceasingly over the pupil:

And this is the reward for all the cares I have taken in your Education; for all my troubles and Anxieties; and Heaven knows how many they have been! All I wished for, was to breed you up virtuously; I never wanted you to play the harpsichord, or draw better than anyone else; but I had hoped to see you respectable and good; to see you able and willing to give an example of Modesty and Virtue to the Young people here abouts. I bought you Blair's Sermons, and Coelebs in Search of a Wife, I gave you the key to my own Library, and borrowed a great many books of my own Neighbours for you, all to this purpose.[28]

Here is the 'anxious educator' voice again, as in 'Letter the First', a voice that harps on the anxiety and responsibility of educating young women. To make the pupil respectable and good, modest and virtuous, without meretricious accomplishments (although one suspects that the speaker would not mind if Kitty could play the harpsichord, draw better than anyone else, *and* be virtuous and modest!), is the goal. It is important, I think, that even a Mrs Percival thinks it necessary to give Kitty the key to her library – even assuming that most of the books are as proper as the two she mentions (prime means for inducting Kitty into the ideology of feminine respectability, modesty and propriety), this is a recognition that Kitty should, through reading, at least quasi-autonomously internalize norms that she will use in turn to regulate her self. Supervision and surveillance here become indirect, but no less powerful for this indirectness – as in Hannah More's *Coelebs in Search of a Wife*,[29] where the model parents, the Stanleys, allow their daughters the same paradoxical sort of carefully supervised autonomy.

Strikingly, in 'The Bower', Mrs Percival is not a sinister figure, nor a morally corrupt one. Camilla Stanley's little selfishnesses and calculations, her silliness and her love of money and rank, are shown as far more serious than the foibles of Mrs Percival, who at least has a mind, old-fashioned though it may be; her discussions of politics with Mr Stanley[30] receive less censure in Austen's hands than Camilla's confusion of history and politics.

Camilla is an antithesis of Kitty in terms of the education she has received. Where Kitty has lived quietly in a village, Camilla has lived for six months every year in London being trained in accomplishments by masters. Mistress of Italian, drawing and music, Camilla has 'an Understanding unimproved by reading and a Mind totally devoid of either Taste or Judgment'.[31] In passages like this (as in her indictment of the ostensibly well-educated Maria and Julia Bertram in *Mansfield Park*), Austen shows her contempt for superficially educated women. Camilla thus, damningly, 'professed a love of Books without Reading, was Lively without Wit, and generally Good humoured without Merit'.[32]

Austen describes a conversation between Kitty and Camilla which vividly points up Kitty's superior education. Camilla, when asked if she has read Charlotte Smith's novels, replies that she is delighted with them, but seems in fact not to have read them at all. She is as ignorant of geography, as becomes evident when she is utterly vague about the route she will take during a projected trip to the

Lakes.³³ Nor does Camilla have any interest in history, unlike Kitty. When Mrs Percival wishes for a return to Elizabethan manners, Kitty intervenes warmly. Kitty is an ardent reader of history, 'partial and prejudiced' like her creator, who wrote the wonderfully biting and prejudiced 'History of England'. Like Austen in the 'History of England', she detests Elizabeth the First:

> 'Queen Elizabeth', said Mrs Stanley, who never hazarded a remark on History that was not well founded, 'lived to a good old age, and was a very Clever Woman.' 'True, Ma'am,' said Kitty; 'but I do not consider either of those Circumstances as meritorious in herself, and they are far from making me wish her return, for if she were to come again with the same Abilities and the same good Constitution She might do as much Mischeif [*sic*] and last as long as she did before.'³⁴

Being clever, on its own (even when combined with a long life!), is obviously not enough for Kitty's or Austen's approbation, not if great abilities lead to 'Mischeif'. Kitty is quite clear about this, and has no inhibitions about articulating her unconventional views on Queen Elizabeth boldly and argumentatively, in a way that unobtrusive, retiring young women were not supposed to do. Camilla, however, makes a great display of her proper, feminine ignorance about anything pertaining to the public sphere: when Kitty asks her friend her opinion on the matter, the answer is, 'Oh! dear . . . I know nothing of Politics, and cannot bear to hear them mentioned.'³⁵ Kitty is startled and displeased to find that her friend cannot distinguish history from politics. In making this distinction, Kitty conforms to the eighteenth-century gendered plan of education, in which women were allowed to learn history (and thus gain a knowledge of politics in the past) but not contemporary politics.

When Kitty meets Camilla's brother, she discusses history with him to discover whether he is better informed than his sister. Kitty's judgement may be guided by her feelings, but she argues with 'spirit and enthusiasm', whereas Stanley (rather like Henry Crawford in *Mansfield Park*) 'had scarcely a fixed opinion on the Subject. He could therefore always take either side, and always argue with temper'³⁶ – again, a marker of his intellectual and moral deficiency.

Catharine learns much that is negative about the fashionable world from Camilla – knowledge of its lack of intelligence, its petty calculations and tyrannies. Thus she learns that her friend Mary Wynne, now companion to the daughter of a rich relation, is looked upon as a poor relation, the fact that she is entirely dependent on her relations bandied about the place:

> But only think how good it is in her to take care of Miss Wynne, for she is a very distant relation, and so poor that, as Miss Halifax told me, her Mother was obliged to find her in Cloathes. . . . Lady Halifax . . . treats her as if she were her Daughter; She does not go out into Public with her to be sure; but then she is always present when her Ladyship gives her Balls . . . she would

have taken her to Cheltenham last year, if there had been room enough at the Lodgings, and therefore I do not think *she* can have anything to complain of.[37]

Treated like a daughter indeed! Kitty also learns that Cecilia Wynne, forced to voyage to India in order to catch a husband, 'is most nobly married and the happiest Creature in the World'.[38] The story of Cecilia's life is in fact one of humiliation and forced choices: after the death of her parents, when she and her sister find themselves without any means of support, Cecilia sails to Bengal in search of a rich husband – and finds one, rather as Austen's aunt Philadelphia Hancock had been forced to do. (We remember Elizabeth Hamilton's letter to her brother Charles, in which she refuses to go to India to catch a husband.) The letters Cecilia writes to Kitty, all show her unhappiness. Thus, Kitty's reply to Camilla is angry:

> But do you call it lucky, for a Girl of Genius and Feeling to be sent in quest of a husband to Bengal, to be married there to a Man of whose Disposition she has no opportunity of judging till her Judgement is of no use to her, who may be a Tyrant, or a Fool or both for what she knows to the Contrary.[39]

'Genius' and 'feeling' are not here ironized; together with Austen's abhorrence of women being forced to hunt for husbands is an awareness that an intelligent, educated woman must know a prospective husband's disposition well before committing herself. Cecilia, who must marry whoever offers for her, thus in a sense suspends her judgement (we remember Mary Hamilton's insistence in *Letters from the Duchess de Crui* that women must make rigorous use of their minds in choosing a husband). Austen never allows Kitty to forget that Cecilia has gone to India only because she has been 'necessitated to embrace the only possibility that was offered to her, of a Maintenance'.[40] As Kitty says, 'to a Girl of any Delicacy, the voyage in itself, since the object of it is so universally known, is a punishment that needs no other to make it severe'.[41]

Kitty's bower is associated in her mind with her two absent friends, a fact that attracts much hostility from her aunt, who, on more than one occasion, threatens to have it pulled down, ostensibly on the grounds that it is too damp and cold[42] but really because she thinks the place is part of Kitty's 'whim and Nonsense', part of Kitty's domain of female friendship and autonomy.[43] Scarcely more acceptable, however, is Mrs Stanley's shallow and fashionable effusion about female friendship, which turns into a eulogy of correspondence between young female friends (Mrs Percival, of course, disapproves of female correspondence since letters between women produce 'imprudence and Error by the effect of pernicious advice and bad Example'!)[44]

> I must think that Catharine's affection for her Bower is the effect of a Sensibility that does her Credit. I love to see a Freindship [sic] between Young Persons and always consider it as a sure mark of an aimiable [sic] affectionate disposition. I have from Camilla's infancy taught her to think the same, and have taken

great pains to introduce her to young people of her own age who were likely to be worthy of her regard. Nothing forms the taste more than sensible and elegant letters.[45]

Mrs Stanley, then, controls even Camilla's friendships, and we realize elsewhere in the novella that she has taken care to make sure that all her daughter's correspondents are rich and fashionable young girls. Thus, while Mrs Percival and Mrs Stanley use very different sorts of rhetoric about female education, *both* believe in exercising a great deal of control over the development of their daughter or niece. Catharine is thus caught between the selfish vapidity and the over-severe limitedness of the Stanleys' and Mrs Percival's respective views on female education. Deftly and lightly sketched as it is, 'The Bower' shows that even a heroine as good-natured and buoyant as Kitty is hard put to find physical, emotional and conversational spaces within the boundaries of her life – whether in dancing at a ball, or discussing novels or arguing about history, rigid and unintelligent assumptions about female conduct and education are foisted on her.

'You Think Me Foolish to Call Instruction a Torment':[46] Catherine Morland's Education

Catherine Morland's resistance to formal education is one of the major areas which signal that she is, as her creator says, 'unpropitious for heroism'.[47] To Henry and Eleanor Tilney, Catherine is eloquent about the pains of instruction.

> [I]f you had been as much used as myself to hear poor little children first learning their letters and then learning to spell, if you had ever seen how stupid they can be for a whole morning together, and how tired my poor mother is at the end of it, as I am in the habit of seeing almost every day of my life at home, you would allow that to *torment* and to *instruct* might sometimes be used as synonimous [*sic*] words.[48]

Catherine here takes a sceptical look at the earliest processes of formal education – instead of the virtuous, intelligent mother eager to induct her children into literacy, we see a tired, harried mother chivvying her small children into learning their letters; yet another Austenian deconstruction of the idealized maternal educator, with the children in turn reluctant to learn. Original as Catherine's remark is, it also indicates Austen's determination to create a heroine who will *not* be a diligent and eager pupil, whose mind is *not* perfectly formed, and who is *not* full of talents and virtuous accomplishments: Richardson's Clarissa or Brunton's Laura would be good examples of the kind of heroine Austen is determined not to create. Catherine, a plain child, is in childhood a romp, enjoys 'boys'' games such as cricket, does not like dolls, and shows no predilection for nurturing 'feminine' pursuits such as 'nursing a dormouse, feeding a canary-bird, or watering a rose-bush'.[49] She is often inattentive or stupid at lessons, gives up learning music after a while, is not good at drawing, nor at writing, accounts or French. By the time she is fifteen, she is still not a pretty girl and still does not like learning lessons. She prefers books which are all story and no reflection, is an avid novel-reader, and even if she dutifully reads sonnets and snippets of sententious poetry, she is still hardly the stuff of which beautiful, accomplished heroines are made.

Catherine's ability to make such original remarks that go against the grain of contemporary precepts on education, female or male, is integral to her general sturdiness and independence in the novel, as well as to the sceptical look Austen takes in *Northanger Abbey* at stereotypical notions about the education of heroines. Catherine, one must remember, in the passage I have quoted, is talking to Henry Tilney, whom she is in love with – yet she can speak openly and originally to him.

Even if Catherine is no lover of many aspects of formal education, she might seem to have, in a larger sense, an eminently 'teachable disposition'. It is possible to argue that Catherine is good-natured and pliable, that because of these qualities she is taken in by Isabella Thorpe for a time, but that eventually she learns more from Henry Tilney's superior good sense, including his point that life in southern England is not the same as life in an Ann Radcliffe novel. Catherine and Henry thus appear to conform to a mentor–pupil romantic model, where the man supplies the intelligence and knowledge of the world, while the woman comes with a feeling heart, an inferior intelligence and a rather charming naïveté and ignorance. Readers of *Mansfield Park* will remember that Fanny Price's cousins think that she is hopelessly stupid at lessons (she cannot put the map of Europe together, does not know the difference between water-colours and crayons, cannot recite the kings and queens of England, and so on and so forth), and that this 'deficiency' is in fact a marker of Fanny's more important ability to acquire a deeper education that teaches her to acquire moral discrimination. Fanny, one can argue, *is* a teachable heroine. What is more important, however, is that she is in fact a pupil who excels her teachers, including *her* mentor–hero, who proves fallible – she learns the lessons her male monitors Sir Thomas Bertram and Edmund teach her much better than her teachers have themselves learnt.

Such a subversion of the idea of a docile pupil who learns obediently from superior teachers is even more strongly present in *Northanger Abbey*. Firstly, Austen is highly sceptical about the model of the teachable heroine and the mentor–hero. Tilney is himself an unusual hero, and a mixed character. He is attracted to Catherine only after he realizes that she is in love with him, a fact that does not lessen her in his opinion. On occasion capable of going beyond facile gendered assumptions (he argues that men read novels with as much pleasure as women), he is, on the other hand, as capable of satirizing women's understanding and use of language. Equally, he is aware of the fact that teachableness of disposition in young ladies is a *convention* (as his remark on the hyacinths demonstrates), and in the novel has his most excessive satirical and mentorial tendencies offset both by his own highly developed sense of irony and lack of pomposity, and by the alternative model of his sister Eleanor, who is arguably a more important character than has been acknowledged so far by critics. Eleanor appreciates that Catherine is rather more than an ignorant young girl, as their conversation on history demonstrates. Eleanor is also, in a good-natured way, critical of her brother's occasional tendency to talk down to and satirize women. And Catherine, in making her judgement on the General at Northanger Abbey, has got her fictional sub-genre wrong, but she is quite right in distrusting the General, who may not be an uxoricide but *is* a selfish, tyrannical father. At the end, Henry must learn about his father what has already been foreshadowed in Catherine's mistaken judgement.

Right from his earliest encounter with Catherine, Tilney lightly makes Catherine question various stereotypes, paradoxically by invoking them. When he first dances with Catherine, he mocks the stereotypical idea that all women keep journals, and that women on the whole write better letters than men. He then goes on to criticize women's use of language, a criticism that is not counter-criticized here but will be later, by his sister. The context is the fascinating conversation between Eleanor, Henry and Catherine during their walk round Beechen Cliff. Eleanor and Catherine have their now-famous conversation about history, where Catherine makes her brilliant comments about the fictionality of history: 'the men all so good for nothing, and hardly any women at all – it is very tiresome: and yet I often think it odd that it should be so dull, for a great deal of it must be invention.'[50]

History, in this reading, is dull fiction, peopled by uninteresting men and very few women – the implication is that there might be a causal link between the masculine nature of most history-writing and its dullness, in contrast to the feminized genre of the novel, which, as I discuss later, Austen defends so ardently in *Northanger Abbey*. In that defence, Austen claims that fiction is a form of knowledge *and* of pleasure. Eleanor is intelligent enough to concede Catherine's inspired insight that much of history is indeed fictional – but she confesses to enjoying a 'well drawn up speech', probably with greater pleasure 'if the production of Mr Hume or Mr Robertson, than if the genuine words of Caractacus, Agricola, or Alfred the Great'.[51]

The conversation between Eleanor and Catherine has an arresting quality all too evident to modern readers, and I do not think it accidental that Henry should not, or should choose not to, participate in it. He joins this part of the conversation only to comment amusedly on Catherine's making 'instruction' in history and 'torment' synonymous – he indulgently disagrees with Catherine's criticism of education, but the intelligent male cannot enter the domain of the two young women's sceptical female look at the discipline of history. At the same time, tha fact that he is not judgmental or pompous about Catherine's lack of respect for formal education is also noteworthy; he neither sermonizes at nor patronizes Catherine.

Later, Henry mediates between Catherine and Eleanor to clarify the 'something . . . shocking' that Catherine says has come out in London (Catherine is referring to a new novel, Eleanor thinks she means a serious public disturbance). Henry concludes with a remark that can be construed as derogatory to female understanding: 'Forgive her stupidity. The fears of the sister have added to the weakness of the woman; but she is by no means a simpleton in general.'[52] In the context, Eleanor has in fact displayed a 'masculine' interpretation of the situation: where Catherine is wandering in the realms of fiction, Eleanor is alarmed by the prospect of a public, perhaps even political, disturbance. Eleanor is quick to notice the implied dig at female weakness and fear, and immediately asks him to clear his character handsomely before Catherine and 'Tell her that you think very highly of the understanding of women.'[53] This, Tilney will not do. 'Miss Morland, no one can think more highly of the understanding of women than I do. In my opinion, nature has given them so much, that they never find it necessary to use more than half.'[54]

Terry Castle has argued that a remark such as this shows that Henry has read his Mary Wollstonecraft, and that he is criticizing the way society conditions women not to use their minds.[55] Castle further says that Henry 'does not so much tell Catherine *what* to think as to show her that she can think',[56] and that 'he . . . knows that Catherine's problem can only be rectified by letting her muddle through on her own. Only by not explaining – by refusing to treat her as anything other than an intellectual equal – can he help her to develop, belatedly, an equivalent sense of autonomy.'[57]

I do not agree with this reading, because it gives to Henry a position of enlightened authority that is not given to him in the text. As we have seen, he cannot always participate in or acknowledge the genuine intellectual insights of his sister and of Catherine. His criticism of female understanding is criticized by his sister, who is testimony to how excellent female understanding can in fact be. Moreover, Henry is not, with all his acuteness, averse on occasion to playing mentor towards Catherine, as becomes evident in his exposition of the picturesque. It is here that Austen comments on the importance of imbecility, or at least of ignorance, in heroines who wish men to fall in love with them.

> To come with a well-informed mind, is to come with an inability of administering to the vanity of others, which a sensible person would always wish to avoid. A woman especially, if she have the misfortune of knowing any thing, should conceal it as well as she can. . . . I will . . . add in justice to men, that though to the larger and more trifling part of the sex, imbecility in females is a great enhancement of their personal charms, there is a portion of them too reasonable and too well informed of themselves to desire any thing more in women than ignorance.[58]

The edge of bitterness in the words 'reasonable and . . . well informed' men, such as Tilney, wishing for ignorance in the women they contemplate marrying, is unmistakable. Ignorance (even if it has to be feigned) and a manifest desire to learn from superior males are 'advantages' for women; to be an apt female pupil is also to take on the role of inferior and ignorant woman, thus strengthening the status quo of inequality in the relation between the sexes.

Thus, it is easy to account for the gentle satire in Austen's account of Henry teaching Catherine the principles of taste, particularly in the picturesque. He is eager to teach, while she is a phenomenally quick scholar. Henry, however, is far too sceptical and uncomplacent to be happy in this role for long, and slowly steers the conversation to government and politics – topics outside the limits of feminine discourse, so that Catherine falls silent. This silence also shows up exactly how limited are the parameters of the mentor–pupil relationship between hero and heroine: Henry can teach Catherine safe subjects such as the principles of the picturesque, but once he ventures outside the limits of permitted feminine discourse, she will have to fall silent. Catherine has learnt that such bounds exist to female conversation, just as Camilla Stanley can score a point off Kitty by saying that she cannot bear to hear politics mentioned. Such bounds appear 'natural' to Catherine or Camilla; nor does it seem strange to Catherine that Henry should, after *instructing* her in the picturesque, be 'perfectly satisfied of her having a great deal of *natural* taste'[59] (emphasis mine). Such moments in Austen pose us with the disturbing question of where the 'natural' ends and where the 'learnt' begins, for women. Austen thus creates a questioning dialectic that does not completely explode the convention of the teachable, pliable young heroine and the mentor–hero – but a deeper reading reveals how she deconstructs the topos.

The same refusal to conform to the mentor–pupil convention holds good for Catherine's misjudgement in Northanger Abbey. Henry *will* gently but firmly tell Catherine that her suspicions about the General are wrong, and this lesson that he teaches her marks a new stage of intimacy in their relationship. At the same time, it is Henry who will have to learn the depth of his father's calculating selfishness, thus vindicating Catherine's distrust of the General.

Catherine also learns to be disillusioned with the Thorpes, especially Isabella, all by herself. Neither Henry nor Eleanor attempts to disillusion her about her 'friends' before she comes to that conclusion herself. There is a native sturdiness about Catherine, a trait that the Tilneys appreciate. Catherine, then, like Kitty or Emma Watson or even Frederica, is not a pliable, malleable, easily teachable heroine. Even though Kitty or Catherine are represented as ordinary girls, Austen shows that this does not preclude their being articulate, intelligent, courageous, inquiring or original. By refusing to focus on 'pictures of perfection' (which, she wrote, 'make me sick and wicked'[60]), Austen also refuses to accept the paradoxical and impossible demand on women that they should be both wonderfully 'well-educated' *and* perpetually willing, docile pupils. In *Pride and Prejudice*, Miss Bingley's and Darcy's idea of the accomplished woman is as follows, for example:

> [N]o one can be really esteemed accomplished, who does not greatly surpass what is usually met with. A woman must have a thorough knowledge of music, singing, drawing, dancing, and the modern languages, to deserve the word;

and besides all this, she must possess a certain something in her air and manner of walking, the tone of her voice, her address and expressions, or the word will be but half deserved.'

'All this she must possess,' added Darcy, 'and to all this she must yet add something more substantial, in the improvement of the mind by extensive reading.'[61]

Elizabeth Bennet, in retorting that she has never met a woman as perfect as this, is in fact criticizing the exorbitancy of such expectations, the reverse side of which is the desirability of female ignorance and inferiority in relation to male power and knowledge. Austen's heroines puncture such expectations throughout her oeuvre. An apparently ignorant and naïve Catherine Morland proves to be morally independent and intellectually original, rather than an obedient pupil of a superior young mentor–hero. A Fanny Price, bad at school-room lessons and apparently a submissive moral pupil of authority-figures, ends up becoming the exemplary educative figure at the centre of *Mansfield Park*. An Elizabeth Bennet squashes the masculine vanity of her suitor, who starts off with arrogant and impossible expectations about women and female education.

Boasting of Being an Unlearned Female Who Dared to be an Authoress: Austen's Artful Self-Circumscription

Austen's early fiction takes a highly sceptical view of the idea of malleable, teachable female dispositions, but, compared with earlier writers such as Mary Hamilton, Clara Reeve and Mary Wollstonecraft, and even contemporaries such as Mary Brunton and Elizabeth Hamilton, she gives us a circumscribed view of female education, losing much of the range of issues, the boldness, the intellect-ualism and the polemics of earlier women's fictions of education, including those of conservative writers. No woman studies mathematics or Latin or Newton in Austen, or complains of the few paid occupations open to women, or plans female seminaries to train women in paid jobs; Austen's heroines do not go off to London shops to sell their own paintings, or make and sell toys, or journey to Scotland to become governesses. We have grown used to thinking that Austen is so much a better writer than Brunton or Reeve precisely because of this 'realist' vision – but this choice owes much, also, to her own conservatism. Within the boundaries that she chooses, Austen is indeed an anatomist of the small difficulties and pleasures of female education in its intellectual and social forms – but we need also to recognize how many of the already available, more ambitious topoi of contemporary women's writing on female education she chooses not to incor-porate in her writing. Austen is particularly sceptical about one of the most important subjects of earlier writings on female education – women earning their own living. While Reeve, Elizabeth Hamilton, Frances Burney and Mary Brunton make this a major subject in their writing, allowing a critique of women's exclusion from or problematic status in the public economic sphere, Austen does not think that working heroines are 'realistic'.

Indeed, reading Austen's early fiction, one is tempted to ask what consti-
tutes women's work in the public *or* the private sphere, given that she is just as
sceptical about another important private vocation for women, that of the
maternal or quasi-maternal educator – a figure which, we have seen, also recurs
in the earlier fiction I analyse. Perhaps the answer to this lies in Austen's awareness
that education, even formal education, can be a double-edged sword, with more
negative than positive connotations for women. Where Mary and Elizabeth
Hamilton express outrage at women being denied any enlightened formal education (even if, as I have argued, they know that formal education in itself is not
enough), or where Clara Reeve formulates proposals for educating women to be
economically independent, Austen, instead, expends much energy is showing up
the limitations, tyrannies and hypocrisies of the demands of education, whether
formal education or social training, on women – in her attacks on manipulative
maternal educators ('Lady Susan'); on anxious, authoritarian guardians
('Catharine, or the Bower'); on the accomplished woman ('Catharine', *Northanger
Abbey*); on the perfectly educated, virtuous heroine (*Northanger Abbey*). In many
ways, Austen is the most conscious, among all my writers, of the dangers that
education can pose, as a form of social and ideological *control*, for young women
poised on the threshold of their entrance into the world.

Austen is the most conservative of my writers in her strict adherence to
the courtship novel structure, and in her view of marriage as the end of female
education. Nevertheless, she shows that it is particularly unfair, given their narrowness of horizons, that young women should face the impossible demand that
they should be both well-educated and accomplished, in terms which the world
has set, *and* be perpetually willing, docile pupils eager to learn from male and
female authority-figures, with such pliable tutelage designed to facilitate marriage.

If Austen limits the range of fictional depictions of female education,
she is simultaneously boldly confident about the status and educative power of
fiction, epitomized by the female-authored, female-centred novel. In *Northanger
Abbey,* she proclaims:

> 'Oh! it is only a novel!' replies the young lady; while she lays down her book
> with affected indifference, or momentary shame. – 'It is only Cecilia, or Camilla,
> or Belinda'; or, in short, only some work in which the greatest powers of the
> mind are displayed, in which the most thorough knowledge of human nature,
> the happiest delineation of its varieties, the liveliest effusions of wit and humour
> are conveyed to the world in the best chosen language.[62]

Austen acknowledges the association of novels with women, pays tribute
to Frances Burney and Maria Edgeworth, the most celebrated contemporary
novelists, and makes a strikingly strong intellectual defence of the novel, with an
implicitly educational base ('greatest powers of the *mind* . . . displayed, the most
thorough *knowledge* of human nature'; emphasis mine). An elimination of what
she sees as absurdities and improbabilities in discussions of female education
empowers Austen's own critical and educative vision. The defence of fiction and

of women's fiction, in a work that itself humorously critiques another kind of female-authored fiction, aligns Austen with the other women writers analysed in this book, most notably Clara Reeve, but also Mary Brunton and Elizabeth Hamilton who, while they write fiction of a kind different from Austen's, also debate the value of fiction and the special relationship that women have to fiction, and who also vindicate the knowledge-value of fiction, particularly fiction written by discerning women.

However, we must also note that Austen's bold vindication of women's fiction, written very early in her career, between 1798 and 1803, remained unpublished till after her death. Indeed, a publisher accepted the manuscript of *Susan*, the original title of *Northanger Abbey*, but refused to publish it. The work had to be rescued by the Austens, and even then publication was posthumous. Until recently, *Northanger Abbey* was considered a very minor part of the Austen canon. I find the struggle for publication and canonization of *Northanger Abbey* telling; the story it tells is intimately related to the contested nature of fiction and the contest for legitimacy that women-authored fiction faced, a struggle in which Austen's defence has a stellar role.

One of my contentions in this book is that it was *because* fiction was in a transitional, relatively marginal state in this period that women writers adopted this mode, using it to explore questions surrounding female development and education. Fiction, viewed as poised between high and low, between knowledge and (illicit) pleasure, became a discursive domain offering knowledge that was compendious, uncategorized and miscellaneous – an implicit alternative to the many domains of formal learning that women had highly limited access to.

Austen occupies a double-edged position in this narrative. When the pompous chaplain to the Prince Regent tried to tell Austen that she should write a novel centred on a clergyman remarkably similar to him, she staved off the unwelcome suggestion by pleading her own ignorance and lack of masculine education:

> Such a Man's Conversation must at times be on subjects of Science & Philosophy of which I know nothing – or at least be occasionally abundant in quotations and allusions which a Woman, who like me, knows only her own Mother-tongue & has read very little in that, would be totally without the power of giving. . . . And I think I may boast myself to be, with all possible Vanity, the most unlearned, & uninformed Female who ever dared to be an Authoress.[63]

The woman writer who affected such modest ignorance and lack of masculine learning was, paradoxically, the same writer who announced that the acme of the novel, itself the zenith of literary achievement, is the woman-authored novel, which has at its centre the experience and education of a young lady such as Belinda, Camilla, Kitty or Catherine, who is *not* as facilely and pliably teachable as she appears at first glance.

There is a characteristically Austenian cunning, irony and self-circumscription behind her simultaneous vindication of the novel, and the kind of novel she chose to write – if one appears to be talking modestly of heroines with a workaday, unremarkable education, one may escape censure; in writing, as in life, an appearance of ignorance was necessary for Austen, particularly since underlying this was a hidden confidence. But Austen had no doubts that for her heroines to succeed, like their author, they must be *confidently and determinedly* self-circumscribed.

The fact that there was to be no 'masculine' learning or wandering in the public sphere (literal or metaphorical – one thinks of Burney's talented female wanderer and of Elizabeth Hamilton's metaphors of mobility to describe female education) for Austen's heroines was thus not merely a matter of their author's eschewing stock topoi. It was a novelistic and intellectual choice that very deliberately refused to grant narratives of female education the intellectual ambition and loose but confident wandering between various domains of knowledge and experience that we have seen in the earlier chapters.

The self-imposed limitedness of Austen's novelistic vision thus marked a definite break and a discontinuity from many of her predecessors and contemporaries – yet, as the passage on the novel in *Northanger Abbey* proclaims, Austen saw herself as very much a part of that earlier distinguished line of women's fiction. This powerful sense of continuity and discontinuity working together is one of the central thrusts of my argument: the assemblage of texts in this book delineates a female-authored novelistic field that resists categorization into reductive, linear models of literary history.

Recent works by Clifford Siskin and Deidre Lynch[64] have read Austen's fiction as contributing to the 'naturalization' (Siskin) of the novel, seen as a form which offers a narrow, deep vision of the world, which epitomizes the emergent discipline of literature, and which delineates characters in terms of inward depth and development – all these, Siskin and Lynch argue, are powerful contributors to the shaping of the modern, disciplined self and to the shaping of literature as a field of knowledge which systematically represents such selves in their 'economy of character'.

Austen's semi-parodic early fiction, however, allows us to see that her fictions are often themselves about fiction, and that heroines such as Kitty Percival and Catherine Morland are inserted into a world where they must negotiate many of the conventions of earlier fiction, particularly in the arena of female education. The ideology of female education that Austen built up through her later oeuvre did contribute powerfully to a canonization of one form of the novel – the well-wrought courtship novel 'realistically' describing a small community, and a female self evolving 'realistically' towards marriage. The self-imposed limitedness of Austen's vision of female education, however, was at least partly shaped by her awareness of female education being a set of conventions, constructions and processes of control, while the 'inner self' of the heroine (as *Northanger Abbey* and 'The Bower' make particularly clear) was not seen as a mystified inner domain of autonomy, but a miscellaneous entity itself constructed by reading and misreading or conventions about courtship between men and women.

In other words, to brand Austen as a neutralizer of a limited view of female education is incorrect, it seems to me: her early fiction yields a trail of clues and pointers to her sharp awareness of how very *un*-natural and difficult any version of education is for heroines, and, one may infer, for real-life women. Demystifying female education is thus the signal achievement of Austen's early oeuvre – yet another among the polyphony of female voices writing in Britain between 1778 and 1814. Austen's early heroines take their place among a huge variety of others – among them mothers, wives, widows, old maids, servants, governesses, painters, botanists, philosophers, shop-keepers, house-keepers and land-owners – who are let loose by their late eighteenth and early nineteenth-century female creators to negotiate a highly gendered dialectic, between control and freedom, fundamental to education and female development.

Notes and References

[1] Jane Austen, *Northanger Abbey, Lady Susan, The Watsons, and Sanditon*, edited by John Davie and with a new introduction by Terry Castle (Oxford: Oxford University Press, 1990), p. 139.

[2] For discussions of the dates of composition of the early writings, see, for example, Mary Gaither Marshall, 'Jane Austen's Manuscripts of the Juvenilia and *Lady Susan*: A History and Description', in *Jane Austen's Beginnings: The Juvenilia and Lady Susan*, edited by J. David Grey (Ann Arbor and London: UMI Research Press, 1989), pp. 107–21; Brian Southam, *Jane Austen's Literary Manuscripts* (Oxford: Oxford University Press, 1964), pp. 14–17.

[3] Jan Fergus, *Jane Austen: A Literary Life* (Basingstoke: Macmillan, 1991), p. 52.

[4] Marilyn Butler, *Jane Austen and the War of Ideas* (Oxford: Clarendon Press, 1987); Claudia Johnson, *Jane Austen: Women, Politics and the Novel* (Chicago and London: University of Chicago Press, 1988).

[5] Discussions of the juvenilia which stress their parodic elements include Sandra Gilbert and Susan M. Gubar, 'Shut Up in Prose: Gender and Genre in Austen's Juvenilia', *The Madwoman in the Attic: The Woman Writer and the Nineteenth Century Literary Imagination* (New Haven and London: Yale University Press, 1979), pp. 107–45; Ellen E. Martin, 'The Madness of Jane Austen: Metonymic Style and Literature's Resistance to Interpretation', in *Jane Austen's Beginnings*, pp. 83–94; Margaret Anne Doody, 'Introduction', in Jane Austen, *Catharine and Other Writings*, edited by Margaret Anne Doody and Douglas Murray (Oxford: Oxford University Press, 1993), pp. ix–xxxviii.

[6] Austen, *Northanger Abbey, Lady Susan, The Watsons, and Sanditon*, pp. 215–16.

[7] Ibid., p. 227.

[8] Ibid., p. 226.

[9] Ibid., p. 218.

[10] Ibid., p. 232.

[11] Ibid., p. 234.

[12] Ibid., p. 236.

[13] Ibid., p. 236.

[14] Ibid., p. 240.

[15] Ibid., p. 278.

[16] Ibid., p. 278.

[17] Jane Austen, *Emma*, edited by James Kinsley, with a new introduction by Terry Castle (Oxford and New York: Oxford University Press, 1995), pp. 270–71.

[18] Austen, *Northanger Abbey, Lady Susan, The Watsons, and Sanditon*, p. 248.

[19] Ibid., p. 256.

[20] Ibid., p. 272.

[21] Austen, *Catharine and Other Writings*, p. 145.

[22] Ibid., p. 146.

23 Ibid., p. 147.
24 Ibid., pp. 145–46.
25 Ibid., p. 186.
26 Ibid., p. 222.
27 Johnson, *Jane Austen: Women, Politics and the Novel*, pp. 53–54.
28 Austen, *Catharine and Other Writings*, p. 222.
29 In a revision made in 1809, Austen substituted the title of More's work for the earlier 'Seccar's Explanation of the Catechism', an indication that she was interested in changing trends in prescribed didactic reading for young women.
30 Austen, *Catharine and Other Writings*, pp. 201–02.
31 Ibid., p. 191.
32 Ibid., p. 191.
33 Ibid., p. 192.
34 Ibid., pp. 193–94.
35 Ibid., p. 194.
36 Ibid., p. 221.
37 Ibid., pp. 195–96.
38 Ibid., p. 196.
39 Ibid., p. 197.
40 Ibid., p. 188.
41 Ibid., p. 198.
42 Ibid., p. 202.
43 Ibid., p. 202.
44 Ibid., p. 202.
45 Ibid., p. 202.
46 Jane Austen, *Northanger Abbey, Lady Susan, The Watsons, and Sanditon*, p. 85.
47 Ibid., p. 1.
48 Ibid., p. 85.
49 Ibid., p. 2.
50 Ibid., p. 84.
51 Ibid., p 85.
52 Ibid., p. 88.
53 Ibid., p. 89.
54 Ibid., p. 89.
55 Ibid., xxiii.
56 Ibid., p. xxii.
57 Ibid., p. xxiii.
58 Ibid., p. 86.
59 Ibid., p. 86.
60 Letter to Fanny Knight, 23–25 March 1817, in *Jane Austen's Letters*, edited by Deirdre Le Faye (Oxford: Oxford University Press, 1997), p. 335.
61 Jane Austen, *Pride and Prejudice*, edited by James Kinsley and Frank W. Bradbrook (Oxford: Oxford University Press, 1980), p. 34. In Austen's parodic 'Plan of a Novel' (written c. 1816), the heroine is 'very highly accomplished, understanding modern Languages and (generally speaking) everything that the most accomplished young Women learn, but particularly excelling in Music – her favourite pursuit – and playing equally well on the Piano Forte and Harp – and singing in the first stile [sic].' Austen, *Catharine and Other Writings*, p. 231.
62 Austen, *Northanger Abbey, Lady Susan, The Watsons, and Sanditon*, p. 22.
63 Letter to James Stanier Clarke, 11 December 1815, *Jane Austen's Letters*, p. 306.
64 Clifford Siskin, *The Work of Writing: Literature and Social Change in Britain, 1700–1830* (Baltimore and London: Johns Hopkins University Press, 1998), pp. 193–209. Deidre Shauna Lynch, *The Economy of Character: Novels, Market Culture, and the Business of Inner Meaning* (Chicago and London: University of Chicago Press, 1998), passim. Lynch sees not just Austen but most Regency-period women novelists participating in a market culture of novel-writing and creating an economy of character based on inner depth.

Conclusion

In the age of late Enlightenment and Romanticism, in the era of the French Revolution and the Industrial Revolution, many British gentlewomen, five of whom are centre-stage in this book, wrote quietly and respectably, at an apparently cosy and safe distance from social clamour and unrest. They were not part of revolutionary circles, did not support the American or French Revolutions, and belonged to old-fashioned gentry formations embedded in established feudal hierarchies. They mostly used the form of fiction – at the time considered an upstart form which was suitable to be patronized and practised by women, and which was also seen as both a potentially educative and potentially licentious form.

These women wrote as uneasy members of the British public sphere, and the powerful world of British letters and print culture. They wrote in a period and a country that were the crucible for the formation of still globally dominant notions of education and development. I have shown in this book that these women and their writings belie their 'cosy', 'old-fashioned', 'conservative' image. They were not at a safe distance from the major social, economic and political cruxes and tensions of their time. They did not create escapist writing in an anodyne genre.

This book was written with a certain devoted and passionate engagement on my part with these voices (the neglected early oeuvre of Austen not excepted) which are in crying need of being heard in their originality, disturbingness, range and adventurousness. It was a deliberate choice to give much space to cited passages – that their voices should continually intersperse with my commentary and analysis, and give the reader a taste of these tomes now, for the most part, locked away in a few exclusive libraries. I made a conscious readerly, critical and political choice, then, in foregrounding close reading and micro-analysis. I did not want these women's creations to get swamped and reduced to untenable reductive narratives of literary and cultural history of the sort I have critiqued in my introduction, *even before* we listen in nuance and detail to the diversity and complexity of what they said.

To reduce and card-index Romantic-era British women's voices in the steel file-cabinet of disciplinary academia, buttressed by a wrong-headed, so-called Historicism, is a major pitfall of contemporary scholarship, it seems to me. It leads to blanket, facile docketing and straitjacketing of women's writing into claustrophobic prison cells of the emergent bourgeois hegemonic subject (Nancy Armstrong), or the disciplined, cultivated modern female self which helps to produce an ideology of novelism (Clifford Siskin). Once we take refuge in such linear, conveniently neat taxonomies, we can then ignore both the energetic adventurousness of women's plots and polemics in the Romantic period, and the disturbing exclusions and disjunctions that are symptomatic of deep-seated social, cultural and economic fractures and fissures in the society which produced these unsettling, eccentric scribbling gentlewomen.

Out of my listening to the voices of these women, and only *after* a prioritization of the detail and complexity of the individual and the particular (the particular has traditionally been the domain of the feminine, since women were not supposed to be capable of the encyclopaedic, the general and the all-subsuming), comes a realization that these women and their writings illuminate and change our grand narratives and broad notions of Romantic-era Britain, its culture, socio-economic dynamics, politics, its sexual and familial history. It also changes our map of the intellectual history of education, development and feminism.

I have argued throughout this book that it was not accidental that the form of the exploring and questioning engaged in by these women was fiction. Nor is it accidental that these compendious, ambitious, unruly, baggy monsters of female-authored fiction should challenge any epistemological enterprise that seeks to contain, tame and render pliable and manageable, the subjectivities, histories and narratives of the women who created them. For, the form of Romantic-era fiction, as much as its content, poses a challenge to still prevalent masculinist modes of creating disciplinary knowledge that seek to iron out the contestations, unsettlingness and fractures in fiction. British Romantic-era gentlewomen, themselves sites of competing, fractured norms and modes of being, attempt to give a shape and contour to their sense of growth and development by using the tension-ridden notion of education in the heuristic form of fiction.

It matters that, at this time, fiction is still in an uncanonized state, though the process of canonization is beginning at the very time in which these women wrote. The canon that was created excluded the majority of these women, and happily ignored the sly or unruly elements in the mature Austen, the only one among them who did gain fame as an exquisite writer of miniatures.

Romantic-era fiction allowed women to inscribe their subjectivities in the kind of knowledge/pleasure compendium of fiction they chose to produce, a kind of knowledge that had not yet itself become an object of study as English literature. The writers used the theme of education, and the space offered by contemporary approval given to didacticism in fiction, to unfold and explore a huge array of questions about female development and about their society. The form of Romantic-era women's fiction, we have seen, is an experimental amalgam of diverse ways of writing about female education and development, with the styles, modes and registers that were used ranging from prescriptions to letters to political polemic to disquisitions on history to discourses on psychology and philosophy.

I shall stick my neck out and say that women's fiction has *always* remained an unruly and uneasy category, and a weapon for women, even in later periods when English literature became a discipline. Fiction by women has remained an arena of heuristic knowledge and an experimental laboratory where women try on and parade many different kinds of selfhood, and course along a variety of paths and journeys of development. And fiction continued, much after the early nineteenth century, to be viewed with suspicion as being particularly dangerously and illicitly related to female subjectivities, as, for example, we find in George Gissing's denunciation of female novel-reading as sickeningly sentimental and corrupting, in his novel *The Odd Women*, published in 1893 (the fact that Gissing put this denunciation into the mouth of the radical feminist Rhoda Nunn, highlights the abiding and tension-ridden relationship between women and novels in British writing and society).[1]

Playing with and plotting their own development and education through fiction was an enterprise engaged in for the first time on a large scale by women such as the ones I analyse. This was recognized by another sympathetic reader of Romantic-era women's fiction, in a conversational, eclectic, virtuoso feminist treatise written for women studying and teaching in pioneering institutions of female education:

> Thus, towards the end of the eighteenth century a change came about which, if I were rewriting history, I should describe more fully and think of greater importance than the Crusades or the Wars of the Roses. The middle-class woman began to write. For if *Pride and Prejudice* matters, and *Middlemarch* and *Villette* and *Wuthering Heights* matter, then it matters far more than I can prove in an hour's discourse that women generally, and not merely the lonely aristocrat shut up in her country house among her folios and her flatterers, took to writing. . . . For masterpieces are not single and solitary births; they are the outcome of many years of thinking in common, of thinking by the body of the people, so that the experience of the mass is behind the single voice.[2]

This is Virginia Woolf, writing in *A Room of One's Own*, a book based on papers read in 1928 at Girton and Newnham, the two Cambridge colleges for women established after an arduous struggle in the nineteenth century.

My view of the relationship between women, fiction and education is, like Woolf's, categorizable as 'Romantic', and this is particularly appropriate when my specific subject is British women writing on education and scripting female selves in the Romantic period. The view is Romantic in the sense that it does not denude women's fictions about their own education and development of dynamism, agency and emancipatory impulses, while it keeps in mind and considers as constitutive, the exclusions, closures, control and discipline in them. This book is also, therefore, one that affirms both the value and the dialectics inherent in Enlightenment notions of education.

This book has also argued that the women I analyzed did *not* write fiction that promoted the idea of Britain as a feminized nation, powerful in good measure because of its women upholding heterosexual, patriarchal family life and virtue. To the question of how invested these writers were in the heterosexual nuclear family that was becoming increasingly influential at the time, my answer has been that their works constantly go beyond the notion that marriage ought to be the purpose or end of female education. Collectivities of women, communities founded and administered by women, in short, the quest and drive for female utopias that serve to critique and question patriarchal heterosexual models of the family, occur and recur powerfully in these women's thought and work, most outstandingly in the works of Mary Hamilton and Reeve, but the impulse is powerful in all the writers.

Nor is it correct to argue that there was a linear development in late eighteenth-century and early nineteenth-century women's fiction, with unruly, baggy, didactic, stylistically non-naturalistic fiction maturing into the realist, miniature, psychologically oriented, domestic, well-formed Austenian novel. This particular narrative of emergence was generated by later literary reception and canonization, but we can see that simultaneously with Austen, such writers as Brunton and Elizabeth Hamilton were continuing to publish influentially a non-Austenian model of fiction.

My analysis of Austen's early fiction shows that reading the great Jane herself through the lens of her sharply parodic, unruly early fiction or juvenilia allows us to deconstruct that mythos of the well-wrought, cosy Austenian realist novel as the hegemonic form of domestic British fiction and British women's fiction. And, I have argued, in terms of range, breadth, ambitions for women and richness of intellectualism, the four writers other than Austen, easily labelled as didactic, prim and conservative, were in fact far *more* radical and bold, far *less* conservative, than Austen herself.

Seeing coercion and control in models of education is a well-known Foucauldian argument. But it is precisely my intention not to argue that only a 'discipline and punish' model emerged at this time. On the contrary, what we learn from these writings is that disjunctions are constitutive and unignorable for all of us who live, work and grapple with post-Enlightenment paradoxes of education. The darkness at the heart of Enlightenment, we see graphically through these works, played constantly with the light, the freedom with the control, the disciplining with the loosening.

There is no panacea that education and development offer when taken for granted as facile, unilinear concepts. Keeping our focus balanced on that needlepoint between freedom and restraint, coercion and autonomy in education is vital, for such models of education and development are the ones we must live and struggle with today. In the Indian reality where I write this conclusion, teaching continues to be the ultimate womanly profession (perhaps most obviously womanly because it is the most low-paid among white-collar professions!), the most important ideological tool for sustaining patriarchy and social hierarchies, and, paradoxically, the profession through which millions of working women carve out dignity, legitimacy and economic freedom.

Why such paradoxes in education and development continue to shape our lives today is better understood by the writings of British gentlewomen in the late eighteenth and early nineteenth century. Women of the great imperial nation, women participating in the public sphere of a rich and powerful country, enshrined with the social legitimacy of being gentry-born, they desperately sought controlled ways out for women. Simultaneously, they were delegitimized in the public sphere as eccentric, they were excluded from the political sphere, and they struggled to find dignified ways of earning a living.

Both dispossessed and legitimized in their own context, both excluded from masculine schemas of dignified formal education and in turn excluding many others from the plots of education they created, they illuminate the double-edgedness of a project of education and development that arose in Enlightenment Europe, in which the promise of knowledge and emancipation went hand in hand with the exclusion and containment of such promises of freedom, rationality and progress. Their critical, questioning voices are destabilizing and revitalizing voices from the past for present-day thinkers and workers in the world of education and development, which spawns its own brood of inequalities and fractures.

Notes and References

1 'All her spare time was given to novel-reading. If every novelist could be strangled and thrown into the sea we should have some chance of reforming women.' George Gissing, *The Odd Women* (New York: Norton, 1977), p. 98.

2 Virginia Woolf, *A Room of One's Own and Three Guineas,* edited with an introduction by Morag Shiach (Oxford: Oxford University Press, 1992), p. 84.

Bibliography

Primary Works

Anon., (Drake, Judith), *An Essay in Defence of the Female Sex*, written by a Lady, in *The Pioneers: Early Feminists*, edited by Marie Mulvey Roberts and Tamae Mizuta, with an introduction by Marie Mulvey Roberts ([1696] 4th edn, London: S. Butler, 1721; rpt, London: Routledge/Thoemmes Press; Tokyo: Kinokuniya Co., 1993).

Astell, Mary, *A Serious Proposal to the Ladies, for the Advancement of Their True and Greatest Interest*, in *The Pioneers: Early Feminists*, edited by Marie Mulvey Roberts and Tamae Mizuta, with an introduction by Marie Mulvey Roberts ([1694] 4th edn, London: R. Wilkin, 1701; rpt, London: Routledge/Thoemmes Press; Tokyo: Kinokuniya Co., 1993).

Austen, Jane, *Catharine and Other Writings*, edited by Margaret Anne Doody and Douglas Murray, with an introduction by Margaret Anne Doody, Oxford World's Classics (Oxford and New York: Oxford University Press, 1993).

——, *Northanger Abbey, Lady Susan, The Watsons, and Sanditon*, edited by John Davie, with an introduction by Terry Castle, Oxford World's Classics (Oxford and New York: Oxford University Press, 1990).

——, *Sense and Sensibility*, edited by James Kinsley, with a new introduction by Margaret Anne Doody, Oxford World's Classics ([1811] Oxford and New York: Oxford University Press, 1990).

——, *Pride and Prejudice*, edited by James Kinsley and F.W. Bradbrook, Oxford World's Classics ([1813] Oxford and New York: Oxford University Press, 1980).

——, *Mansfield Park*, edited by James Kinsley, with a new introduction by Marilyn Butler, Oxford World's Classics ([1814] Oxford and New York: Oxford University Press, 1990).

——, *Emma*, edited by James Kinsley, with a new introduction by Terry Castle, Oxford World's Classics ([1816] Oxford and New York: Oxford University Press, 1995).

——, *Persuasion*, edited by John Davie, with a new introduction by Claude Rawson, Oxford World's Classics ([1818] Oxford and New York: Oxford University Press, 1990).

Backscheider, Paula, and John Richetti, eds, *Popular Fiction by Women 1660–1730: An Anthology* (Oxford: Clarendon Press, 1996).

Baillie, Joanna, *A Series of Plays: In Which It Is Attempted to Delineate the Stronger Passions of the Mind*, with a new introduction by Caroline Franklin (London:

Cadell and Davies 1798; rpt, London: Routledge/ Thoemmes Press, 1996).

Barbauld, Anna Laetitia, *Works*, with a memoir by Lucy Aikin and a new introduction by Caroline Franklin, 2 vols (London: Longman, Hurst, Rees, Orme, Brown and Green, 1825; rpt, London: Routledge/ Thoemmes Press, 1996).

———, *A Legacy for Young Ladies, Consisting of Miscellaneous Pieces, in Prose and Verse* (London: Longman, Hurst, Rees, Orme, Brown and Green, 1826).

Barbauld, Anna Laetitia, ed., *The British Novelists: With an Essay, and Prefaces, Biographical and Critical*, 50 vols (London: Rivington, 1810).

Barker, Jane, *The Galesia Trilogy and Selected Manuscript Poems*, edited by Carol Shiner Wilson (Oxford: Oxford University Press, 1997)

Behn, Aphra, *Love-Letters Between a Nobleman and His Sister*, edited with an introduction and notes by Janet Todd, Penguin Classics ([1684–87] Harmondsworth: Penguin Books, 1996).

———, *Oroonoko and Other Writings*, edited with an introduction and notes by Paul Salzman, Oxford World's Classics (Oxford and New York: Oxford University Press, 1994).

Benger, Miss [Elizabeth], *Memoirs of the Late Mrs Elizabeth Hamilton, With a Selection from Her Correspondence and Other Unpublished Writings*, 2 vols (London: Longman, Hurst, Rees, Orme and Brown, 1818).

———, *The Female Geniad* (London: Hookham and Carpenter, 1791; reprinted with repagination, Providence: Brown Women Writers Project, 1993).

Boaden, James, ed., *Memoirs of Mrs Inchbald, Including Her Correspondence with the Most Distinguished Persons of Her Time*, 2 vols (London: Richard Bentley, 1833).

Brontë, Charlotte, *Jane Eyre*, edited by Margaret Smith, Oxford World's Classics ([1847] Oxford and New York: Oxford University Press, 1993).

Brooke, Frances, *The Excursion*, edited by Paula R. Backscheider and Hope D. Cotton ([1777] Lexington: University Press of Kentucky, 1997).

Brunton, Mary, *Self-Control: A Novel* (Edinburgh: Manners and Miller; London: Longman, Hurst, Rees, Orme and Brown, 1811).

———, *Discipline* (Edinburgh: Manners and Miller, 1814).

———, *Self-Control*, introduced by Sara Maitland (London: Pandora, 1986).

———, *Discipline*, introduced by Fay Weldon (London: Pandora, 1986).

———, *Emmeline: With Some Other Pieces*, with a new introduction by Caroline Franklin (Edinburgh: Manners and Miller, 1819; rpt, London: Routledge/Thoemmes Press, 1992).

Burney, Frances, *Evelina*, edited with an introduction by Edward A. Bloom, with the assistance of Lillian D. Bloom, Oxford World's Classics ([1778] Oxford and New York: Oxford University Press, 1982).

———, *Cecilia*, edited by Margaret Anne Doody and Peter Sabor, with an introduction by Margaret Anne Doody, Oxford World's Classics ([1782] Oxford and New York: Oxford University Press, 1988).

———, *Camilla*, edited with an introduction by Edward A. Bloom and Lillian D. Bloom, Oxford World's Classics ([1796] Oxford and New York: Oxford University Press, 1983).

———, *The Wanderer, or Female Difficulties*, edited by Margaret Anne Doody, Robert

L. Mack and Peter Sabor, with an introduction by Margaret Anne Doody, Oxford World's Classics ([1814] Oxford and New York: Oxford University Press, 1991).

Byron, Lord, *Complete Poetical Works* (Oxford and New York: Oxford University Press, 1970).

Chapone, Hester, *Letters on the Improvement of the Mind*, in *Female Education in the Age of the Enlightenment*, Vol. 2 (Dublin: J. Exshaw and others, 1773; rpt, London: William Pickering, 1996).

Charke, Charlotte, *A Narrative of the Life of Mrs Charlotte Charke* (London: Reeve, Dodd and Cook, 1755).

Chesterfield, Lord, *Letters*, edited with an introduction by David Roberts, Oxford World's Classics (Oxford: Oxford University Press, 1998).

Cowper, William, *Poems*, edited by John D. Baird and Charles Ryskamp, 3 vols. (Oxford: Clarendon Press, 1995).

Darwin, Erasmus, *A Plan for the Conduct of Female Education in Boarding Schools* (London: Joseph Johnson, 1797).

Davys, Mary, *The Reform'd Coquet, Familiar Letters Betwixt a Gentleman and a Lady, and The Accomplish'd Rake*, edited by Martha Bowden (Lexington: University Press of Kentucky, 1999).

Edgeworth, Maria, *Letters for Literary Ladies, to Which Is Added an Essay on the Noble Science of Self-Justification*, edited by Claire Connolly ([1795] London: Dent, 1993).

———, *The Parent's Assistant, or Stories for Children*, with an introduction by Anne Thackeray Ritchie ([1796–1800] London: Macmillan, 1907).

———, *Belinda*, edited with an introduction and notes by Kathryn Kirkpatrick, Oxford World's Classics ([1801] Oxford and New York: Oxford University Press, 1994).

———, *Early Lessons* ([1801–25] London: Simpkin, Marshall and Co. and others, 1855).

———, *Patronage*, introduced by Eva Figes ([1814] London: Pandora, 1986).

———, *Helen*, introduced by Maggie Gee ([1834] London: Pandora, 1987).

———, *Tales and Novels by Maria Edgeworth*, 18 vols, including *Tales of Fashionable Life*, 5 vols (London: Baldwin and Cradock and others, 1833).

———, *The Novels and Selected Works of Maria Edgeworth*, general editors: Marilyn Butler and Mitzi Myers, 9 vols (London: Pickering and Chatto, 1999).

Edgeworth, Maria, and Richard Lovell, *Practical Education*, 3 vols ([1798] London: Joseph Johnson, 1801; rpt, Poole and New York: Woodstock Books, 1996).

Fénelon, François de, *Telemachus, Son of Ulysses*, edited and translated by Patrick Riley (Cambridge: Cambridge University Press, 1994).

Fenwick, Eliza, *Secresy*, edited by Isobel Grundy ([1795] Peterborough, Ontario: Broadview Press, 1994).

Ferguson, Moira, ed., *First Feminists: British Women Writers 1578–1799* (Bloomington: Indiana University Press; Old Westbury, N.Y.: Feminist Press, 1985).

Ferrier, Susan, *Marriage*, edited with an introduction by Herbert Foltinek ([1818] London: Oxford University Press, 1971).

Fielding, Sarah, *The Governess, or Little Female Academy*, with an introduction and bibliography by Jill Grey (London: the author, 1749; rpt, London: Oxford University Press, 1968).

————, *The Adventures of David Simple*, edited with an introduction by Malcolm Kelsall, Oxford World's Classics ([1744] Oxford and New York: Oxford University Press, 1994).

Fleetwood, William, *The Relative Duties of Parents and Children, Husbands and Wives, Masters and Servants* (London: Charles Harper, 1705; rpt, New York and London: Garland Publishing, 1985).

Fraser, Sir William, *The Melvilles Earls of Melville and the Leslies Earls of Leven*, 3 vols (Edinburgh: printed privately, 1890).

Genlis, Stephanie de, *Adelaide and Theodore; or, Letters on Education: Containing All the Principles Relative to Three Different Plans of Education; to that of Princes, and to Those of Young Persons of Both Sexes*, 3 vols ([1782] Dublin: Luke White, 1783).

Gisborne, Thomas, *An Enquiry into the Duties of the Female Sex*, in *Female Education in the Age of the Enlightenment*, Vol. 2 (London: Cadell and Davies, 1797; rpt, London: William Pickering, 1996).

Gissing, George, *The Odd Women* ([1893] New York: Norton, 1977).

Godwin, William, *The Political and Philosophical Writings of William Godwin*, general editor: Mark Philp, 7 vols (London: Pickering and Chatto, 1993).

Goethe, Johann Wolfgang von, *The Sorrows of Young Werther; Elective Affinities; Novella*, edited by David E. Wellbery, translated by Victor Lange and Judith Ryan ([1774] Princeton, New Jersey: Princeton University Press, 1988).

Gregory, Dr, *A Father's Legacy to His Daughters*, in *The Young Lady's Pocket Library, or Parental Monitor*, with an introduction by Vivien Jones (Dublin: John Archer, 1790; rpt, Bristol: Thoemmes Press, 1995).

Griffith, Elizabeth, *The Delicate Distress*, edited by Cynthia Booth Ricciardi and Susan Staves ([1769] Lexington: University Press of Kentucky, 1997).

Hamilton, Elizabeth, *Translation of the Letters of a Hindoo Rajah*, 2 vols (Dublin: H.Colbert, 1797).

————, *Translation of the Letters of a Hindoo Rajah*, edited by Pamela Perkins and Shannon Russell (Peterborough: Broadview Press, 1999).

————, *Memoirs of the Life of Agrippina, the Wife of Germanicus* (London: G. and J. Robinson, 1804).

————, *A Series of Popular Essays, Illustrative of Principles Essentially Connected with the Improvement of the Understanding, the Imagination, and the Heart*, 2 vols (Edinburgh: Manners and Miller; London: Hurst, Rees, Orme and Brown and others, 1813).

————, *Letters Addressed to the Daughter of a Nobleman on the Formation of the Religious and Moral Principles*, 2 vols (London: Cadell and Davies, 1806; rpt, New York and London: Garland Press, 1974).

————, *The Cottagers of Glenburnie: A Tale for the Farmer's Inglenook* (Edinburgh: Manners and Miller; London: Cadell, Davies and Miller, 1808).

————, *Memoirs of Modern Philosophers*, 3 vols. (London: Robinson, 1800; rpt, London: Routledge/Thoemmes Press, 1992).

————, *Hints Addressed to the Patrons and Directors of Schools*, introduced by Jeffrey Stern (London: Longman, Hurst, Rees, Orme, and Brown, 1815; rpt, Bristol: Thoemmes Press; Taipei: Unifacmanu Trading Co. Ltd., 1994).

————, *Letters on Education* (Dublin: Colbert and Kelly, 1801).

Hamilton [Walker], Lady Mary, *Letters from the Duchess de Crui and Others, on Subjects Moral and Entertaining, wherein the Character of the Female Sex, with Their Rank, Importance, and Consequence, Is Stated, and Their Relative Duties in Life Are Enforced*, 2 vols ([1776] 3rd edn, Dublin: S. Price and others, 1779).

————, *Memoirs of the Marchioness de Louvoi*, 3 vols (London: Robson, Walter and Robinson, 1777).

————, *Munster Village: A Novel*, 2 vols (London: Robson, Walter, and Robinson, 1778).

————, *Munster Village*, introduced by Sarah Baylis ([1778] London: Pandora, 1987).

————, *La Famille du Duc de Popoli*, 2 vols (Paris: the author, 1810).

Hays, Mary, *An Appeal to the Men of Great Britain in Behalf of Women*, in *The Radicals: Revolutionary Women*, edited by Marie Mulvey Roberts and Tamae Mizuta, introduced by Marie Mulvey Roberts (London: Joseph Johnson, 1798; rpt, London: Routledge/Thoemmes Press, 1994).

————, *Memoirs of Emma Courtney*, edited with an introduction by Eleanor Ty, Oxford World's Classics ([1796] Oxford and New York: Oxford University Press, 1996).

————, *The Victim of Prejudice*, with a new introduction by Caroline Franklin, 2 vols (London: Joseph Johnson, 1799; rpt, London: Routledge/ Thoemmes Press, 1995).

————, *Letters and Essays, Moral and Miscellaneous* (London: T. Knox, 1793; rpt, New York and London: Garland Publishing, 1974).

Haywood, Eliza, *The History of Miss Betsy Thoughtless*, edited with an introduction by Beth Fowkes Tobin, Oxford World's Classics ([1751] Oxford and New York: Oxford University Press, 1997).

Hill, Bridget, edited and introduced by, *The First English Feminist: Reflections upon Marriage and Other Writings by Mary Astell* (Aldershot: Gower/Maurice Temple Smith, 1986).

Inchbald, Elizabeth, *A Simple Story*, edited by J.M.S. Tompkins, with an introduction by Jane Spencer, Oxford World's Classics ([1791] Oxford and New York: Oxford University Press, 1988).

————, *Nature and Art*, with a new introduction by Caroline Franklin, 2 vols. ([1794] London: Robinson, 1797; rpt, London: Routledge/Thoemmes Press, 1995).

Jones, Vivien, ed., *Women in the Eighteenth Century: Constructions of Femininity* (London: Routledge, 1990).

Kelly, Gary, general editor, *Bluestocking Feminism: Writings of the Bluestocking Circle, 1738–1785*, 6 vols (London: Pickering and Chatto, 1999). Vol. I, Elizabeth Montagu, edited by Elizabeth Eger; Vol. II, Elizabeth Carter, edited by Judith Hawley; Vol. III, Catherine Talbot, edited by Rhoda Zuk; Vol. IV, Anna Seward, edited by Jennifer Kelly; Vol. V, Sarah Scott, edited by Gary Kelly; Vol. VI, Sarah Scott and Clara Reeve, edited by Gary Kelly.

Le Faye, Deirdre, ed., *Jane Austen's Letters* (Oxford: Oxford University Press, 1997).

Lennox, Charlotte, *The Life of Harriot Stuart, Written by Herself*, edited with an introduction by Susan Kubica Howard ([[1750] Madison: Fairleigh Dickinson University Press; London: Associated University Presses, 1995).

————, *The Female Quixote*, edited by Margaret Dalziel, with an introduction by Margaret Anne Doody, Oxford World's Classics ([1752] Oxford and New York: Oxford University Press, 1997).

Llandover, Lady, ed., *The Autobiography and Correspondence of Mary Granville, Mrs Delany*, 3 vols (London: Richard Bentley, 1861).

Locke, John, *Some Thoughts Concerning Education and Of the Conduct of the Understanding*, edited with an introduction by Ruth W. Grant and Nathan Tarcov (Indianapolis and Cambridge: Hackett, 1996).

Lonsdale, Roger, ed., *Eighteenth-Century Women Poets: An Oxford Anthology* (Oxford and New York: Oxford University Press, 1990).

Macaulay, Catharine, *Letters on Education* (London: C. Dilly, 1790; rpt, Oxford and New York: Woodstock Books, 1994).

———, *The History of England from the Ascension of James I to that of the Brunswick Line* (London: Nourse, Dodsley, Johnston and others, 1763–83).

Marcet, Jane, *Conversations on Political Economy* (5th edn, London: Longman etc., 1824).

Moore, Edward, *Fables for the Female Sex, in The Young Lady's Pocket Library, or Parental Monitor*, with a new introduction by Vivien Jones (Dublin: John Archer, 1790; rpt, Bristol: Thoemmes Press, 1995).

More, Hannah, *Hints Towards Forming the Character of a Young Princess*, 2 vols. (London: Cadell and Davies, 1805).

———, *Selected Writings of Hannah More*, edited with an introduction and notes by Robert Hole, Pickering Women's Classics (London: William Pickering, 1996).

———, *Coelebs in Search of a Wife*, with a new introduction by Mary Waldron ([1808] London: James Blackwood and Co., n.d; rpt, Bristol: Thoemmes Press, 1995)

Morgan, Lady (Sydney Owenson), *The Wild Irish Girl*, introduced by Brigid Brophy ([1806] London: Pandora, 1986).

Opie, Mrs [Amelia], *Adeline Mowbray, or the Mother and Daughter*, introduced by Jeannette Winterson ([1804] London: Pandora, 1986).

Pennington, Lady [Sarah], *An Unfortunate Mother's Advice to Her Absent Daughters*, in *The Young Lady's Pocket Library, or Parental Monitor*, introduced by Vivien Jones (Dublin: John Archer, 1790; rpt, Bristol: Thoemmes Press, 1995).

Radcliffe, Ann, *The Mysteries of Udolpho*, edited with an introduction by Bonamy Dobrée, explanatory notes by Frederick Garber, Oxford World's Classics ([1794] Oxford and New York: Oxford University Press, 1980).

———, *The Italian*, edited with an introduction by Frederick Garber, Oxford World's Classics ([1797] Oxford and New York: Oxford University Press, 1981).

Radcliffe, Mary Anne, *The Female Advocate; or an Attempt to Recover the Rights of Woman from Male Usurpation*, in *The Radicals: Revolutionary Women*, edited by Marie Mulvey Roberts and Tamae Mizuta, with an introduction by Marie Mulvey Roberts (London: Vernor and Hood, 1799; rpt, London: Routledge/ Thoemmes Press, 1994).

'Randall, Anne Frances' [Mary Robinson], *A Letter to the Women of Great Britain on the Injustice of Mental Subordination*, in *The Radicals: Revolutionary Women*, edited by Marie Mulvey Roberts and Tamae Mizuta, introduced by Marie Mulvey Roberts (London: Longman and Rees, 1799; rpt, London: Routledge/ Thoemmes Press, 1994).

Reeve, Clara, *The Progress of Romance and the History of Charoba, Queen of Egypt*, with a bibliographical note by Esther M. McGill (Colchester: Keymer; London: Robinson, 1785; rpt, New York: The Facsimile Text Society, 1930).

———, *The School for Widows*, 2 vols (Dublin: Wogan and nine others, 1791).

———, *Plans of Education, With Remarks on the Systems of Other Writers*, with an introduction by Gina Luria (London: Hookham and Carpenter, 1792; rpt, New York and London: Garland Publishing, 1974).

———, *Original Poems on Several Occasions* (London: T. and J.W. Pasham, 1769).

———, *The Two Mentors: A Modern Story* (London: C. Dilly, 1783).

———, *Destination: Or the Memoirs of a Private Family*, 3 vols. (London: Longman and Rees, 1799; Microfiche, Wildberg: Edition Corvey Ser.3-628-45160-4).

———, *The Phoenix; or, the History of Polyarchus and Argenis*, translated by George Barclay, 4 vols (London: John Bell and C. Etherington, 1772).

Richardson, Samuel, *Pamela*, introduced by M. Kinkead-Weekes, 2 vols ([1740] London: Dent, 1991).

———, *Clarissa, or the History of a Young Lady*, edited by Angus Ross, Penguin Classics ([1747–48] Harmondsworth: Penguin Books, 1985).

———, *The History of Sir Charles Grandison*, edited with an introduction by Jocelyn Harris, Oxford World's Classics ([1753–54] Oxford and New York: Oxford University Press, 1986).

Roberts, Marie Mulvey, and Tamae Mizuta, eds., *The Pioneers: Early Feminists*, with an introduction by Marie Mulvey Roberts (London: Routledge/Thoemmes Press; Tokyo: Kinokuniya Co., 1993).

———, *The Radicals: Revolutionary Women*, with an introduction by Marie Mulvey Roberts (London: Routledge/Thoemmes Press, 1994).

Robinson, Mary, *Perdita: The Memoirs of Mary Robinson*, edited by M.J. Levy ([1801] London and Chester Springs: Peter Owen, 1994).

Rousseau, Jean-Jacques, *Eloisa, or A Series of Original Letters*, translated by William Kenrick ([1760] London: Vernor, Hood and others, 1803; rpt, Oxford: Woodstock Books, 1989).

———, *Emile, or On Education*, translated with an introduction and notes by Allan Bloom, Penguin Classics ([1762] Harmondsworth: Penguin Books, 1979).

Scott, Sarah, *Millenium Hall*, edited by Gary Kelly ([1762] Peterborough: Broadview Press, 1997).

———, *The History of Sir George Ellison*, edited by Betty Rizzo ([1766] Lexington: The University Press of Kentucky, 1996).

Scott, Sir Walter, *Lives of the Novelists* ([1821–24] London: Oxford University Press, 1906).

Sheridan, Frances, *Memoirs of Miss Sidney Bidulph*, edited by Patricia Köster and Jean Coates Clery, Oxford World's Classics ([1761] Oxford and New York: Oxford University Press, 1995).

Staël, Madame de, *Corinne, or Italy*, edited and translated by Sylvia Raphael, introduced by John Isbell ([1807] Oxford and New York: Oxford University Press, 1998).

Taylor, Jane, *Display: A Tale for Young People* (London: Taylor and Hessey, 1815).

Thomas, Antoine, *Essay on the Character, Manners, and Genius of Women in Different Ages*, enlarged from the French of M. Thomas, by Mr Russell, 2 vols (London: G. Robinson, 1773).

Wakefield, Priscilla, *Reflections on the Present Condition of the Female Sex* (London: Joseph Johnson and others, 1798).

———, *Mental Improvement*, edited with an introduction and notes by Ann B. Shteir

([1794] East Lansing: Colleagues Press; Woodbridge: Boydell and Brewer, 1995).

West, Jane, *Letters to a Young Lady*, in *Female Education in the Age of the Enlightenment*, Vols 4–6 (London: Longman, Hurst, Rees, Orme and Brown, 1811; rpt, London: William Pickering, 1996).

Wollstonecraft, Mary, *Works*, edited by Janet Todd and Marilyn Butler, 7 vols (London: William Pickering, 1989).

——, *A Vindication of the Rights of Woman*, edited by Carol H. Poston (New York and London: W.W. Norton and Co., 1988).

——, *Mary and Maria*, and Mary Shelley, *Matilda*, edited by Janet Todd, 1 vol. (Harmondsworth: Penguin, 1992.

Wollstonecraft, Mary, and William Godwin, *A Short Residence in Sweden and Memoirs of the Author of 'The Rights of Woman'*, edited with an introduction and notes by Richard Holmes, Penguin Classics (Harmondsworth: Penguin Books, 1987).

Secondary Works

Alic, Margaret, *Hypatia's Heritage: A History of Women in Science from Anti-quity to the Late Nineteenth Century* (London: Women's Press, 1986).

Altick, Richard, *The English Common Reader: A Social History of the Mass Reading Public, 1800–1900* (Chicago and London: University of Chicago Press, 1963).

Armstrong, Isobel, '"The Gush of the Feminine": How Can We Read Women's Poetry of the Romantic Period?', in *Romantic Women Writers: Voices and Counter-voices*, edited by Paula Feldman and Theresa M. Kelley (Hanover and London: University Press of New England, 1995), pp. 13–32.

Armstrong, Nancy, *Desire and Domestic Fiction: A Political History of the Novel* (New York and Oxford: Oxford University Press, 1987).

Armstrong, Nancy and Leonard Tennenhouse, eds, *The Ideology of Conduct: Essays on Literature and the History of Sexuality* (New York and London: Methuen, 1987).

Bakhtin, M.M., *The Dialogic Imagination: Four Essays*, edited by Michael Holquist, translated by Caryl Emerson and Michael Holquist (Austin: University of Texas Press, 1981).

Ballaster, Ros, *Seductive Forms: Women's Amatory Fiction from 1684–1740* (Oxford: Clarendon Press; New York: Oxford University Press, 1992).

Barker, Hannah, and Elaine Chalus, eds, *Gender in the Eighteenth Century: Roles, Representations and Responsibilities* (London and New York: Longman, 1997).

Barker-Benfield, G.J., *The Culture of Sensibility: Sex and Society in Eighteenth-century Britain* (Chicago and London: University of Chicago Press, 1992).

Barry, Jonathan, and Christopher Brooks, eds, *The Middling Sort of People: Culture, Society and Politics in England, 1550–1800* (Basingstoke: Macmillan, 1994).

Beer, John, ed., *Questioning Romanticism* (Baltimore and London: Johns Hopkins University Press, 1995).

Benedict, Barbara M., *Making the Modern Reader: Cultural Mediation in Early Modern Literary Anthologies* (Princeton, New Jersey: Princeton University Press, 1996).

Benjamin, Marina, ed., *A Question of Identity: Women, Science, and Literature* (New Brunswick: Rutgers University Press, 1993).

Benkovitz, Miriam, 'Some Observations on Woman's Concept of Self in the Eighteenth

Century', in *Woman in the Eighteenth Century, and Other Essays*, edited by Paul Fritz and Richard Morton (Toronto and Sarasota: Samuel Stevens Hakkert and Co., 1976), pp. 37–54.

Bennett, Judith M., '"History that Stands Still": Women's Work in the European Past', *Feminist Studies*, 14:2 (Summer 1988), pp. 269–83.

Berg, Maxine, *The Age of Manufactures 1700–1820: Industry, Innovation and Work in Britain* (London and New York: Routledge, 1994).

Bermingham, Ann, 'Elegant Females and Gentlemen Connoisseurs: The Commerce in Culture and Self-Image in Eighteenth-Century England', in *The Consumption of Culture 1600–1800*, edited by Ann Bermingham and John Brewer (London and New York: Routledge, 1995).

Bermingham, Ann, and John Brewer, eds, *The Consumption of Culture 1600–1800* (London and New York: Routledge, 1995).

Blain, Virginia, Patricia Clements and Isobel Grundy, eds, *The Feminist Companion to Literature in English: Women Writers from the Middle Ages to the Present* (London: Batsford, 1990).

Blakey, Dorothy, *The Minerva Press: 1790–1820* (London: The Bibliographical Society, 1939).

Bloch, Jean, 'Contrasting Voices: Male and Female Discourse on the Education of Women in Eighteenth-Century France', *Studies on Voltaire and the Eighteenth Century*, 303 (1992), pp. 276–79.

Bolla, Peter de, *The Discourse of the Sublime: Readings in History, Aesthetics, and the Subject* (Oxford and New York: Basil Blackwell, 1989).

Bonnel, Roland, and Catherine Rubinger, eds, *Femmes Savantes et Femmes d'Esprit: Women Intellectuals of the French Eighteenth Century* (New York: Peter Lang, 1994).

Bowers, Toni, *The Politics of Motherhood: British Writing and Culture 1680–1760* (Cambridge: Cambridge University Press, 1996).

Brant, Claire, 'Speaking of Women: Scandal and the Law in the Mid-Eighteenth-Century', in *Women, Texts and Histories 1575–1760*, edited by Claire Brant and Diane Purkiss (London and New York: Routledge, 1992), pp. 242–70.

Brant, Claire, and Diane Purkiss, eds, *Women, Texts and Histories 1575–1760* (London and New York: Routledge, 1992).

Brewer, John, 'Reconstructing the Reader: Prescriptions, Texts and Strategies in Anna Larpent's Reading', in *The Practice and Representation of Reading in England*, edited by James Raven, Helen Small and Naomi Tadmor (Cambridge: Cambridge University Press, 1996), pp. 226–45.

Briedenthal, Renate, and Claudia Koonz, eds, *Becoming Visible: Women in European History* (Boston: Houghton Mifflin, 1977).

Brophy, Elizabeth Bergen, *Women's Lives and the Eighteenth-Century English Novel* (Tampa: University of South Florida Press, 1991).

Browne, Alice, *The Eighteenth Century Feminist Mind* (Brighton: Harvester, 1989).

Browning, J.D., ed., *Education in the Eighteenth Century* (London: Garland Publishing, 1979).

Burlin, Katrin R., '"At the Crossroads": Sister Authors and the Sister Arts,' in *Fetter'd or Free? British Women Novelists, 1670–1815*, edited by Mary Anne Schofield and Cecilia Macheski (Athens, Ohio: Ohio University Press, 1986), pp. 60–84.

Butler, Marilyn, *Maria Edgeworth: A Literary Life* (Oxford: Clarendon Press, 1972).

——, *Jane Austen and the War of Ideas* (Oxford: Clarendon Press, 1987).

——, 'Edgeworth's Stern Father: Escaping Thomas Day, 1795–1801', in *Tradition in Transition: Women Writers, Marginal Texts and the Eighteenth-Century Canon*, edited by Alvaro Ribeiro and James G. Basker (Oxford: Clarendon Press, 1996), pp. 75–93.

Campbell, Mary, *Lady Morgan: The Life and Times of Sydney Owenson* (London: Pandora, 1988).

Castle, Terry, *Masquerade and Civilization: The Carnivalesque in Eighteenth-Century English Culture and Fiction* (London: Methuen, 1986).

——, *The Female Thermometer: Eighteenth-Century Culture and the Invention of the Uncanny* (New York and Oxford: Oxford University Press, 1995).

Chapman, R.W., *Jane Austen: Facts and Problems* (Oxford: Oxford University Press, 1948).

Chitnis, Anand, *The Scottish Enlightenment: A Social History* (London: Croom Helm; Totawa: Rowman and Littlefield, 1976).

Clery, E.J., *The Rise of Supernatural Fiction, 1762–1800*, Cambridge Studies in Romanticism 12 (Cambridge: Cambridge University Press, 1995).

Clinton, Katherine, 'Femme et Philosophe: Enlightenment Origins of Feminism', *Eighteenth Century Studies*, 8 (1975), pp. 185–99.

Colley, Linda, *Britons: Forging the Nation 1707–1837* (London: Pimlico, 1992).

Conger, Syndy M., *Mary Wollstonecraft and the Language of Sensibility* (Rutherford: Fairleigh Dickinson University Press; London: Associated University Presses, 1994).

Copeland, Edward, *Women Writing about Money: Women's Fiction in England, 1790–1820*, Cambridge Studies in Romanticism 9 (Cambridge: Cambridge University Press, 1995).

Copley, Stephen, and John Whale, eds, *Beyond Romanticism: New Approaches to Texts and Contexts, 1780–1832* (London and New York: Routledge, 1992).

Copley, Stephen, and Kathryn Sutherland, eds, *Adam Smith's Wealth of Nations: New Interdisciplinary Essays*, Texts in Culture (Manchester and New York: Manchester University Press, 1995).

Craft-Fairchild, Catherine, *Masquerade and Gender: Disguise and Female Identity in Eighteenth-Century Fictions by Women* (University Park: Pennsylvania State University Press, 1993).

Crossley Evans, M.J., 'The English Evangelicals and the Enlightenment: The Case of Hannah More', *Studies on Voltaire and the Eighteenth Century*, 303 (1992), pp. 458–62.

Dabundo, Laura, ed., *Encyclopaedia of Romanticism: Culture in Britain, 1780s–1830s* (London and New York: Routledge, 1992).

Dales, Joanna Clare, 'The Novel as Domestic Conduct-Book: Richardson to Jane Austen' (unpublished doctoral thesis, University of Cambridge, 1970).

Davidoff, Leonore, and Catherine Hall, *Family Fortunes: Men and Women of the English Middle Class 1780–1850* (London: Hutchinson, 1987).

Davis, Gwenn, and Beverly A. Joyce, *Personal Writings by Women to 1900: A Bibliography of American and British Writers* (London: Mansell, 1989).

Davis, Natalie Zemon, and Arlette Farge, eds, *A History of Women in the West:*

Renaissance and Enlightenment Paradoxes (Cambridge, Massachusetts, and London: The Belknap Press, 1993).

Davison, Rosena, 'Madame d'Epinay's Contribution to Girls' Education', in *Femmes Savantes et Femmes d'Esprit: Women Intellectuals of the French Eighteenth Century*, edited by Roland Bonnel and Catherine Rubinger (New York: Peter Lang, 1994), pp. 219–41.

Day, Aidan, *Romanticism*, The New Critical Idiom (London: Routledge, 1996).

Deane, Seamus, *The French Revolution and Enlightenment in England, 1789–1832* (Cambridge, Massachusetts, and London: Harvard University Press, 1988).

Deguise, Alix, 'Madame Leprince de Beaumont: Conteuse ou Moraliste?', in *Femmes Savantes et Femmes d'Esprit: Women Intellectuals of the French Eighteenth Century*, edited by Roland Bonnel and Catherine Rubinger (New York: Peter Lang, 1994), pp. 155–82.

DeJean, Joan, and Nancy K. Miller, eds, *Displacements: Women, Tradition, Literatures in French* (Baltimore and London: Johns Hopkins University Press, 1991).

Donoghue, Emma, *Passions between Women: British Lesbian Culture, 1688–1801* (London: Scarlet Press, 1993).

Doody, Margaret, *A Natural Passion: A Study of the Novels of Samuel Richardson* (Oxford: Clarendon Press, 1974).

———, *Frances Burney: The Life in the Works* (Cambridge: Cambridge University Press, c.1988).

———, *The True Story of the Novel* (New Brunswick, New Jersey: Rutgers University Press, 1996).

Dwyer, John, *Virtuous Discourse: Sensibility and Community in Late Eighteenth-Century Scotland* (Edinburgh: John Donald, 1987).

Dwyer, John, and Richard B. Sher, eds, *Sociability and Society in Eighteenth-Century Scotland* (Edinburgh: The Mercat Press, 1993).

Ellis, Markman, *The Politics of Sensibility: Race, Gender, and Commerce in the Sentimental Novel*, Cambridge Studies in Romanticism 18 (Cambridge: Cambridge University Press, 1996).

Epstein, Julia, *The Iron Pen: Frances Burney and the Politics of Women's Writing* (Bristol: Bristol Classical Press, 1989).

Favret, Mary A., *Romantic Correspondence: Women, Fiction and the Politics of Letters*, Cambridge Studies in Romanticism (Cambridge: Cambridge University Press, 1993).

Feather, John, *A History of British Publishing* (London: Croom Helm, 1988).

Feldman, Paula, and Theresa M. Kelley, eds, *Romantic Women Writers: Voices and Countervoices* (Hanover and London: University Press of New England, 1995).

———, *Jane Austen: A Literary Life* (Basingstoke: Macmillan, 1991).

———, 'Women Readers: A Case Study', in *Women and Literature in Britain 1700–1800*, edited by Vivien Jones (Cambridge University Press, 2000), pp. 155–76.

Ferguson, Moira, *Subject to Others: British Women Writers and Colonial Slavery, 1670–1834* (New York and London: Routledge, 1992).

Ferris, Ina, *The Achievement of Literary Authority: Gender, History and the Waverley Novels* (Ithaca and London: Cornell University Press, 1991).

Forster, Antonia, *Index to Book Reviews in England 1775–1800* (London: British Library, 1997).

Foucault, Michel, *The History of Sexuality*, translated by Robert Hurley, Vol. 1, An Introduction (London: Allen Lane, 1979).

Fraiman, Susan, *Unbecoming Women: British Women Writers and the Novel of Development* (New York: Columbia University Press, 1993).

Fritz, Paul, and Richard Morton, eds, *Woman in the Eighteenth Century and Other Essays* (Toronto and Sarasota: Samuel Stevens Hakkert and Co., 1976).

Gallagher, Catherine, *Nobody's Story: The Vanishing Acts of Women Writers in the Marketplace, 1670–1820* (Oxford: Clarendon Press, 1994).

Gallagher, Catherine, and Thomas Laqueur, eds, *The Making of the Modern Body: Sexuality and Society in the Nineteenth Century* (Berkeley, Los Angeles, and London: University of California Press, 1989).

Gardiner, Dorothy, *English Girlhood at School: A Study of Women's Education through Twelve Centuries* (London: Oxford University Press, 1929).

Garside, Peter, and Anthony Mandal, 'Producing Fiction in Britain, 1800–1829' (Internet, Cardiff Corvey website: http://www.cf.ac.uk/uwcc/secap/corvey/articles.html), accessed 15 April 1998.

Garside, Peter, James Raven and Rainer Schöwerling, general editors, *The English Novel 1770–1829: A Bibliographical Survey of Prose Fiction Published in the British Isles*, 2 vols. Vol. I, edited by James Raven and Antonia Forster; Vol. II, edited by Peter Garside and Rainer Schöwerling (Oxford: Oxford University Press, 2000).

Gifford, Douglas, and Dorothy McMillan, eds, *A History of Scottish Women's Writing* (Edinburgh: Edinburgh University Press, 1997).

Gilbert, Sandra, and Susan M. Gubar, *The Madwoman in the Attic: The Woman Writer and the Nineteenth Century Literary Imagination* (New Haven and London: Yale University Press, 1979).

Goldsmith, Elizabeth C., and Dena Goodman, eds, *Going Public: Women and Publishing in Early Modern France* (Ithaca and London: Cornell University Press, 1995).

Gonda, Caroline, *Reading Daughters' Fictions, 1709–1834: Novels and Society from Manley to Edgeworth*, Cambridge Studies in Romanticism 19 (Cambridge: Cambridge University Press, 1996).

Goodman, Dena, 'Enlightened Salons: The Convergence of Female and Philosophic Ambitions', *Eighteenth Century Studies*, 22 (1989), pp. 329–50.

———, *The Republic of Letters: A Cultural History of the French Enlightenment* (Ithaca and London: Cornell University Press, 1994).

Grey, J. David, ed., *Jane Austen's Beginnings: The Juvenilia and Lady Susan* (Ann Arbor and London: UMI Research Press, 1989).

Grieder, Josephine, *Translations of French Sentimental Prose Fiction in Late Eighteenth-Century England: The History of a Literary Vogue* (Durham, North Carolina: Duke University Press, 1975).

Guest, Harriet, 'The Wanton Muse: Politics and Gender in Gothic Theory after 1760', in *Beyond Romanticism: New Approaches to Texts and Contexts 1780–1832*, edited by Stephen Copley and John Whale (London and New York: Routledge, 1992), pp. 118–39.

Habermas, Jürgen, *The Structural Transformation of the Public Sphere: An Inquiry into a Category of Bourgeois Society*, translated by Thomas Burger (Cambridge, Polity Press, 1989).

Hardin, James, ed., *Reflection and Action: Essays on the Bildungsroman* (Columbia: University of South Carolina Press, 1991).

Heafford, Michael, *Pestalozzi: His Thought and Its Relevance Today* (London: Methuen, 1967).

Hecht, J. Jean, *The Domestic Servant Class in Eighteenth-Century England* (London: Routledge and Kegan Paul, 1956).

Henderson, Andrea, *Romantic Identities: Varieties of Subjectivity, 1774–1830*, Cambridge Studies in Romanticism 20 (Cambridge: Cambridge University Press, 1996).

Henry-Rosier, Marguerite, *La Vie de Charles Nodier*, Vie des Hommes Illustrées, nr. 73 (Paris: Libraririe Gallimard, 1931).

Hill, Bridget, 'A Refuge from Men: The Idea of a Protestant Nunnery', *Past and Present*, 117 (1987), pp. 107–30.

——, *Women, Work and Sexual Politics in Eighteenth-Century England* (London: UCL Press, 1994).

——, 'Priscilla Wakefield as a Writer of Children's Books', *Women's Writing*, 4:1 (1997), pp. 3–14.

Hobby, Elaine, *Virtue of Necessity: English Women's Writing 1649–1688* (London: Virago, 1988).

Hofkosh, Sonia, *Sexual Politics and the Romantic Author*, Cambridge Studies in Romanticism 29 (Cambridge: Cambridge University Press, 1998).

Horwitz, Barbara, *Jane Austen and the Question of Women's Education* (New York: Peter Lang, 1991).

Howe, Bea, *A Galaxy of Governesses* (London: Derek Verschoyle, 1954).

Hufton, Olwen, *The Prospect Before Her: A History of Women in Western Europe*, Vol. 1, 1500–1800 (London: Harper Collins, 1995).

Hunter, J. Paul, *Before Novels: The Cultural Contexts of Eighteenth-Century English Fiction* (New York and London: Norton, 1990).

Jacobus, Mary, *First Things: The Maternal Imaginary in Literature, Art and Psychoanalysis* (New York and London: Routledge, 1995).

——, '"The Science of Herself": Scenes of Female Enlightenment', in *Romanticism, History, and the Possibilities of Genre, Re-forming Literature 1789–1837*, edited by Tilottama Rajan and Julia Wright (Cambridge: Cambridge University Press, 1998), pp. 240–69.

Janowitz, Anne, *Romanticism and Gender: Essays and Studies 1998* (Cambridge: D.S. Brewer, 1998).

Jelinek, Estelle C., *The Tradition of Women's Autobiography: From Antiquity to the Present* (Boston: Twayne Publishers, 1986).

Johnson, Claudia L., *Jane Austen: Women, Politics and the Novel* (Chicago and London: University of Chicago Press, 1988).

——, *Equivocal Beings: Politics, Gender and Sentimentality in the 1790s: Wollstonecraft, Radcliffe, Burney, Austen* (Chicago and London: University of Chicago Press, 1995).

Jones, Ann, *Ideas and Innovations: Best Sellers of Jane Austen's Age* (New York: AMS Press, 1986).

Jones, Vivien, 'Placing Jemima: Women Writers of the 1790s and the Eighteenth-Century Prostitution Narrative', *Women's Writing*, 4:2 (1997), pp. 201–20.

Jones, Vivien, ed., *Women and Literature in Britain, 1700–1800* (Cambridge: Cambridge University Press, 2000).

Jump, Harriet Devine, *Women's Writing of the Romantic Period, 1789–1836* (Edinburgh: Edinburgh University Press, 1997).

Kamm, Josephine, *Hope Deferred: Girls' Education in English History* (London: Methuen, 1965).

Kelly, Gary, 'Discharging Debts: The Moral Economy of Amelia Opie's Fiction', *The Wordsworth Circle*, 11:4 (Autumn 1980), pp. 198–203.

———, 'Amelia Opie, Lady Caroline Lamb and Maria Edgeworth: Official and Unofficial Ideology', *Ariel*, 12:4 (1981), pp. 3–24.

———, *Revolutionary Feminism: The Mind and Career of Mary Wollstonecraft* (Basingstoke: Macmillan, 1992).

———, *Women, Writing and Revolution, 1790–1827* (Oxford: Clarendon Press, 1993).

———, 'Feminine Romanticism, Masculine History, and the Founding of the Modern Liberal State', in *Romanticism and Gender: Essays and Studies*, edited by Anne Janowitz (Cambridge: D.S. Brewer, 1998), pp. 1–18.

Kern, Jean B., 'The Old Maid, or "To Grow Old and Be Poor, and Laughed at"', in *Fetter'd or Free? British Women Novelists 1670–1815*, edited by Mary Anne Schofield and Cecilia Macheski (Athens and London: Ohio University Press, 1986), pp. 201–14.

Klancher, Jon P., *The Making of English Reading Audiences, 1790–1832* (Madison: University of Wisconsin Press, 1987).

Klein, Lawrence, 'Gender, Conversation, and the Public Sphere in Early Eighteenth-Century England', in *Textuality and Sexuality: Reading Theories and Practices*, edited by Judith Still and Michael Worton (Manchester and New York: Manchester University Press, 1993), pp. 100–15.

Landes, Joan B., ed., *Feminism, the Public and the Private* (Oxford and New York: Oxford University Press, 1998).

Langford, Paul, *A Polite and Commercial People: England, 1727–1783* (Oxford and New York: Oxford University Press, 1992).

Laqueur, Thomas Walter, *Religion and Respectability: Sunday Schools and Working Class Culture 1780–1850* (New Haven and London: Yale University Press, 1976).

———, 'Orgasm, Generation, and the Politics of Reproductive Biology', in *The Making of the Modern Body: Sexuality and Society in the Nineteenth Century*, edited by Catherine Gallagher and Thomas Laqueur (Berkeley, Los Angeles and London: University of California Press, 1987), pp. 1–41.

Leranbaum, Miriam, '"Mistresses of Orthodoxy": Education in the Lives and Writings of Late Eighteenth-Century English Women Writers', *Proceedings of the American Philosophical Society*, 121 (1977), pp. 281–301.

Lewis, Jayne Elizabeth, *The English Fable: Aesop and Literary Culture, 1651–1740* (Cambridge: Cambridge University Press, 1996).

London, April, 'Jane West and the Politics of Reading', in *Tradition in Transition: Women Writers, Marginal Texts and the Eighteenth-Century Canon*, edited by Alvaro Ribeiro and James Basker (Oxford: Clarendon Press, 1996), pp. 56–74.

Lorch, Jennifer, *Mary Wollstonecraft: The Making of a Radical Feminist* (New York and Oxford: Berg, 1990).

Lovell, Terry, *Consuming Fiction* (London: Verso, 1987).

Luke, Carmen, ed., *Feminisms and Pedagogies of Everyday Life* (Albany: State University of New York Press, 1996).

Lynch, Deidre, 'Domesticating Fictions and Nationalizing Women: Edmund Burke, Property, and the Reproduction of Englishness', in *Romanticism, Race and Imperial Culture, 1780–1834*, edited by Alan Richardson and Sonia Hofkosh (Bloomington and Indianapolis: Indiana University Press, 1996), pp. 40–71.

——, *The Economy of Character: Novels, Market Culture, and the Business of Inner Meaning* (Chicago and London: University of Chicago Press, 1998).

Lynch, Deidre, and William B. Warner, eds, *Cultural Institutions of the Novel* (Durham and London: Duke University Press, 1996).

MacCarthy, B.G., *The Later Women Novelists 1744–1818*, Vol. 2 of *The Female Pen* (Cork: Cork University Press; Oxford: Basil Blackwell, 1944).

Marshall, Mary Gaither, 'Jane Austen's Manuscripts of the Juvenilia and Lady Susan: A History and Description', in *Jane Austen's Beginnings: The Juvenilia and Lady Susan*, edited by J. David Grey (Ann Arbor and London: UMI Research Press, 1989), pp. 107–21.

Martin, Ellen E., 'The Madness of Jane Austen: Metonymic Style and Literature's Resistance to Interpretation', in *Jane Austen's Beginnings: The Juvenilia and Lady Susan*, edited by J. David Grey (Ann Arbor and London: UMI Research Press, 1989), pp. 83–94.

Martin, Fritz, 'Bildungsroman: Term and Theory', in *Reflection and Action: Essays on the Bildungsroman*, edited by James Hardin (Columbia: University of South Carolina Press, 1991), pp. 1–25.

Martin, Mary Patricia, '"High and Noble Adventures": Reading the Novel in *The Female Quixote*', *Novel*, 31:1 (Fall 1997), pp. 45–62.

Mayo, Robert D., *The English Novel in the Magazines, 1740–1815* (Evanston: Northwestern University Press; London: Oxford University Press, 1962).

McDermid, Jane, 'Conservative Feminism and Female Education in the Eighteenth Century', *History of Education*, 18:4 (1989), pp. 309–22.

McGann, Jerome, *The Poetics of Sensibility: A Revolution in Literary Style* (Oxford: Clarendon Press, 1996).

McGavran, James Holt, ed., *Romanticism and Children's Literature in Nineteenth-Century England* (Athens and London: University of Georgia Press, 1991).

McKendrick, Neil, John Brewer and J.H. Plumb, *The Birth of a Consumer Society: The Commercialization of Eighteenth-Century England* (London: Europa Publications, 1982).

McKeon, Michael, *The Origins of the English Novel, 1600–1740* (Baltimore: Johns Hopkins University Press, 1987).

Meehan, Johanna, ed., *Feminists Read Habermas: Gendering the Subject of Discourse* (New York and London: Routledge, 1995).

Mellor, Anne K., *Romanticism and Gender* (New York and London: Routledge, 1993).

——, 'Joanna Baillie and the Counter-Public Sphere', *Studies in Romanticism*, 33:4 (Winter 1994), pp. 559–67.

——, '"Am I not a Woman, and a Sister?": Slavery, Romanticism, and Gender', in *Romanticism, Race, and Imperial Culture, 1780–1834*, edited by Alan Richardson and Sonia Hofkosh (Bloomington and Indianapolis: Indiana University Press, 1995), pp. 311–29.

——, 'A Criticism of Their Own: Romantic Women Literary Critics', in *Questioning*

Romanticism, edited by John Beer (Baltimore and London: Johns Hopkins University Press, 1995), pp. 29–48.

Mews, Hazel, *Frail Vessels: Woman's Role in Women's Novels from Fanny Burney to George Eliot* (London: Athlone Press, 1969).

Miller, Nancy K., 'Men's Reading, Women's Writing: Gender and the Rise of the Novel', in *Displacements: Women, Tradition, Literatures in French*, edited by Joan DeJean and Nancy K. Miller (Baltimore and London: Johns Hopkins University Press, 1991), pp. 37–54.

Miller, P.J., 'Women's Education, 'Self-Improvement' and Social Mobility—A Late 18th Century Debate', *British Journal of Educational Studies*, 20:3 (October 1972), pp. 302–14.

Moers, Ellen, *Literary Women* (London: W.H. Allen, 1977).

Moretti, Franco, *The Way of the World: The Bildungsroman in European Culture* (London: Verso, 1987).

Mücke, Dorothea E. von, *Virtue and the Veil of Illusion: Generic Innovation and the Pedagogical Project in Eighteenth-Century Literature* (Stanford: Stanford University Press, 1991).

Mullan, John, *Sentiment and Sociability: The Language of Feeling in the Eighteenth Century* (Oxford: Clarendon Press, 1988).

——, 'Gendered Knowledge, Gendered Minds: Women and Newtonianism, 1690–1760', in *A Question of Identity: Women, Science and Literature*, edited by Marina Benjamin (New Brunswick: Rutgers University Press, 1993), pp. 41–56.

Myers, Mitzi, 'Reform or Ruin: "A Revolution in Female Manners"', *Studies in Eighteenth-Century Culture*, 11 (1982), pp. 199–216.

——, 'Hannah More's Tracts for the Times: Social Fiction and Female Ideology', in *Fetter'd or Free? British Women Novelists 1670–1815*, edited by Mary Anne Schofield and Cecilia Macheski (Athens and London: Ohio University Press, 1986), pp. 264–84.

——, 'The Dilemmas of Gender as Double-Voiced Narrative; or Maria Edgeworth Mothers the *Bildungsroman*', in *The Idea of the Novel in the Eighteenth Century*, edited by Robert W. Uphaus (East Lansing: Colleagues Press, 1988), pp. 67–96.

——, 'Romancing the Moral Tale: Maria Edgeworth and the Problematics of Pedagogy', in *Romanticism and Children's Literature in Nineteenth-Century England*, edited by James Holt McGavran (Athens and London: University of Georgia Press, 1991), pp. 96–128.

——, 'Aufklärung für Kinder? Maria Edgeworth and the Genders of Knowledge Genres; Or "The Genius of Nonsense" and "The Grand Panjandrum"', *Women's Writing*, 2:2 (1995), pp. 113–40.

——, '"We Must Grant a Romance Writer a Few Impossibilities": "Unnatural Incident" and Narrative Motherhood in Maria Edgeworth's "Emilie de Coulanges"', *The Wordsworth Circle*, 27:3 (Summer 1996), pp. 151–57.

Myers, Sylvia Harcstark, *The Bluestocking Circle: Women, Friendship, and the Life of the Mind in Eighteenth-Century England* (Oxford: Clarendon Press, 1990).

Nelson, T.G.A., *Children, Parents, and the Rise of the Novel* (London: Associated University Presses; Newark: University of Delaware Press, 1995).

Nussbaun, Felicity, *The Autobiographical Subject: Gender and Ideology in Eighteenth-*

Century England (Baltimore and London: Johns Hopkins University Press, 1989).

———, *Torrid Zones: Maternity, Sexuality, and Empire in Eighteenth-Century English Narratives* (Baltimore and London: Johns Hopkins University Press, 1995).

Oakleaf, David, 'The Name of the Father: Social Identity and the Ambition of Evelina', *Eighteenth-Century Fiction*, 3:4 (July 1991), pp. 341–58.

O'Day, Rosemary, *Education and Society 1500–1800: The Social Foundations of Education in Early Modern Britain* (London and New York: Longman, 1982).

Okin, Susan Moller, 'Women and the Making of the Sentimental Family', *Philosophy and Public Affairs*, 11:1 (Winter 1982), pp. 65–88.

Orr, Clarissa Campbell, ed., *Wollstonecraft's Daughters: Womanhood in England and France 1780–1920* (Manchester: Manchester University Press, 1996).

Pawl, Amy J., '"And What Other Name May I Claim?" Names and Their Owners in Frances Burney's Evelina', *Eighteenth-Century Fiction*, 3:4 (July 1991), pp. 283–99.

Pearson, Jacqueline, *Women's Reading in Britain 1750–1850: A Dangerous Occupation* (Cambridge: Cambridge University Press, 1998).

Perry, Ruth, *Women, Letters and the Novel* (New York: AMS Press, 1980).

———, *The Celebrated Mary Astell. An Early English Feminist* (Chicago and London: University of Chicago Press, 1986).

———, 'Women in Families: the Great Disinheritance', in *Women and Literature in Britain, 1700–1800*, edited by Vivien Jones (Cambridge: Cambridge University Press, 2000), pp. 111–31.

Pfau, Thomas, '"Positive Infamy": Surveillance, Ascendancy, and Pedagogy in Andrew Bell and Mary Wollstonecraft', *Romanticism*, 2:2 (1996), pp. 220–42.

Phillipson, N., and R. Mitchison, eds, *Scotland in the Age of Improvement: Essays in Scottish History in the Eighteenth Century* (Edinburgh: Edinburgh University Press, 1970).

Phillipson, Nicholas, 'The Scottish Enlightenment', in *The Enlightenment in National Context*, edited by Roy Porter and Mikulas Teich (Cambridge: Cambridge University Press, 1981), pp. 19–40.

Pollin, Burton, 'Mary Hays on Women's Rights in the *Monthly Magazine*', *Etudes Anglaises*, 24:3 (1971), pp. 271–82.

Poovey, Mary, *The Proper Lady and the Woman Writer: Ideology as Style in the Works of Mary Wollstonecraft, Mary Shelley and Jane Austen* (Chicago and London: University of Chicago Press, 1984).

Porter, Elizabeth, 'Women and Friendships: Pedagogies of Care and Relationality', in *Feminisms and Pedagogies of Everyday Life*, edited by Carmen Luke (Albany: State University of New York Press, 1996), pp. 56–79.

Porter, Roy, and Mikulas Teich, eds, *The Enlightenment in National Context* (Cambridge: Cambridge University Press, 1981).

Prévot, Jacques, *La Première Institutrice de France, Madame de Maintenon*, (Paris: Editions Belin, 1981).

Prochaska, F.K., 'Women in English Philanthropy 1790–1830', *International Review of Social History*, 19 (1974), pp. 426–45.

Raftery, Deirdre, *Women and Learning in English Writing, 1600–1900* (Dublin: Four Courts Press, 1997).

Rajan, Balachandra, 'Feminizing the Feminine: Early Women Writers on India', in *Romanticism, Race, and Imperial Culture, 1780–1834*, edited by Alan Richardson and Sonia Hofkosh (Bloomington and Indianapolis: Indiana University Press, 1996), pp. 149–72.

Rajan, Tilottama, and Julia Wright eds, *Romanticism, History, and the Possibilities of Genre, Re-forming Literature 1789–1837* (Cambridge: Cambridge University Press, 1998).

Raven, James, *Judging New Wealth: Popular Publishing and Responses to Commerce in England, 1750–1800* (Oxford: Clarendon Press, 1992).

Raven, James, Helen Small and Naomi Tadmor, eds, *The Practice and Representation of Reading in England* (Cambridge: Cambridge University Press, 1996).

Redfield, Marc, *Phantom Formations: Aesthetic Ideology and the Bildungsroman* (Ithaca and London: Cornell University Press, 1996).

Rees, Christine, *Utopian Imagination and Eighteenth-Century Fiction* (London and New York: Longman, 1996).

Rendall, Jane, *The Origins of Modern Feminism: Women In Britain, France, and the United States, 1780–1860* (Basingstoke and London: Macmillan, 1985).

——, 'Writing History for Women: Elizabeth Hamilton and the *Memoirs of Agrippina*', in Clarissa Campbell Orr, ed., *Wollstonecraft's Daughters: Womanhood in England and France 1780–1920* (Manchester: Manchester University Press, 1996), pp. 79–93.

Ribeiro, Alvaro, and James Basker, eds, *Tradition in Transition: Women Writers, Marginal Texts, and the Eighteenth-Century Canon* (Oxford: Clarendon Press, 1996).

Richardson, Alan, *Literature, Education, and Romanticism: Reading as Social Practice, 1780–1832*, Cambridge Studies in Romanticism 8 (Cambridge: Cambridge University Press, 1994).

Richardson, Alan, and Sonia Hofkosh, eds, *Romanticism, Race, and Imperial Culture, 1780–1834* (Bloomington and Indianapolis: Indiana University Press, 1995).

Rizzo, Betty, *Companions without Vows: Relationships among Eighteenth-Century British Women* (Athens and London: University of Georgia Press, 1994).

Roper, Derek, *Reviewing before the Edinburgh 1788–1802* (London: Methuen, 1978).

Runge, Laura, *Gender and Language in British Literary Criticism* (Cambridge: Cambridge University Press, 1997).

Sanderson, Michael, *Education, Economic Change and Society in England 1780–1870* (Basingstoke and London: Macmillan, 1983).

Schnorrenberg, Barbara, 'A Paradise Like Eve's: Three Eighteenth Century English Female Utopias', *Women's Studies*, 9:3 (1982), pp. 263–73.

Schofield, Mary Anne, *Masking and Unmasking the Female Mind: Disguising Romances in Feminine Fiction, 1713–1799* (Newark: University of Delaware Press; London and Toronto: Associated University Presses, 1990).

Schofield, Mary Anne, and Cecilia Macheski, eds, *Fetter'd or Free? British Women Novelists 1670–1815* (Athens and London: Ohio University Press, 1986).

Schwarz, Joel, *The Sexual Politics of Jean-Jacques Rousseau* (Chicago: University of Chicago Press, 1984).

Shevelow, Kathryn, *Women and Print Culture: The Construction of Femininity in the Early Periodical* (London: Routledge, 1989).

Showalter, Elaine, *A Literature of Their Own: from Charlotte Brontë to Doris Lessing* (London: Virago, 1995).

Shteir, Ann B., *Cultivating Women, Cultivating Science: Flora's Daughters and Botany in England, 1760–1860* (London: Johns Hopkins University Press, 1996).

Silver, Harold, *English Education and the Radicals 1780–1850* (London: Routledge and Kegan Paul, 1975).

Simon, Brian, *Studies in the History of Education 1780–1870* (London: Lawrence and Wishart, 1960).

Siskin, Clifford, *The Historicity of Romantic Discourse* (Oxford and New York: Oxford University Press, 1988).

——, *The Work of Writing: Literature and Social Change in Britain, 1700–1830* (Baltimore and London: Johns Hopkins University Press, 1998).

Skedd, Susan, 'Women Teachers and the Expansion of Girls' Schooling in England, *c.* 1760–1820', in *Gender in the Eighteenth Century, Roles, Representations and Responsibilities*, edited by Hannah Barker and Elaine Chalus (London and New York: Longman, 1997), pp. 101–25.

Smallwood, Angela, *Fielding and the Woman Question: The Novels of Henry Fielding and Feminist Debate 1700–1750* (Hemel Hampstead: Harvester Wheatsheaf; New York: St. Martin'e Press, 1989).

Smith, Hilda, *Reason's Disciples: Seventeenth-Century English Feminists* (Urbana: University of Illinois Press, 1982).

Smith, Sarah W.R., 'Men, Women, and Money: the Case of Mary Brunton', in *Fetter'd or Free? British Women Novelists 1670–1815*, edited by Mary Anne Schofield and Cecilia Macheski (Athens and London: Ohio University Press, 1986), pp. 40–48.

Smout, T.C., 'The Landowner and the Planned Village in Scotland, 1730–1830', in *Scotland in the Age of Improvement: Essays in Scottish History in the Eighteenth Century*, edited by N. Phillipson and R. Mitchison (Edinburgh: Edinburgh University Press, 1970), pp. 73–106.

Sonnet, Martine, 'A Daughter to Educate', in *A History of Women in the West: Renaissance and Enlightenment Paradoxes*, edited by Natalie Zemon Davis and Arlette Farge (Cambridge, Massachusetts and London: The Belknap Press, 1993), pp. 101–31.

Southam, Brian, *Jane Austen's Literary Manuscripts* (Oxford: Oxford University Press, 1964).

Spacks, Patricia Meyer, *Imagining a Self: Autobiography and Novel in Eighteenth-Century England* (Cambridge, Massachusetts, and London: Harvard University Press, 1976).

Spencer, Jane, *The Rise of the Woman Novelist: From Aphra Behn to Jane Austen* (Oxford: Basil Blackwell, 1986).

Spender, Dale, *Mothers of the Novel: 100 Good Women Writers before Jane Austen* (London: Pandora, 1986).

Springborg, Patricia, 'Mary Astell and John Locke', in *The Cambridge Companion to English Literature 1650–1740*, edited by Steven Zwicker (Cambridge: Cambridge University Press, 1998), pp. 276–306.

Stewart, Dugald, *The Collected Works of Dugald Stewart*, edited by Sir William Hamilton, with an introduction by Knud Haakonssen, 11 vols (Edinburgh: Thomas Constable and Co., 1854–60; Bristol: Thoemmes Press, 1994).

Still, Judith, and Michael Worton, eds, *Textuality and Sexuality: Reading Theories and Practices* (Manchester and New York: Manchester University Press, 1993).

Stone, Lawrence, *The Family, Sex, and Marriage in England, 1500–1800* (Harmondsworth: Penguin Books, 1979).

Sudan, Rajani, 'Mothering and National Identity in the Works of Mary Wollstonecraft', in *Romanticism, Race, and Imperial Culture, 1780–1834*, edited by Alan Richardson and Sonia Hofkosh (Bloomington and Indiana: Indiana University Press, 1996), pp. 72–89.

Summerfield, Geoffrey, *Fantasy and Reason: Children's Literature in the Eighteenth Century* (London: Methuen, 1984).

Sutherland, Kathryn, 'Adam Smith's Master Narrative: Women and the *Wealth of Nations*', in *Adam Smith's Wealth of Nations: New Interdisciplinary Essays*, edited by Stephen Copley and Kathryn Sutherland, Texts in Culture (Manchester and New York: Manchester University Press, 1995), pp. 97–121.

Symes, Ruth Alexandra, 'Educating Women: The Preceptress and Her Pen, 1780–1820' (unpublished D.Phil. thesis, University of York, 1996).

Tadmor, Naomi, '"In the Even My Wife Read to Me": Women, Reading, and Household Life in the Eighteenth century', in *The Practice and Representation of Reading in England*, edited by James Raven, Helen Small and Naomi Tadmor (Cambridge: Cambridge University Press, 1996), pp. 162–74.

Thaddeus, Janice Farrar, 'Elizabeth Hamilton's Domestic Politics', *Studies in Eighteenth-Century Culture*, 23 (1994), pp. 265–84.

Tobin, Beth Fowkes, *Superintending the Poor: Charitable Ladies and Paternal Landlords in British Fiction, 1770–1860* (New Haven and London: Yale University Press, 1993).

Todd, Janet, *Dictionary of British and American Women Writers, 1660–1800* (London: Methuen, 1984).

———, *Sensibility: An Introduction* (London and New York: Methuen, 1986).

———, *Feminist Literary History: A Defence* (Cambridge: Polity Press, in association with Basil Blackwell, 1988).

———, *The Sign of Angellica: Women, Writing, and Fiction, 1660–1800* (London: Virago, 1989).

Tomaselli, Sylvana, 'The Enlightenment Debate on Women', *History Workshop Journal*, 19 (1985), pp. 101–24.

———, 'Reflections on the History of the Science of Woman', in *A Question of Identity: Women, Science, and Literature*, edited by Marina Benjamin (New Brunswick: Rutgers University Press, 1993), pp. 25–40.

Tompkins, J.M.S., *The Popular Novel in England, 1770–1800* (London: Constable, 1932; rpt, London: Methuen, n.d.).

———, *The Polite Marriage* (Cambridge: Cambridge University Press, 1938).

Topliss, Iain, 'The Novels of Maria Edgeworth: Enlightenment and Tutelage' (Ph.D. thesis, University of Cambridge, 1985).

Trouille, Mary, 'Eighteenth-Century Amazons of the Pen: Stephanie de Genlis and Olympe de Gouges,' in *Femmes Savantes et Femmes d'Esprit: Women Intellectuals of the French Eighteenth Century*, edited by Roland Bonnel and Catherine Rubinger (New York: Peter Lang, 1994), pp. 341–70.

———, 'Sexual/ Textual Politics in the Enlightenment: Diderot and D'Epinay Respond to Thomas's *Essay on Women*', *British Journal for Eighteenth-Century Studies*, 19:1 (Spring 1996), pp. 1–15.

Trumbach, Randolph, *The Rise of the Egalitarian Family: Aristocratic Kinship and Domestic Relations in Eighteenth-Century England* (New York: Academic Press, 1978).

Tuchman, Gaye, and Nina E. Fortin, *Edging Women Out: Victorian, Novelists, Publishers, and Social Change* (London: Routledge, 1989).

Turner, Cheryl, *Living by the Pen: Women Writers in the Eighteenth Century* (London: Routledge, 1994).

Ty, Eleanor, 'Female Philosophy Refunctioned: Elizabeth Hamilton's Parodic Novel', *Ariel*, 22:4 (1991), pp. 111–29.

———, *Unsex'd Revolutionaries: Five Women Novelists of the 1790s* (Toronto, Buffalo and London: Toronto University Press, 1993).

Utter, R.P., and G.B. Needham, *Pamela's Daughters* (London: Lovat Dickson, 1937).

Vallone, Lynne, *Disciplines of Virtue: Girls' Culture in the Eighteenth and Nineteenth Centuries* (New Haven and London: Yale University Press, 1995).

Vickery, Amanda, 'The Neglected Century: Writing the History of Eighteenth-Century Women', *Gender and History*, 3:2 (Summer 1991), pp. 211–19.

———, 'Golden Age to Separate Spheres? A Review of the Categories and Chronology of English Women's History', *The Historical Journal*, 36:2 (June 1993), pp. 383–414.

———, *The Gentleman's Daughter* (New Haven and London: Yale University Press, 1998).

Vincent, David, *Literacy and Popular Culture: England 1750–1914* (Cambridge: Cambridge University Press, 1993).

Watson, Nicola, *Revolution and the Form of the British Novel 1790–1825: Intercepted Letters, Interrupted Seductions* (Oxford: Clarendon Press, 1994).

Watt, Ian, *The Rise of the Novel: Studies in Defoe, Richardson and Fielding* (London: Pelican Books, 1972).

Wiesner, Merry E., *Women and Gender in Early Modern Europe*, New Approaches to European History 1 (Cambridge: Cambridge University Press, 1993).

Williams, Ioan, ed., *Novel and Romance, 1700–1800: A Documentary Record* (London: Routledge and Kegan Paul, 1970).

Woolf, Virginia, *A Room of One's Own and Three Guineas*, edited with an introduction by Morag Shiach (Oxford and New York: Oxford University Press, 1992).

Wright, Julia, '"I Am Ill Fitted": Conflicts of Genre in Eliza Fenwick's *Secresy*', in *Romanticism, History, and the Possibilities of Genre, Re-forming Literature 1789–1837*, edited by Tilottama Rajan and Julia Wright (Cambridge: Cambridge University Press, 1998), pp. 149–75.

Yeazell, Ruth, *Fictions of Modesty: Women and Courtship in the English Novel* (Chicago and London: University of Chicago Press, 1991).

Zaragoza, Georges, *Charles Nodier: le Dériseur Sensé* (n.p.: Klincksieck, 1992).

Zomchick, John P., *Family and the Law in Eighteenth-Century Fiction: The Public Conscience in the Private Sphere*, Cambridge Studies in Eighteenth-Century English Literature and Thought 15 (Cambridge: Cambridge University Press, 1993).

Index